Solid Edge ST6 Synchronous Modeling

Larneasy.com

© Copyright 2014

This book may not be duplicated in any way without the express written consent of the publisher, except in the form of brief excerpts or quotations for the purpose of review. The information contained herein is for the personal use of the reader and may not be incorporated in any commercial programs, other books, database, or any kind of software without written consent of the publisher. Making copies of this book or any portion for purpose other than your own is a violation of copyright laws.

Limit of Liability/Disclaimer of Warranty:
The author and publisher make no representations or warranties with respect to the accuracy or completeness of the contents of this work and specifically disclaim all warranties, including without limitation warranties of fitness for a particular purpose. The advice and strategies contained herein may not be suitable for every situation. Neither the publisher nor the author shall be liable for damages arising here from.

Trademarks:
All brand names and product names used in this book are trademarks, registered trademarks, or trade names of their respective holders. The author and publisher are not associated with any product or vendor mentioned in this book.

Contents

Introduction xiii
Topics covered in this Book xiii

Chapter 1: Getting Started with Solid Edge ST6 1

Introduction to Solid Edge ST6 1
   Starting Solid Edge ST6 2
   File Types 4
   User Interface 4
      Environments in Solid Edge 4
      Part environment (Synchronous and Ordered) 5
      Assembly environment 5
      Draft environment 6
      Sheet Metal environment 6
      Application Menu 6
      Quick Access Toolbar 7
      Graphics Window 7
      Prompt Bar 7
      Status Bar 8
      Command bar 8
      Changing the display of the Ribbon 9
      Dialog Boxes 10
      Radial Menus 10
      Shortcut Menus 10
   Starting a new document 10
      The New dialog box 11
   Solid Edge Options 11
   View Overrides dialog box 12
   Solid Edge Help 12
   Questions 13

Chapter 2: Sketch Techniques 15

   Create Sketches in the Synchronous mode 15

Create Sketches in the Ordered mode 16
Draw Commands 17
    The Line command 17
    Using Grid and Snap settings 18
    The Tangent Arc command 18
    The Arc by 3 Points command 19
    The Arc by Center Point command 19
    The Rectangle by Center command 20
    The Rectangle by 2 Points command 20
    The Rectangle by 3 Points command 20
    The Polygon by Center command 20
    The Circle by Center Point command 21
    The Circle by 3 Points command 21
    The Tangent Circle command 22
    The Ellipse by Center Point command 22
    The Ellipse by 3 Points command 22
    The Curve command 23
    The Smart Dimension command 24
    The Distance Between command 25
    The Angle Between command 26
    Driving Vs Driven dimensions 26
    IntelliSketch Auto-Dimensions 27
Geometric Relations 27
    Connect 28
    Parallel 28
    Concentric 28
    Lock 28
    Horizontal/Vertical 29
    Equal 29
    Perpendicular 30
    Rigid Set 30
    Tangent 31
    Symmetric 32

    Collinear 32
  Maintain Relationships 33
  Relationship Handles 33
  Relationship Assistant 34
  The Construction command 35
  The Symmetric Diameter command 35
  The Fillet command 35
  The Chamfer command 36
  The Split command 37
  The Extend to Next command 37
  The Trim command 38
  The Trim Corner command 38
  The Offset command 39
  The Symmetric Offset command 39
  The Move command 40
  The Rotate command 41
  The Mirror command 41
  The Scale command 42
  The Stretch command 42
  Example 1 (Millimetres) 42
    Example 2 (Inches) 49
    Example 3 (Millimetres) 54
  Questions 58
  Exercise 1 59
  Exercise 2 59
  Exercise 3 59

Chapter 3: Extrude and Revolve Features 61
  Extrude Features (Synchronous) 61
  Extrude Features (Ordered) 61
  Revolve Features (Synchronous) 62
  Revolve Features (Ordered) 63
  Creating Planes (Synchronous) 64

- Coincident Plane ... 65
- Normal to Curve ... 66
- By 3 Points ... 66
- Tangent ... 66

Coordinate System ... 67

Creating Planes (Ordered) ... 67
- Parallel ... 67
- Angled ... 68
- Perpendicular ... 68
- Coincident by Axis ... 68

Additional options of the Extrude command ... 69
- Selection Type options ... 69
- Include Internal Loops ... 69
- Exclude Internal Loops ... 69
- Use Only Internal Loops ... 70
- Add ... 70
- Remove ... 70
- Open ... 71
- Closed ... 71
- Side Step ... 71
- Extent Type options ... 71
- Treatments options ... 72

Example 1 (Millimetres) ... 73

Example 2 (Inches) ... 77

Questions ... 79

Exercise 1 (Millimetres) ... 80

Exercise 2 (Inches) ... 80

Exercise 3 (Millimetres) ... 81

Chapter 4: Placed Features ... 82

Hole ... 82
- Create a Simple Hole feature ... 83
- Create a Threaded Hole feature ... 84

    Create a Tapered Hole feature 85

    Create a Counterbore Hole feature 85

    Create a Countersink Hole feature 86

  Modify Holes 87

  Recognize Holes 87

  Thread 88

  Round 88

  Blend 90

    Variable Radius Blend 90

    Blend between faces 91

  Chamfer Equal Setbacks 92

  Chamfer Unequal Setbacks 93

  Draft 93

  Thin Wall 94

  Example 1 (Millimetres) 95

  Questions 100

  Exercise 1 (Millimetres) 101

  Exercise 2 (Inches) 101

Chapter 5: Patterned Geometry 103

  Mirror 104

  Rectangular Pattern 105

  Circular Pattern 106

  Along Curve Pattern 106

  Fill Pattern 107

    Rectangular Fill Pattern 107

    Staggered Fill Pattern 109

    Radial Fill Pattern 109

    Recognize Hole Patterns 110

  Example 1 (Millimetres) 111

  Questions 116

  Exercise 1 (Millimetres) 117

  Exercise 2 (Inches) 117

Chapter 6: Sweep Features 118

Single path and cross-section sweeps 119

    Face Merging 121

    Section Alignment 122

    Face Continuity 122

    Scale 122

    Twist 123

    Axis Step 124

Multiple paths and cross-sections sweeps 124

Swept Cutout 125

Helix 126

Helical Cutout 128

Example 1 (Inches) 129

Questions 134

Exercise1 134

Chapter 7: Loft Features 137

Loft 137

    Tangency Controls 138

    Loft Cross-sections 139

    Closed Extent 139

    Guide Curves 139

    Section Geometry 140

Loft Cutout 142

Example 1 (Millimetres) 143

Questions 146

Exercise 1 146

Chapter 8: Additional Features and Multibody Parts 147

Rib 147

Web Network 148

Mounting Boss 149

Lip 149

Vent 150

Slot 151
Multi-body Parts 152
    Creating Multibodies 153
    Split 153
    Union 155
    Intersect 155
    Subtract 155
    Multi Body Publish 156
Emboss 156
Example 1 (Millimetres) 157
Questions 161
Exercise 2 163
Face Relations 165
    Coplanar 165
    Concentric 165
    Symmetric 166
    Offset 166
    Parallel 167
    Coplanar Axis 167
    Equal Radius 168
    Tangent 168
    Horizontal/Vertical 168
Using the Steering Wheel Tool to Modify Models 169
    Move faces 169
    Rotate faces 171
Dealing with Live Rules 171
Modify the Part dimensions 173
Live Sections 173
Example 1 (Millimetres) 174
Questions 176
Exercise 1 177

Chapter 10: Assemblies 179

Starting an Assembly	179
Inserting Parts	181
Adding Relationships	181
Drag Components	182
Mate Relationship	184
Planar Align Relationship	185
Axial Align Relationship	185
Insert Relationship	186
Angle Relationship	186
Tangent Relationship	186
Connect Relationship	187
Parallel Relationship	187
Center-Plane Relationship	188
Match Coordinate Systems Relationship	189
Rigid Set Relationship	189
Ground Relationship	190
Path Relationship	190
Cam Relationship	190
Check Interference	191
Capture Fit	192
Editing and Updating Assemblies	193
Replace Part	194
Pattern	195
Mirror Components	196
Sub-assemblies	196
Rigid and Adjustable Sub-Assemblies	197
Transfer	197
Disperse	198
Assembly Features	198
Assembly-Driven Part Features	200
Part Features	201
Top Down Assembly Design	201
Inserting a New Part	201

Assembly Relationship Assistant 203

Exploding Assemblies 204

Example 1 (Bottom Up Assembly) 208

Example 2 (Top Down Assembly) 214

Questions 222

Exercise 1 222

Chapter 11: Drawings 225

Starting a Drawing 225

View Creation 226

Principal View 227

Auxiliary View 228

Section View 228

Detail View 231

Add Break Lines 232

Broken Out 232

Exploded View 233

Display Options 234

View Alignment 235

Parts List and Balloons 236

Dimensions 238

Coordinate Dimensions 239

Center Marks and Centerlines 240

Bolt Hole Circle 241

Callouts and Leaders 241

Notes 242

Example 1 243

Example 2 254

Questions 256

Exercise 1 256

Exercise 2 257

Chapter 12: Sheet Metal Design 259

Starting a Sheet Metal part 259

Tab	260
Flange	262
Close 2-Bend Corner	264
Contour Flange	266
Hem	267
Bend	269
Jog	269
Dimple	270
Drawn Cutout	271
Bead	272
Louver	272
Gusset	274
Cut	275
Creating Cut across Bends	276
Break Corner	276
Flat Pattern	276
Lofted Flange	277
Transition to Synchronous Sheet Metal	278
Sheet Metal Drawings	280
Export to DWF	282
Example 1	282
Questions	291
Exercise 1	291
Exercise 2	292

Introduction

Welcome to the *Solid Edge ST6 Synchronous Modeling* book. This book is written to assist students, designers, and engineering professionals. It covers the important features and functionalities of Solid Edge using relevant examples and exercises.

This book is written for new users, who can use it as a self-study resource to learn Solid Edge. In addition, it can also be used as a reference for experienced users. The main focus of this book is part modeling, assembly modeling, drawings, and sheet metal design.

Topics covered in this Book

- Chapter 1, "Getting Started with Solid Edge ST6", gives an introduction to Solid Edge. The user interface and terminology are discussed in this chapter.

- Chapter 2, "Sketch Techniques", explores the sketching commands in Solid Edge. You will learn to create parametric sketches.

- Chapter 3, "Extrude and Revolve features", teaches you to create basic 3D geometry using the Extrude and Revolve commands.

- Chapter 4, "Placed Features", covers the features which can be created without using sketches.

- Chapter 5, "Patterned Geometry", explores the commands to create patterned and mirrored geometry.

- Chapter 6, "Sweep Features", covers the commands to create swept and helical features.

- Chapter 7, "Loft Features", covers the Loft command and its core features.

- Chapter 8, "Additional Features and Multibody Parts", covers additional commands to create complex geometry. In addition, the multibody parts are also covered.

- Chapter 9, "Modifying Parts", explores the commands and techniques to modify the part geometry.

- Chapter 10, "Assemblies", explains you to create assemblies using the bottom-up and top-down design approaches.

- Chapter 11, "Drawings", covers how to create 2D drawings from 3D parts and assemblies.

- Chapter 12, "Sheet Metal Design", covers how to create sheet metal parts and flat patterns.

Chapter 1: Getting Started with Solid Edge ST6

Introduction to Solid Edge ST6

Solid Edge ST6 is a parametric and feature-based system that allows you to create 3D parts, assemblies, and 2D drawings. The design process in Solid Edge is shown below.

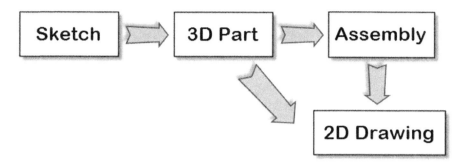

In Solid Edge, everything is controlled by parameters, dimensions, or relationships. For example, if you want to change the position of the hole shown in figure, you need to change the dimension or relation that controls its position.

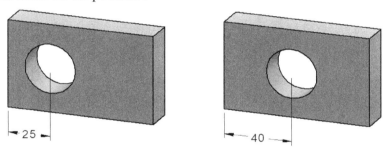

The parameters and relationships that you set up allow you to have control over the design intent. The design intent describes the way your 3D model will behave when you apply dimensions and relationships to it. For example, if you want to position the hole at the center of the block, one way is to add dimensions between the hole and the adjacent edges. However, when you change the size of the block, the hole will not be at the center.

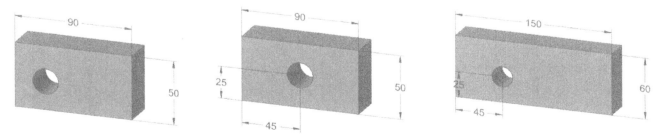

You can make the hole to be at the center, even if the size of the block changes. You need to apply the **Horizontal/Vertical** relationships between the hole and midpoints of the adjacent edges. Now, even if you change the size of the block, the hole will always remain at the center.

Getting Started with Solid Edge ST6

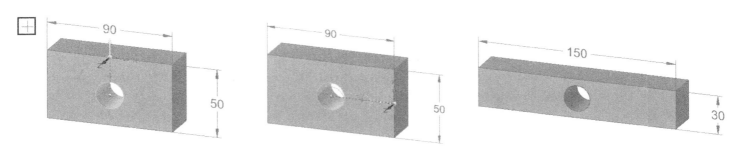

The other big advantage of Solid Edge is the associativity between parts, assemblies and drawings. When you make changes to the design of a part, the changes will take place in any assembly that it's a part of. In addition, the 2D drawing will update automatically.

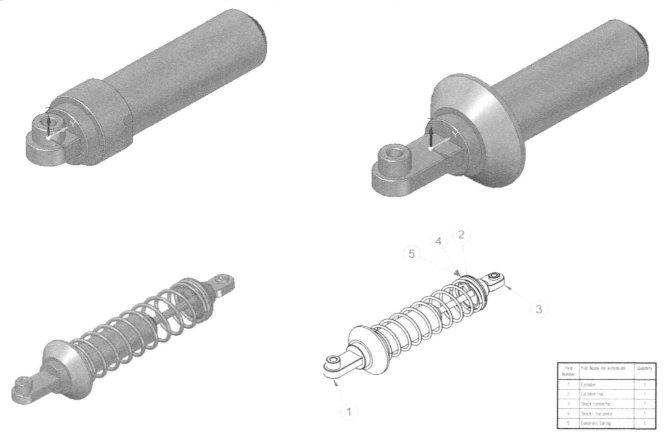

Starting Solid Edge ST6

To start **Solid Edge ST6**, click the **Solid Edge ST6** icon on your computer screen; the theme selection window appears. A theme is a predefined user-interface layout which suits your working style. This window displays four user-interface themes: **Some Assistance**, **Maximum Assistance**, **Maximum Workspace**, and **Balanced (Solid Edge Default)**. The **Some Assistance** theme can be used by users who are familiar with other CAD packages. The **Maximum Assistance** theme can be used by users who are new to CAD. The **Maximum Workspace** theme is for users who have already used Solid Edge. The

Getting Started with Solid Edge ST6

Balanced (Solid Edge Default) theme is the predefined workspace which is similar to the previous versions of Solid Edge.

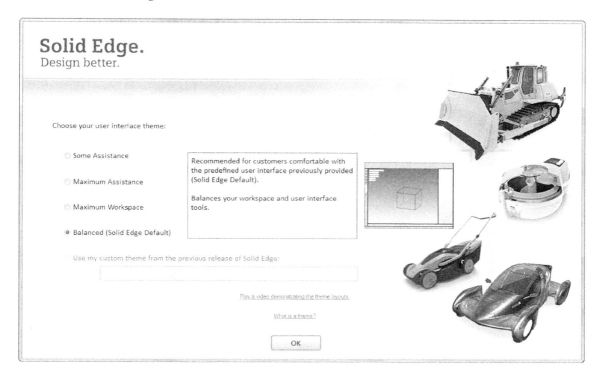

Select the **Balanced (Solid Edge Default)** theme and click **OK**. The **Solid Edge ST6** application window appears. You can use this window to start a new document, open an existing one, start Solid Edge test drive (Hands-On tutorial), get help, learn about the user-interface, and get technical support. You can also add more links to the window. Click **ISO Part** under the **Create** section to start a new part document.

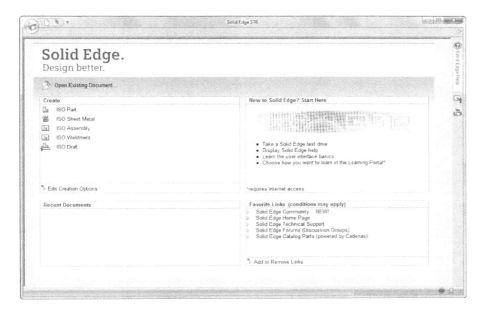

Getting Started with Solid Edge ST6

File Types
Various file types that can be created in Solid Edge are given below.

- Part (.par)
- Assembly (.asm)
- Draft (.dft)
- Sheet Metal (.psm)
- Weldment (.pwd)

User Interface
The following image shows the **Solid Edge ST6** application window.

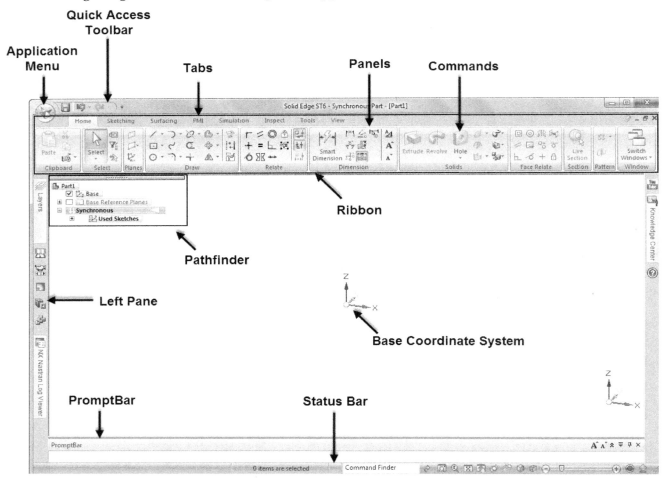

Environments in Solid Edge
There are main five environments available in Solid Edge: **Part (Synchronous** and **Ordered)**, **Assembly**, **Draft**, **Weldment**, and **Sheet Metal (Synchronous** and **Ordered)**. Also, there some additional environments to create exploded views, renderings, structures, piping, wire harnesses, and so on.

Part environment (Synchronous and Ordered)

This environment has all the commands to create a 3D part model. It is available in two modes: **Synchronous** and **Ordered**. The **Synchronous** mode allows you to create and edit models directly. The **Ordered** mode allows you to create History-based models. In this mode, every feature or sketch that you create is stored in the Pathfinder. You can always go back and edit the feature or sketch. It has a ribbon located at the top of the screen. The ribbon is arranged in a hierarchy of tabs, panels, and commands. Panels such as **Draw**, **Relate**, and **Dimension** consists of commands, which are grouped based on their usage. Panels in turn are grouped into various tabs. For example, the panels such as **Draw**, **Relate**, and **Dimension** are located in the **Home** tab.

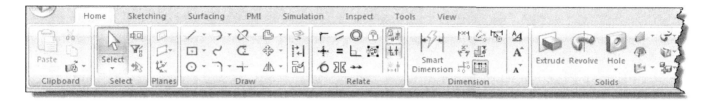

Assembly environment

This environment is used to create assemblies. The **Home** tab of the Ribbon has various commands, which will allow you to assemble and modify the components.

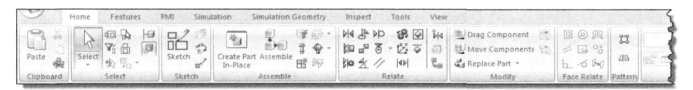

The **Feature** tab has commands, which will help you to create cutouts, holes and other features at the assembly level.

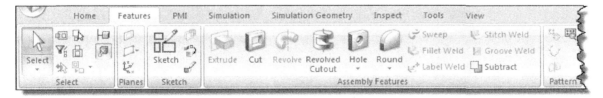

The **Inspect** tab helps you to inspect the assembly geometry.

The **Tools** tab has some advanced commands, which will help you to switch to other environments.

Getting Started with Solid Edge ST6

Draft environment
This environment has all the commands to generate 2D drawings of parts and assemblies.

Sheet Metal environment
This environment has commands to create sheet metal parts.

The other components of the user interface are discussed next.

Application Menu
The **Application Menu** appears when you click on the icon located at the top left corner of the window. The **Application Menu** consists of a list of self-explanatory menus. You can see a list of recently opened documents by clicking the **Recent Documents** menu.

Quick Access Toolbar

This is located at the top left corner of the window. It consists of commonly used commands such as **New**, **Save**, **Open**, **Save As**, and so on. You can add more commands to the **Quick Access Toolbar** by clicking on the down-arrow next to it, and then selecting commands from the pop-up menu.

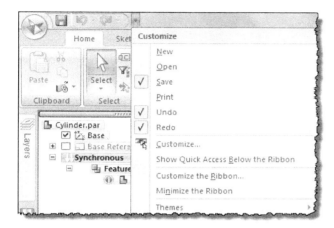

Graphics Window

Graphics window is the blank space located below the ribbon. You can draw sketches and create 3D geometry in the Graphics window. The left corner of the graphics window has a **Pathfinder**. Using the **Pathfinder**, you can access the features of the 3D model.

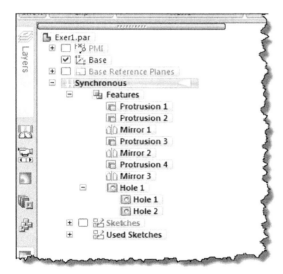

Prompt Bar

Prompt Bar is located below the Graphics Window. It is useful when you activate a command. It displays various prompts while working with any command. These prompts are series of steps needed to successfully create a feature.

Status Bar

Status Bar is located at the bottom of the Solid Edge window. It contains many icons, which help you to visualize the 3D model. You can use the **Record** and **Upload to Youtube** icons to create and upload videos. To add more icons to the Status Bar, click the right mouse button on it and select options from the pop-up menu.

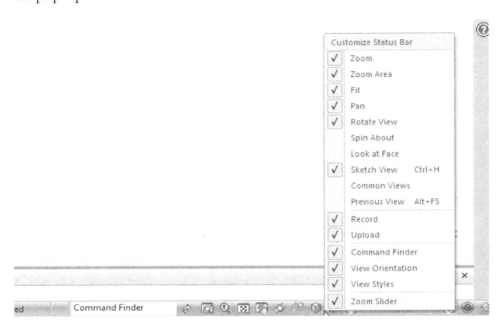

The **Command Finder** bar is used to search for any command. You can type any keyword in the **Command Finder** bar and find a list of commands related to it.

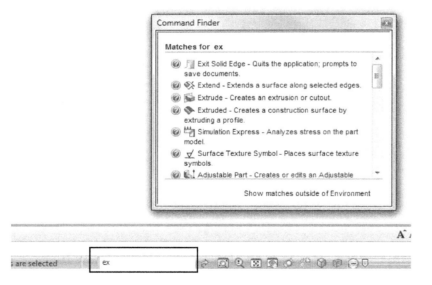

Command bar

When you activate any command in Solid Edge, a contextual productivity tool called the command bar pops up on the screen. It displays the options and steps to complete the execution of the command.

Changing the display of the Ribbon

You can add or remove more commands to the ribbon by clicking the right mouse button on it and selecting **Customize the Ribbon**. On the **Customize** dialog box, click on the options in the right-side box, and then click **Add** or **Remove**. After making the required changes, close the dialog box and click **Yes** to save the changes.

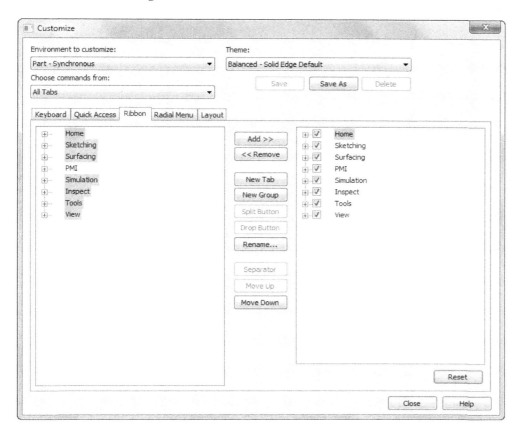

You can minimize the ribbon by clicking the right mouse button on the ribbon and selecting **Minimize the Ribbon**.

Getting Started with Solid Edge ST6

Dialog Boxes

Dialog boxes are part of Solid Edge user interface. Using a dialog box, you can easily specify many settings and options. Examples of dialog boxes are a shown below.

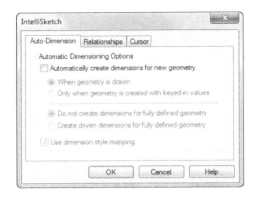 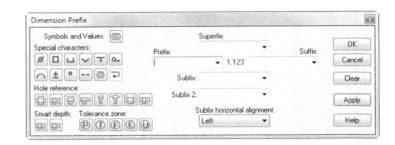

Radial Menus

Radial Menus provide you with another way of activating commands. You can display Radial Menus by clicking the right mouse button and dragging the cursor. A Radial Menu has various commands arranged in a redial manner. You can add or remove commands to the Radial Menu by using the **Customize** dialog box.

Shortcut Menus

Shortcut Menus are displayed when you right-click in the graphics window. Solid Edge provides various shortcut menus in order to help you access some options very easily and quickly. The options in shortcut menus vary based on the environment.

Starting a new document

You can start a new document directly from the initial screen or by using the **New** dialog box. On the initial screen, click on the required option to start a part, assembly, drawing, weldment or sheet metal document.

Getting Started with Solid Edge ST6

The New dialog box

To start a new document using the **New** dialog box, click the **New** button on anyone of the following:

- **Quick Access Toolbar**
- **Application Menu**

The **New** dialog box appears when you click the **New** button. In this dialog box, select the **iso part.par** template for starting a part document. Select the **iso assembly.asm** template for creating assembly models. Click the **More** tab, if you want to start a new document using other templates.

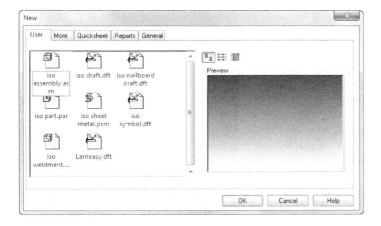

Solid Edge Options

You can customize Solid Edge as per your requirement. On the **Application Menu**, click **Solid Edge Options** to open the **Solid Edge Options** dialog box. On this dialog box, you can set options on each of the pages. The options on this dialog box vary depending upon the environment that you are in.

Getting Started with Solid Edge ST6

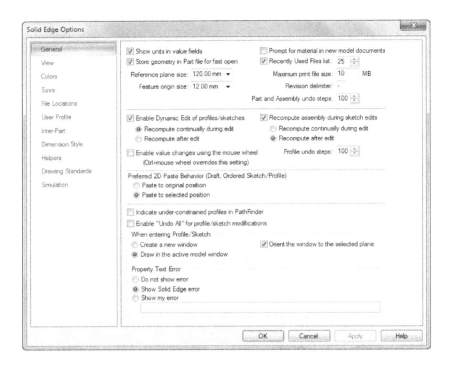

View Overrides dialog box

The **View Overrides** dialog box helps you to change the background color, rendering, and light settings. On the ribbon, click **View > Style > View Overrides** to open this dialog box. On this dialog box, click the **Background** tab and set the **Type** to **Solid Edge default**. The background color changes to white.

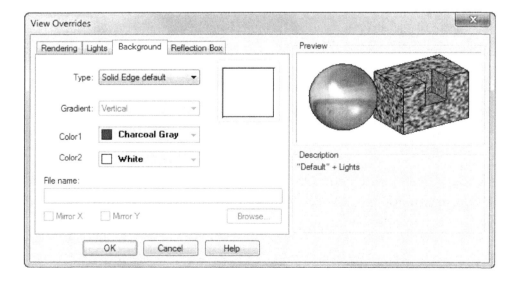

Solid Edge Help

Solid Edge offers you with the help system that goes beyond basic command definition. You can access Solid Edge help by using any of the following methods:

- Press the F1 key.
- Click on the **Solid Edge Help** option on the right-side of the window.
- On any dialog box, click the **Help** button.

Questions

1. Explain how to customize the Ribbon.
2. What is the design intent?
3. Give one example of where you would establish a relationship between a part's features.
4. Explain the term 'associativity' in Solid Edge.
5. List any two procedures to access Solid Edge Help.
6. How can you change the background color of the graphics window
7. How can you activate the Radial Menu?
8. How is Solid Edge a parametric modeling application?

Chapter 2: Sketch Techniques

This chapter covers the methods and commands to create sketches in the part environment. The commands and methods are discussed in context to part environment. In Solid Edge, the part environment is divided into two separate modes: Synchronous and Ordered.

In Solid Edge, you create a rough sketches, and then apply dimensions and constrains that define its shape and size. The dimensions define the length, size, and angle of a sketch element, whereas constrains define the relations between sketch elements.

The topics covered in this chapter are:

- Create sketches in the Part environment (Synchronous and Ordered mode)
- Use relationships and dimensions to control the shape and size of a sketch
- Learn sketching commands
- Learn commands and options that help you to create sketches easily

Create Sketches in the Synchronous mode

Synchronous is the default mode activated in the Part environment. The process to create sketches in this mode is very simple. You need to select a sketch command, and then define a plane on which you want to create the sketch. The sketch commands are available in the **Sketching** or **Home** tab of the ribbon. To create a sketch, check the **Base Reference Planes** option under the **PathFinder** to display the **Base Reference Planes**. Next, select any of the sketch command (For example, the **Line** command) from **Sketching > Draw** panel and place the cursor on anyone of the Base Reference Planes. You will notice that a lock symbol appears on the plane. Click on the lock symbol to lock the plane. You can now start drawing sketches on the locked plane. After creating the sketch, press the Esc key and click on the lock icon at the top right corner. The plane will be unlocked.

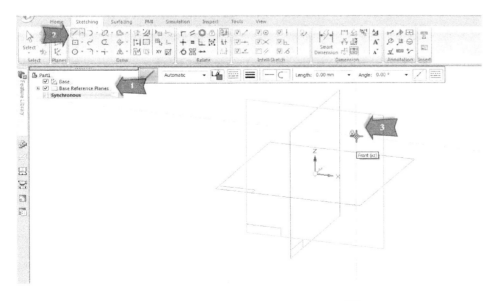

Sketch Techniques

Create Sketches in the Ordered mode

Ordered mode was previously called as traditional environment. You can activate this mode by right-clicking and selecting **Transition to Ordered** or by selecting **Tools > Model > Ordered** on the ribbon.

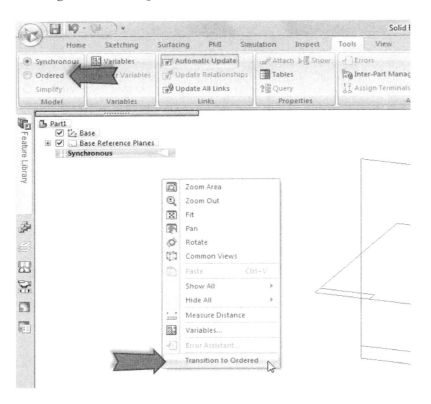

For creating sketches, this mode offers a separate environment called the Sketching environment. To open this environment, select **Home > Sketch > Sketch** on the ribbon, and then click on a **Base Reference Plane** from the graphics window. You will notice that the **Line** command is activated, by default. You can start sketching lines or select any other sketching command. After completing the sketch, select **Home > Close > Close Sketch** on the ribbon. Next, click the **Finish** button on the **Sketch** command bar.

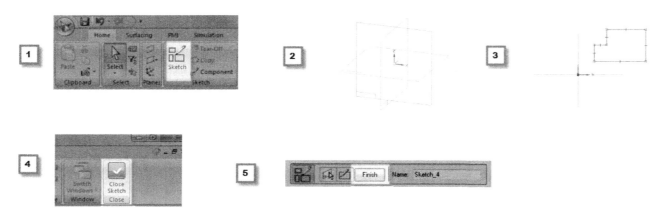

Sketch Techniques

Draw Commands

Solid Edge provides you with a set of commands to create sketches. These commands are located on the **Draw** panel of the **Home** ribbon.

The Line command

This is the most commonly used command while creating a sketch. To activate this command, you need to click **Home > Draw > Line** on the ribbon. As you move the cursor in the graphics window, you will notice that it is changed to a set of crosshairs. This indicates that the command is active. To create a line, click in the graphics window, move the cursor and click again. After clicking for the second time, you can see an end point is added and another line segment is started. This is a convenient way to create a chain of lines. Continue to click to add more line segments. You can right-click in the graphics window, if you want to end the chain. You will notice that the **Line** command is still active. You can create another chain of line segments or press Esc to deactivate this command. You can also click **Home > Select > Select** on the ribbon to deactivate a command.

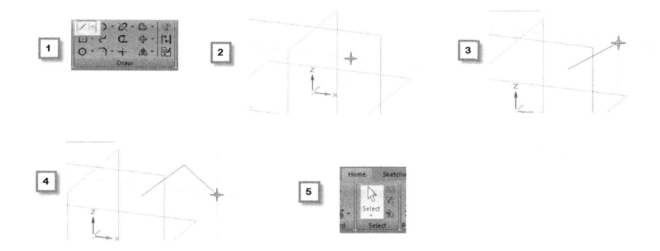

The **Line** command can also be used to draw arcs continuous with lines. Click the **Arc** icon from the command bar to draw this type of arc. The figure below shows the procedure to draw arcs connected to lines.

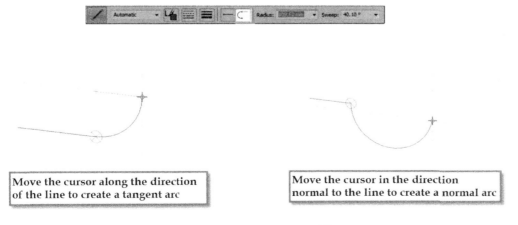

Move the cursor along the direction of the line to create a tangent arc

Move the cursor in the direction normal to the line to create a normal arc

Sketch Techniques

To delete a line, select it and press the **Delete** key. To select more than one line, press and hold the **Ctrl** key and then click on the line segments; the lines will be highlighted. You can also select multiple lines by dragging a box from left to right. Press and hold the left mouse button and drag a box from left to right; the lines inside or crossing the box boundary will be selected. Dragging a box from right to left will only select the lines that are inside the box.

Using Grid and Snap settings

If you are new to Solid Edge, the grid and snap settings will help you to create sketches easily. A grid is similar to a graph paper on your computer screen, whereas the snap mode forces the cursor to select the grid points. You can locate sketch points easily and accurately using the grid and snap settings. To use these settings, you need to activate the **Show Grid** and **Snap to Grid** icons on the **Draw** panel of the **Sketching** tab. Next, activate a drawing command and start drawing the sketch. You will notice that you can select only the grid points. This makes it easy to create sketches.

You can change the spacing between the grid points using the **Grid Options** dialog box. Select **Sketching > Draw > Grid Options** on the ribbon to open this dialog box. Next, modify the **Major line spacing value** to change the distance between the dark grid lines. Change the **Minor spaces per major** value to change the number of lighter grid lines between two major lines (dark lines). Examine the other options in this dialog box. Most of them are self-explanatory.

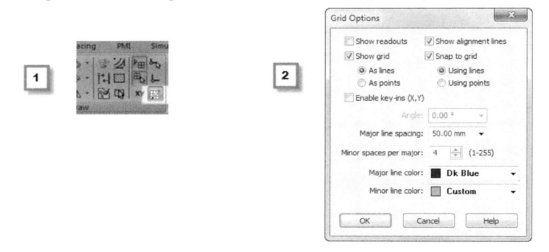

The Tangent Arc command

This command creates an arc tangent to another entity. The working of this command is same as the **Arc** icon on the **Line** command bar. You have to select the end point of a line and create a tangent or normal arc.

Sketch Techniques

The Arc by 3 Points command

This command creates an arc by defining its start, end, and radius. Activate this command (click **Home > Draw > Tangent Arc > Arc by 3 Points** on the ribbon) and click to define the start point of the arc. Click again to define the end point. After defining the start and end of the arc, you have to the define size and position of the arc. Move the mouse cursor and click to define the radius and position of the arc.

The Arc by Center Point command

This command creates an arc by defining its center, start and end points. Activate this command (click **Home > Draw > Tangent Arc > Arc by Center Point** on the ribbon) and click to define the center point. Next, move the cursor and you will notice that a line appears between center and the mouse cursor. This line is the radius of the arc. Now, click to define the start point of the arc and move the cursor; you will notice that an arc is drawn from the start point. Once the arc appears the way you want, click to define its end point.

Sketch Techniques

The Rectangle by Center command
This command creates a rectangle by defining its center and one corner point.

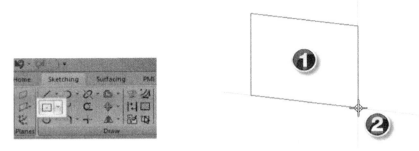

The Rectangle by 2 Points command
This command creates a rectangle by defining its diagonal corners.

The Rectangle by 3 Points command
This command creates an inclined rectangle. The first two points define the length and inclination angle of the rectangle. The third point defines its width.

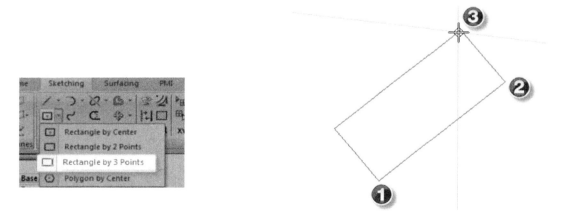

The Polygon by Center command
This command provides a simple way to create a polygon with any number of sides. As soon as you activate this command, a command bar pops up. Now, click in the graphics window to define the center of the polygon. As you move the cursor away from the center, you will see a preview of the polygon. To change the number of sides of the polygon, just click in the **Sides** field on the command bar and type a new number. Next, press the ENTER key to update the preview. You will notice that

Sketch Techniques

there are two icons available on the command bar: **By Vertex** and **By Midpoint**. If you select the **By Vertex** icon, a vertex of the polygon will be attached to the cursor. If you select the **By Midpoint** icon, the cursor will be on one of the flat sides of the polygon. Next, click in the window to define the size and angle of the polygon. You can also define the size and angle of the polygon by entering values in the **Distance** and **Angle** fields on the command bar. After creating a polygon, you will notice that a dashed circle is created touching its vertices. You can change the polygon size by changing the size of this circle.

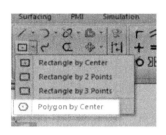 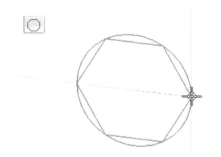 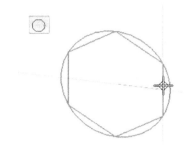

The Circle by Center Point command

This command is the common way to draw a circle. Activate this command (click **Home > Draw > Circle by Center Point** on the ribbon) and click to locate the center of the circle. Next, move the cursor, and then click again to define the diameter of the circle.

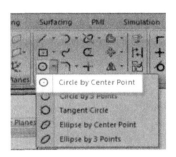 

The Circle by 3 Points command

This command creates a circle by using three points. Activate this command and the select three points from the graphics window. You can also select existing points from the sketch geometry. The first two points define the location of the circle and the third point defines its diameter.

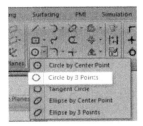 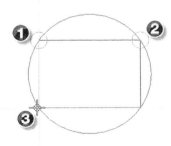

Sketch Techniques

The Tangent Circle command

This command creates a circle by using two tangent points. Activate this command and select two lines; a circle will be drawn tangent to them.

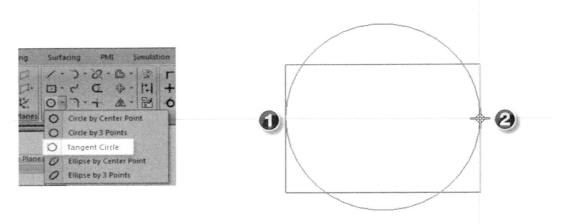

The Ellipse by Center Point command

This command creates an ellipse using a center point, and major and minor axes. Activate this command and click to define the center of the ellipse. As you move the cursor away from the center, you will notice that an axis is displayed. This can be either the major or minor axis of the ellipse. When you click to place it, a preview of the ellipse appears and you can define the other axis. Click to define the other axis; the ellipse will be drawn.

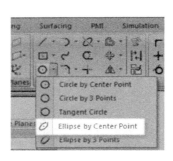 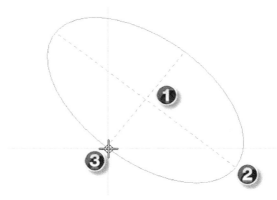

The Ellipse by 3 Points command

This command creates an ellipse by using three points. The first two points define the location and angle of the first axis of the ellipse. The third point defines the second axis of the ellipse.

Sketch Techniques

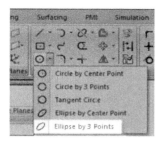 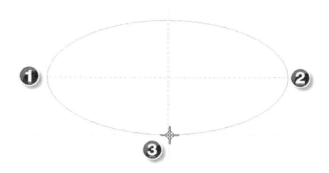

The Curve command

This command creates a smooth B-spline curve along the selected points. B-Splines are non-uniform curves which are used to create irregular shapes. You can select points or press the left mouse button and drag to create a curve.

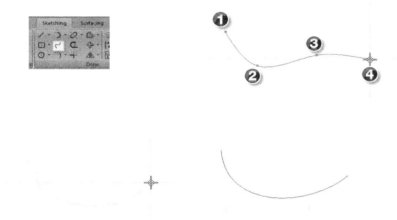

You also use the **Close Curve** option to create a closed curve.

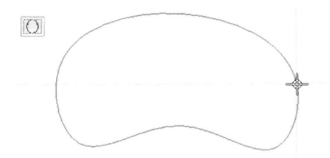

Press Esc to deactivate this command, and then select curve; you will notice that control vertices are displayed on the curve. Click and drag the control vertices to edit the curve shape. You can use the **Add/Remove points** option on the command bar to add more points or remove points from the curve.

Sketch Techniques

The Smart Dimension command

It is generally considered a good practice to ensure that every sketch you create is fully-constrained before moving on to create features. The term, 'fully-constrained' means that the sketch has a definite shape and size. You can fully-constrain a sketch by using dimensions and relations. You can add dimensions to a sketch by using the **Smart Dimension** command. You can use this command to add all types of dimensions such as length, angle, and diameter and so on. This command creates a dimension based on the geometry you select. For instance, to dimension a circle, activate the **Smart Dimension** command, and then click on the circle. Next, move the cursor and click again to position the dimension; you will notice that a box pops up. You can type-in a value in this box, and then press Enter to update the dimension.

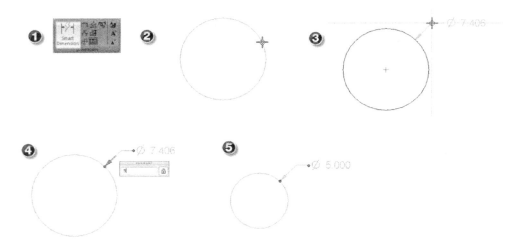

If you click a line, this command automatically creates a linear dimension. Click once more to position the dimension, and then type-in a value and press Enter; the dimension will be updated.

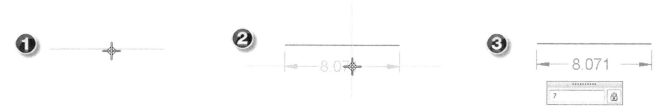

You can use the **Angle** option on the **Smart Dimension** command bar to add an angle dimension.

Sketch Techniques

The Distance Between command

This command creates a linear dimension between two points. Activate this command and select the **Horizontal/Vertical** option on the command bar. Select the end points of a line and move the cursor to establish a vertical or horizontal dimension.

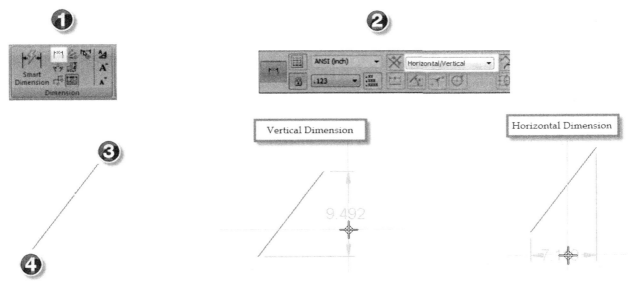

If you want the true length of the line, select the **By 2 Points** option on the command bar. Next, select the end points of a line, and the move the cursor and position the dimension. Type-in a value in the box and press Enter to update the dimension.

Sketch Techniques

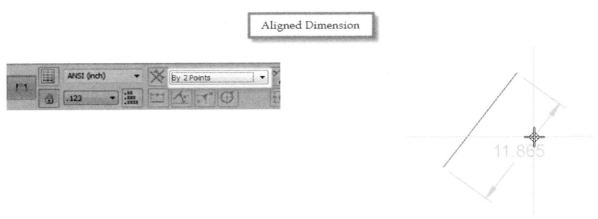

The Angle Between command

This command creates an angle dimension between two selected elements. Activate this command and select the elements. Next, move the cursor and position the dimension. Type-in a value and press Enter to update it.

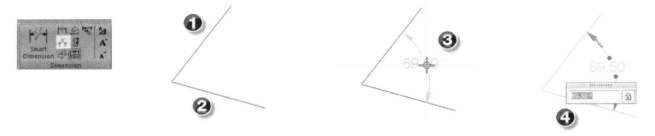

Driving Vs Driven dimensions

When creating sketches for a part, Solid Edge will not allow you to over-constrain the geometry. The term 'over-constrain' means adding more dimensions than required. The following figure shows a fully constrained sketch. If you add another dimension to this sketch (e.g. diagonal dimension), it appears in blue color. This type of dimension is a driven dimension. You cannot double-click and edit this dimension because it is redundant.

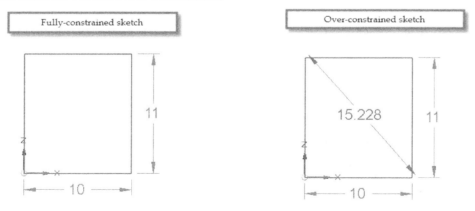

The sketch geometry is already defined by existing driving dimensions (dimensions in red color). Driving dimensions are so named because they drive the geometry of the sketch. Double-clicking one of the driving dimensions and changing the value will change the geometry of the sketch. For example,

Sketch Techniques

if you change the value of the width the driven dimension along the diagonal updates, automatically. Also, note that the dimensions which are initially created will be driving dimensions, whereas the dimensions created after fully defining the sketch are driven dimensions.

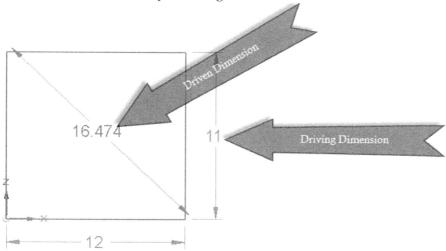

IntelliSketch Auto-Dimensions

Solid Edge provides you with an option to create dimensions, automatically. You can do it using the **IntelliSketch Options** dialog box. Click **Sketching > IntelliSketch > IntelliSketch Options** to activate this dialog box. On this dialog box, select the **Auto-Dimension** tab, and then select the **Automatically create dimensions for new geometry** option.

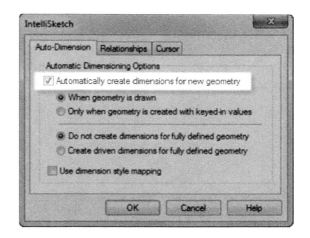

Also, there are other options to define the conditions to create automatic dimensions. These options are self-explanatory. Click **OK** after defining the settings in this dialog box.

Geometric Relations

Geometric Relations are used to control the shape of a sketch by establishing relationships between the sketch elements. These geometric relations are available on the **Relate** panel of the **Home** tab and are explained next.

Sketch Techniques

Connect
This relation connects a point to another point or element. Activate this button, and then select two points; the selected points will be connected.

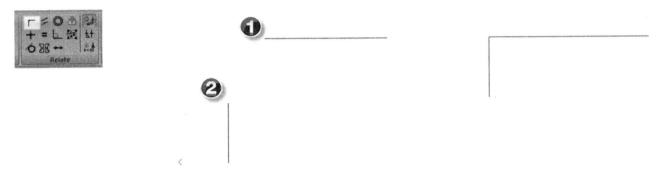

Parallel
This relation makes two lines parallel to each other. Activate this button, and then select two lines from the sketch; the first line is made parallel to the second line.

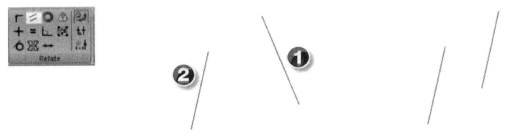

Concentric
This relation makes the center points of arcs, circles or ellipses coincident. Activate this button and select a circle or arc from the sketch. Select another circle or arc. The first circle/arc will be concentric with the second circle/arc.

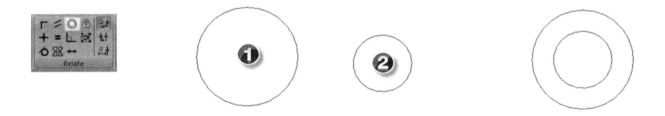

Lock
This relation locks a sketch element or dimension so that it cannot be moved or modified. Activate this button and select an element or dimension; it will be locked at its current position. Also, you cannot change the shape and size of the element.

Sketch Techniques

Horizontal/Vertical

This relation makes a line horizontal or vertical. The lines positioned at an angle below 45-degrees will be made horizontal. The lines positioned at an angle above 45-degrees will be made vertical. You can also make two points horizontally or vertically aligned.

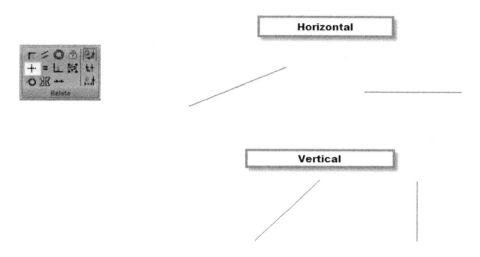

Equal

This relation makes two objects equal. For example, if you select two circles, the diameter of the selected circles will become equal. If you select two lines, the length of the two lines will be equal.

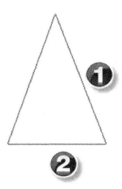
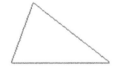

Sketch Techniques

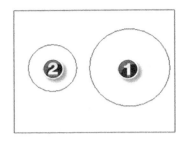 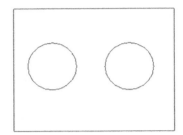

Perpendicular

This relation makes two lines perpendicular to each other. Activate this button and select two lines from the sketch. The first line will be made perpendicular to the second line.

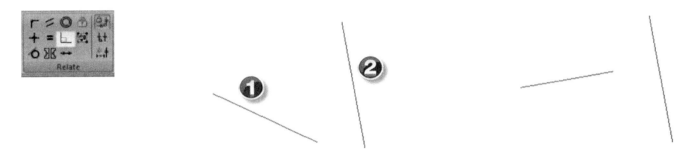

Rigid Set

This relation makes the selected objects act as a single unit. Activate this button and select two or more objects from the sketch. Click the green check on the command bar. The selected objects will be made into a rigid set.

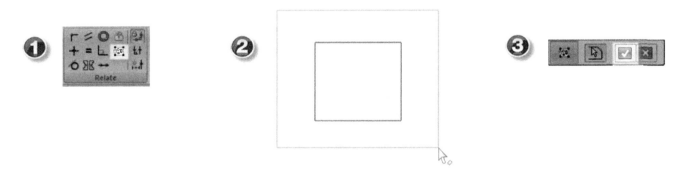

Now, click and drag anyone of the object from the rigid set. You will notice that entire set will be dragged.

Sketch Techniques

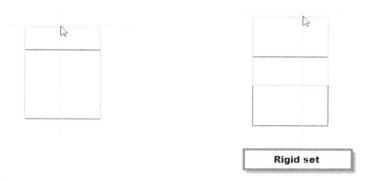

Tangent

This relation makes an arc, circle, or line tangent to another arc or circle. Activate this button and select a circle, arc, or line. Select another circle, arc, or line. The first object will be tangent to the second object.

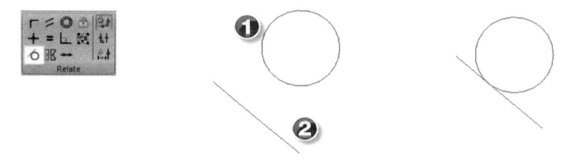

You can also make a curve continuous with another curve or arc using the **Tangent** relation.

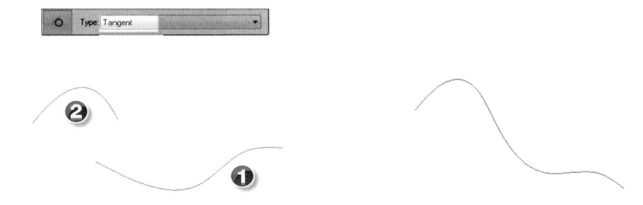

Sketch Techniques

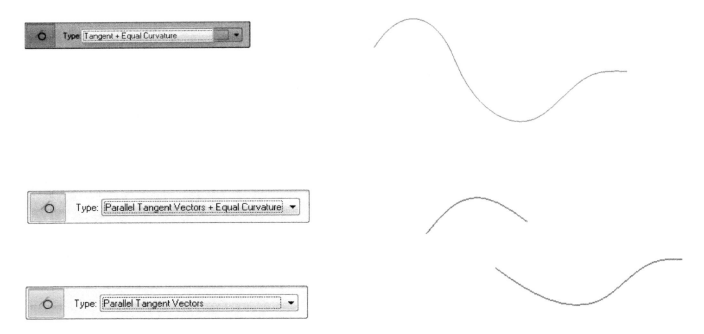

Symmetric

This relation makes two objects symmetric about a line. The objects will have same size, position and orientation about a line. Activate this button and select the symmetry line. Select two objects from the sketch. They will be made symmetric about the selected line.

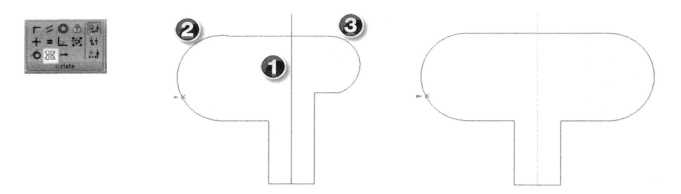

Collinear

This relation forces a line to be collinear to another line. The lines are not required to touch each other.

Sketch Techniques

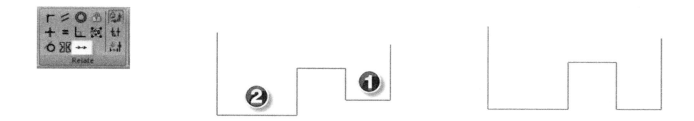

Maintain Relationships

Relations can also be applied automatically by activating the **Maintain Relationships** command. Activate or deactivate **Maintain Relationships** by picking the **Maintain Relationships** button on the **Relate** panel. With this command on, relations are applied automatically when the sketch elements are created. You can define which relations to apply automatically by using the **IntelliSketch Options** dialog box. Click **Sketching > IntelliSketch > IntelliSketch Options**, and then select the **Relationships** tab on the **IntelliSketch Options** dialog box. In this tab, select the relations to be created while sketching elements, and then click **OK**.

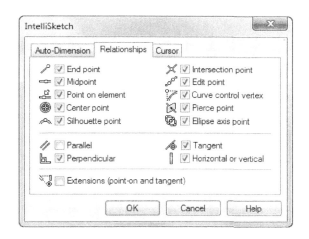

Relationship Handles

As relations are created, they can be viewed using the **Relationship Handles** button located on the **Relate** panel. When dealing with complicated sketches involving numerous relations, you can deactivate this button to turn off all relationship handles.

Sketch Techniques

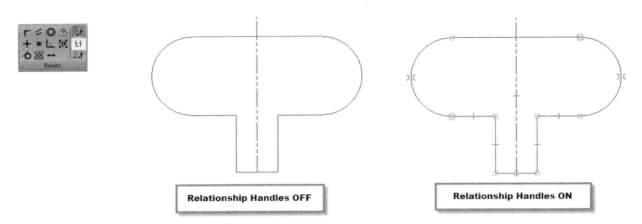

Relationship Assistant

In addition to the **Smart Dimension** command and other geometric relations, Solid Edge provides you with the **Relationship Assistant** command. This command automatically applies relations and dimensions to fully-constrain a sketch. To activate this command, click **Home > Relate > Relationship Assistant** on the ribbon. A command bar pops up. Select the **Options** icon on the command bar to open the **Relationship Assistant** dialog box. On this dialog box, click the **Geometry** tab, and then select the relations to be applied. Similarly, click the **Dimension** tab and select the dimensions to be applied. You can also select the **Dimension Scheme** such as **Stack**, **Chain**, and **Coordinate**. Click **OK** on the **Relationship Assistant** dialog box and select the objects to apply relations and dimensions. Next, click the green check on the command bar and then select the horizontal and vertical dimension origins. The relations and dimensions will be created, automatically.

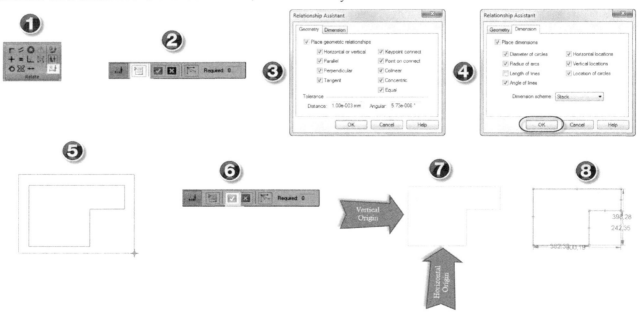

Sketch Techniques

The Construction command

This command converts a sketch element into a construction element. Construction elements are reference elements which support you to create a sketch of desired shape and size. Activate the **Construction** command from the **Draw** panel and click on a sketch element. The selected element will be converted to a construction element. You can also convert back the construction element to a sketch element by activating this command and selecting it.

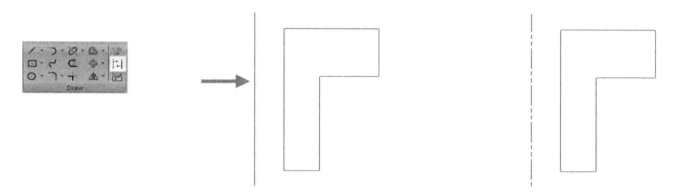

The Symmetric Diameter command

This command is very useful while creating a sketch for a revolved feature. It creates a dimension by measuring the distance between two lines or points, and then multiplying it by two. Activate this command from the **Dimension** panel, and then select the dimension origin. You need to ensure that the dimension origin it locked at its location. Now, select the line upto which the dimension is to be created. Click to position the dimension, and then change the value.

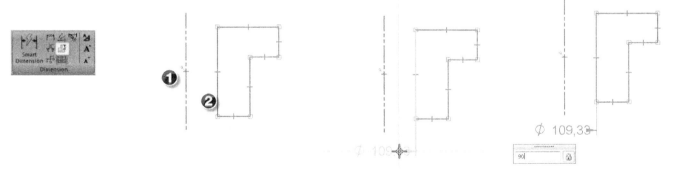

The Fillet command

This command rounds a sharp corner created by intersection of two lines, arcs, circles, and rectangle or polygon vertices. Activate this command from the **Draw** panel and select the elements' ends to be filleted. Type-in a radius value in the **Radius** box of the command bar and press Enter. The elements to be filleted are not required to form an intersection.

Sketch Techniques

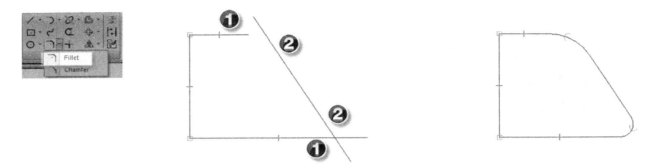

You can also drag the cursor across the elements to fillet the corner.

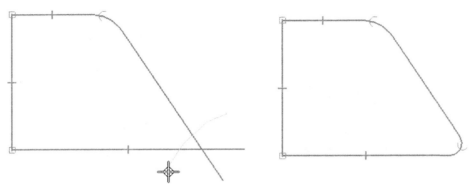

By default, the elements are automatically trimmed or extended to meet the end of the new fillet radius. You can use the **No Trim** option on the command bar, if you do not want to trim or extend the elements as necessary.

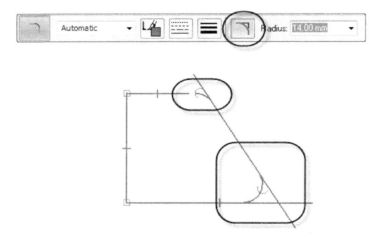

The Chamfer command

This command replaces a sharp corner with an angled line. Activate this command from the **Fillet** drop-down on the **Draw** panel and select the elements' ends to be chamfered. Type-in the chamfer angle in the **Angle** box on the command bar and press Enter. Next, move the cursor and click to create the chamfer. Instead, you can also use **Setback A** and **Setback B** on the command bar to define the chamfer size.

36

Sketch Techniques

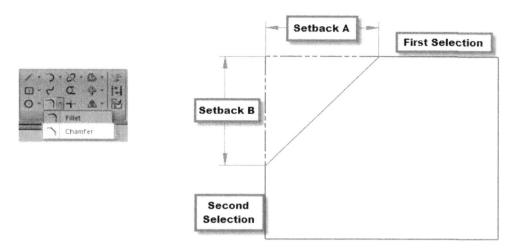

The Split command

This command splits an element into two elements. Activate this command from the **Draw** panel and click the element to split. Next, select a split point on the element. In case of a circle or ellipse, you must select two split points.

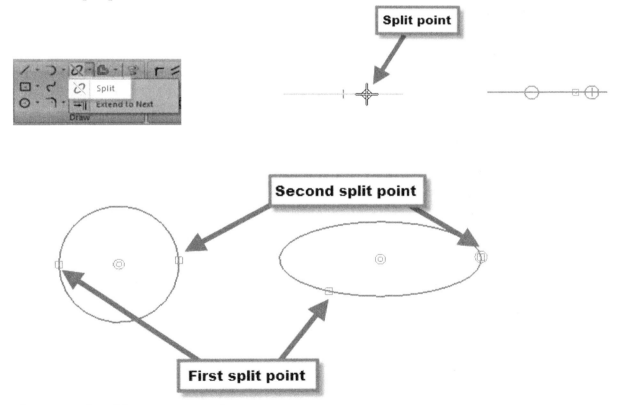

The Extend to Next command

This command extends elements such as lines, arcs, and curves until they intersect another element called a boundary edge. Activate this command from the **Split** drop-down on the **Draw** panel and click on the element to extend. It will extend upto the next element.

Sketch Techniques

The Trim command

This command trims the end of an element back to the intersection of another element. Activate this command from the **Draw** panel and select the element or elements to trim. You can also drag the cursor across the elements to trim.

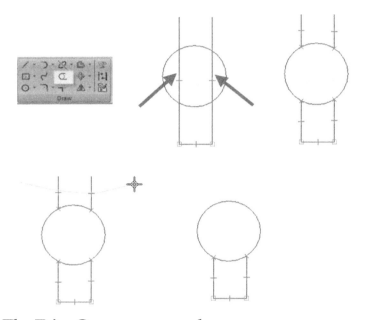

The Trim Corner command

This command trims and extends elements to form a corner. Activate this command from the **Draw** panel and select two intersecting elements. The elements will be trimmed and extended to form a closed corner.

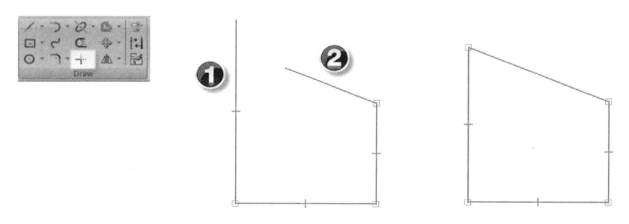

Sketch Techniques

The Offset command

This command creates a parallel copy of a selected element or chain of elements. Activate this command from the **Draw** panel and select an element or chain of elements to offset. You can use the **Single** or **Chain** option from the **Select** drop-down on the command bar to select a single element or chain of elements. After selecting the element, type-in a value in the **Distance** field on the command bar and click the green check. Click to define the side of the offset. The parallel copy of the elements will be created and you can click again to create another parallel copy. Click the right mouse button to deactivate this command after creating parallel copies.

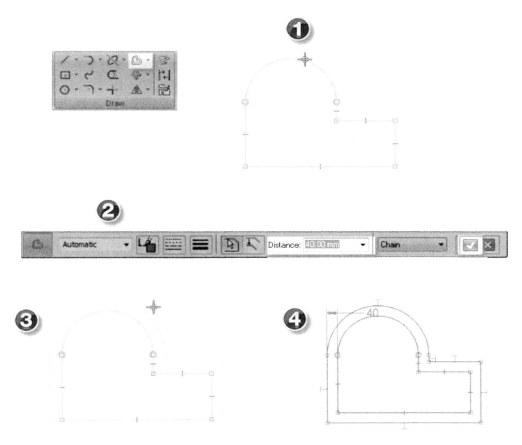

The Symmetric Offset command

This command creates a parallel copy on both sides of a selected element or chain of elements. It is helpful while creating a sketch slot. Activate this command from the **Offset** drop-down on the **Draw** panel. The **Symmetric Offset Options** dialog box pops ups on the screen.

Sketch Techniques

 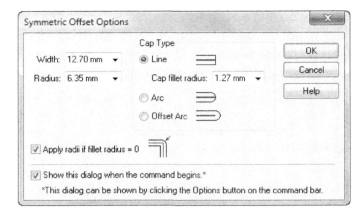

The options on this dialog are explained below. Set the required options on the dialog box and click **OK**. Next, select an open sketch and click the green check to create the symmetric offset.

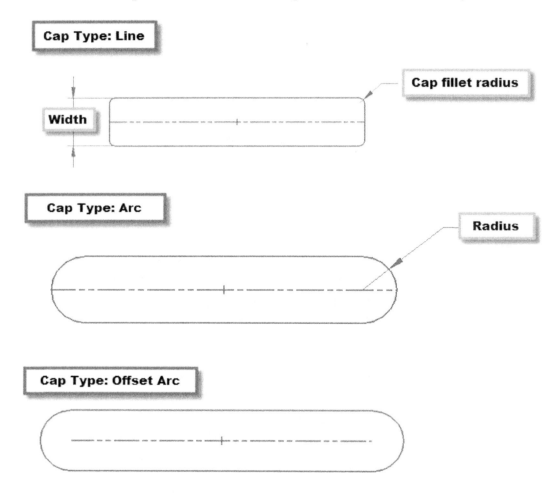

The Move command

This command relocates one or more elements from one position in the sketch to any other position you specify. Activate this command from the **Draw** panel, and then click on the elements to move. Next, you must select a base point and click at a new location.

Sketch Techniques

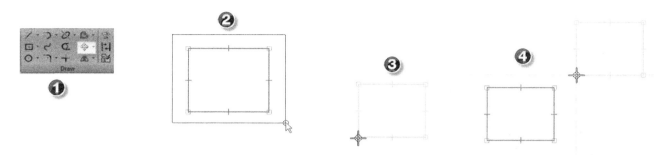

The **Copy** option on the **Move** command bar can be used to copy and move the selected elements.

The Rotate command

This command rotates the selected elements to any position. Activate this command from the **Draw** panel, and then select the elements to rotate. Next, you must define a base point and a point to rotate from. Move the cursor and click to define the rotation angle. You can use the **Copy** option on the command bar to copy and rotate the selected elements.

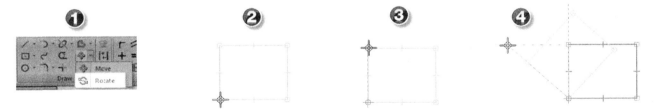

The Mirror command

This command creates a mirror image of the selected elements. You have the option to retain or delete the original elements. Activate this command from the **Draw** panel, and then select the elements to mirror. Next, you have to create two points defining the mirror-line. To retain the original elements, you must ensure that the **Copy** option is active on the command bar.

Sketch Techniques

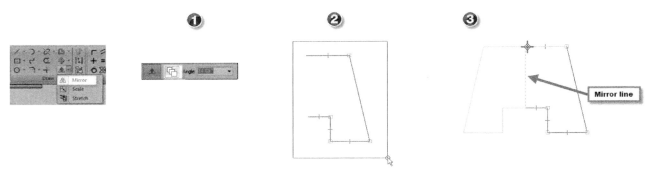

The Scale command

This command increases or decreases the size of elements in a sketch. Activate this command from the **Mirror** drop-down of **Draw** panel, and then select the elements to scale. After selecting the elements, you must select a base point. You can then scale the size of the selected elements by moving the cursor or entering a scale value in the **Scale** field on the command bar.

The Stretch command

This command moves a portion of the sketch while still preserving other parts of it. Activate this command from the **Mirror** drop-down on the **Draw** panel, and then drag a box to select the elements to be stretched. Select a base point and move the cursor to stretch the selected elements.

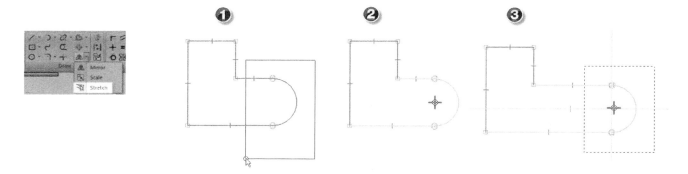

Examples

Example 1 (Millimetres)

In this example, you will draw the sketch shown below.

Sketch Techniques

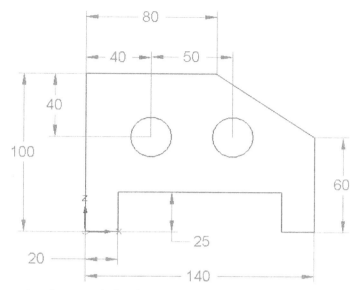

1. Start **Solid Edge ST6** by clicking the **Solid Edge ST6** icon on your desktop.
2. On the initial screen, click **ISO Part**; a new part file is opened.

3. To start a new sketch, click **Home > Draw > Line** on the ribbon.
4. Place the mouse cursor on the coordinate system; the XZ plane gets highlighted.
5. Click the lock icon on the XZ plane to lock the plane.
6. Click the **Sketch View** icon located at the bottom of the window; this orients the sketch plane normal to the screen.

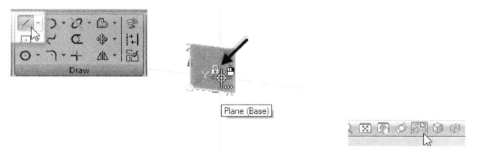

7. Click on the origin point to define the first point of the line.
8. Create a closed loop by selecting points in the sequence, as shown below.

Sketch Techniques

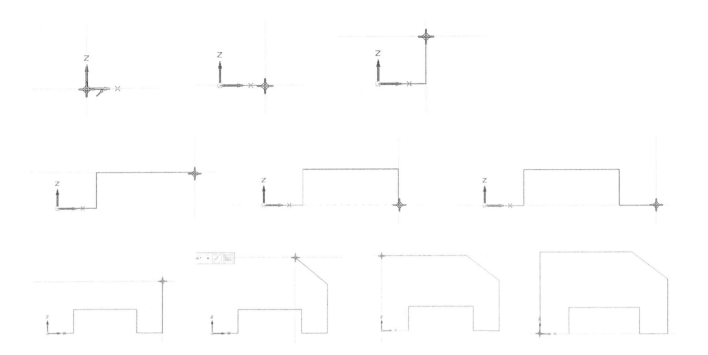

9. Click **Home > Relate > Collinear** on the ribbon and click on the two horizontal lines at the bottom; they become collinear.

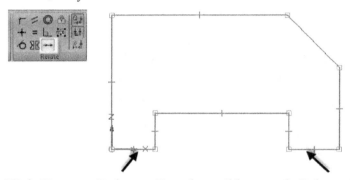

10. Click **Home > Relate > Equal** on ribbon and click on the two horizontal lines at the bottom; they become equal in length.

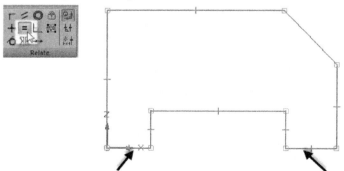

11. Select the small vertical lines to make their lengths equal.

Sketch Techniques

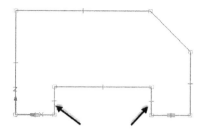

12. Click **Home > Dimension > Smart Dimension** on the ribbon and click on the lower left horizontal line. Move the mouse cursor downward and click to locate the dimension.
13. Type-in **20** in the dimension box and press Enter.

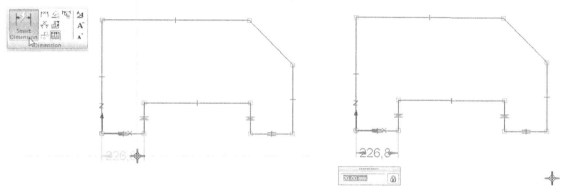

14. Click on the small vertical line located at the left side. Move the mouse cursor towards right and click to position the dimension.
15. Type-in **25** in the dimension box and press Enter.

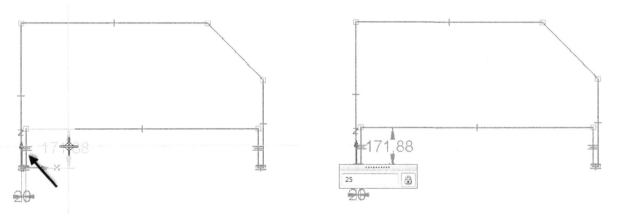

16. Create other dimensions in the sequence, shown below.

45

Sketch Techniques

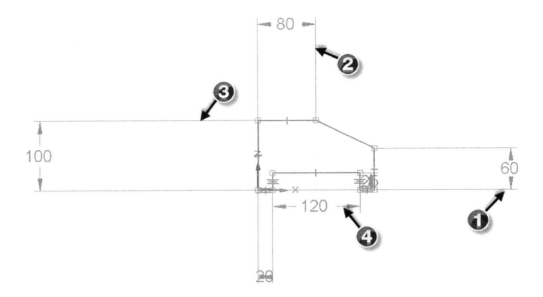

17. On any dimension, click on the portion between the dimension value and the arrow. Press the left mouse button and drag the dimension near to the sketch.

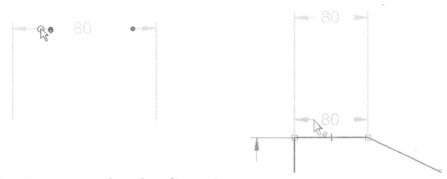

18. Likewise, arrange the other dimensions.

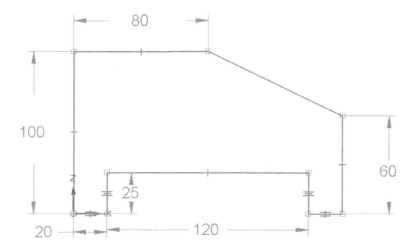

Sketch Techniques

19. On the ribbon, click **Home > Draw > Circle by Center Point**. Click inside the sketch region to define the center point of the circle. Move the mouse cursor and click to define the diameter. Likewise, create another circle.

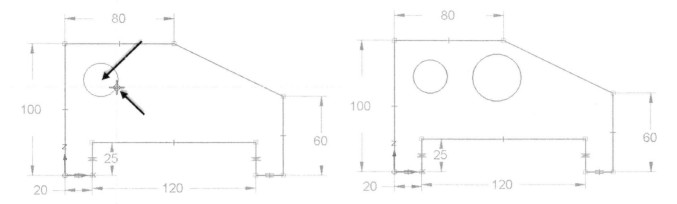

20. On the ribbon, click **Home > Relate > Horizontal/Vertical**. Click on the center points of the two circles to make them horizontally aligned.

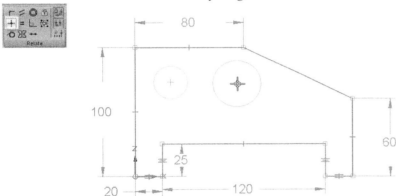

21. On the ribbon, click **Home > Relate > Equal** and click on the two circles. The diameters of the circles will become equal.

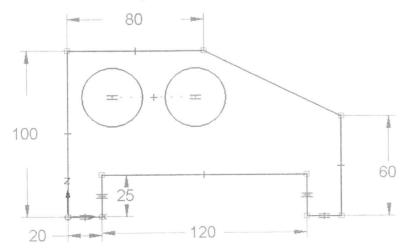

Sketch Techniques

22. Activate the **Smart Dimension** command and click on anyone of the circles. Move the mouse cursor and click to position the dimension. Type 25 in the dimension box and press Enter.

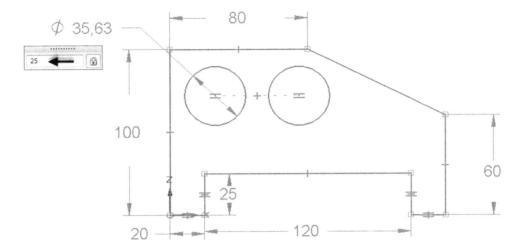

23. Create other dimensions between the circles and the adjacent lines, shown below.

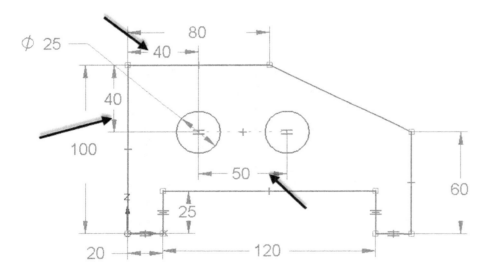

24. Click the Lock icon on the right-side to unlock the sketch plane.

25. Click the **Save** icon on the **Quick Access Toolbar**. Define the location and file name and click **Save** to save the part file.

26. Click **Close Window** on the top right corner to close the part file.

Sketch Techniques

Example 2 (Inches)

In this example, you will draw the sketch shown below.

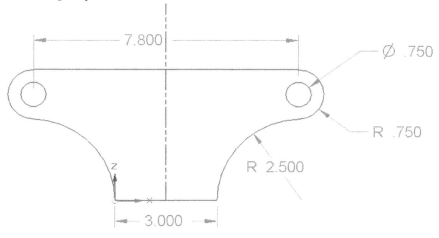

1. Start **Solid Edge ST6** by clicking the **Solid Edge ST6** icon on your desktop.
2. On the **Quick Access Toolbar**, click the **New** icon; the **New** dialog box is opened.

3. On the **New** dialog box, click the **More** tab and select the **ansi part.par** template. Click **OK** to start a new part file.

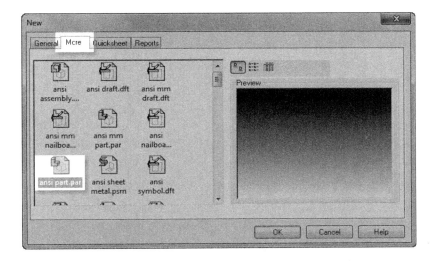

Sketch Techniques

4. To start a new sketch, click **Home > Draw > Line** on the ribbon.
5. Place the mouse cursor on the coordinate system; the XZ plane gets highlighted and a mouse icon appears.
6. Click the right mouse button to display the **QuickPick** box.
7. On the **QuickPick** box select the XY plane.

8. On your keyboard, press the F3 key to lock the sketch plane.
9. Click the **Sketch View** icon located at the bottom of the window; this orients the sketch plane normal to the screen.
10. Click on the origin point to define the first point of the line. Move the mouse cursor horizontally and click to draw a line.

11. On the **Line** command bar, click the **Arc** icon.
12. Take the mouse cursor to the end point of the line and move it upwards right.
13. Click to create the arc.

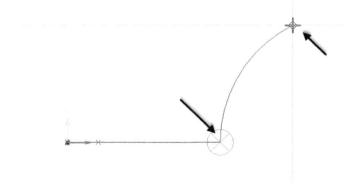

14. Again, click the **Arc** icon the command bar.
15. Take the mouse cursor to the end point of the arc and move it upwards right.
16. Move the cursor toward left and click when a vertical dotted line appears, as shown below.

Sketch Techniques

17. Move the mouse cursor toward left and click to create a horizontal line.
18. Click the **Arc** icon the command bar. Take the mouse cursor to the end point of the arc and move it downward left.
19. Move the cursor toward right and click when a vertical dotted line appears, as shown below.

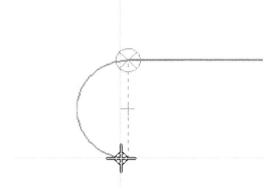

20. Click the **Arc** icon on the command bar. Move the mouse cursor toward downward right and click on the origin to close the sketch.

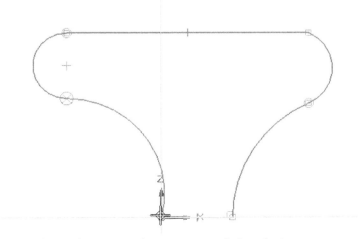

21. Click the right mouse button to end the chain.

51

Sketch Techniques

22. Click on the midpoint of the lower horizontal line. Move the mouse cursor vertically up and click to create a vertical line.

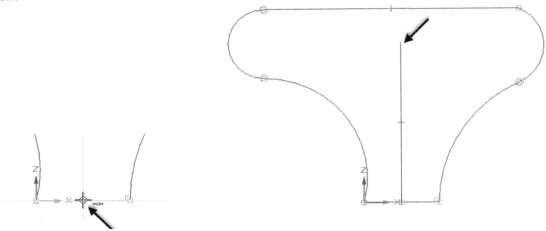

23. On the ribbon, click **Home > Draw > Construction**. Click on the vertical line located at the center. The line is converted into a construction element.

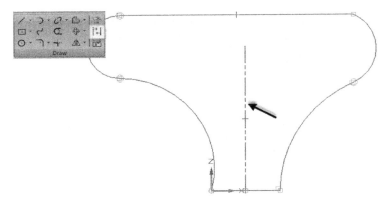

24. Activate the **Circle by Center Point** command and draw a circle on the right side of the construction line.
25. On the ribbon, click **Home > Relate > Concentric.** Click on the circle and the small arc. The circle and arc are made concentric.

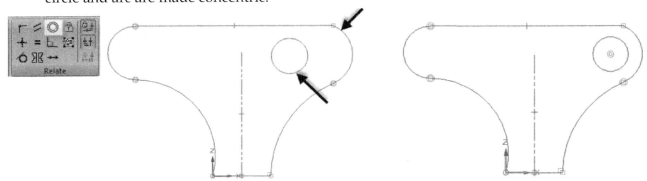

26. Likewise, create another circle concentric to the small arc located on the left side of the construction line.

Sketch Techniques

27. On the ribbon, click **Home > Relate > Symmetric**. Click on the construction line located at the center. The line will act as a symmetry line.
28. Click on the large arcs on both sides of the symmetry line. The arcs are made symmetric about the construction line.
29. Likewise, make the small arcs and circles symmetric about the construction line.

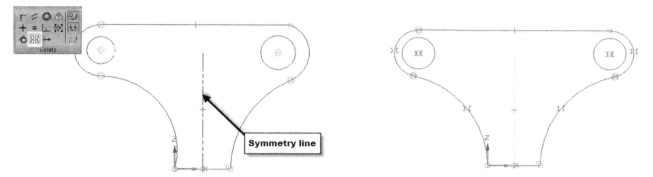

30. Activate the **Smart Dimension** command and apply dimensions to the sketch in the sequence, as shown below.

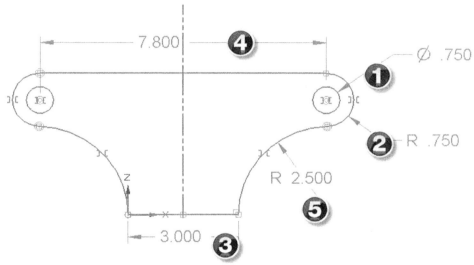

31. On the status bar, click the **Fit** icon to fit the drawing in the graphics window.
32. To save the file, click **Application Menu > Save**. Define the location and file name and click **Save** to save the part file.

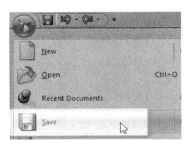

33. To close the file, click **Application Menu > Close**.

Sketch Techniques

Example 3 (Millimetres)

In this example, you will draw the sketch shown below.

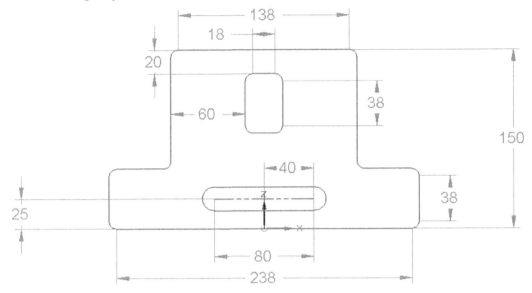

1. Start **Solid Edge ST6** by clicking the **Solid Edge ST6** icon on your desktop.
2. To start a new part file click **Application Menu > New > ISO Part**.

3. To start sketching, activate the **Line** command and click on the XZ plane. Press F3 to lock the sketch plane.
4. Click the **Sketch View** icon located at the bottom of the window; this orients the sketch plane normal to the screen.
5. Place the mouse cursor on the origin and move it toward left; a dotted line appears.

6. Click to define the first point. Move the mouse cursor horizontally toward right and click to define the second point.
7. Create a closed loop by clicking points in the sequence shown below.

Sketch Techniques

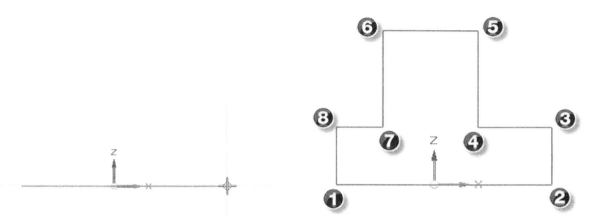

8. Click **Home > Relate > Symmetric** on the ribbon. Click on the Z axis to define the symmetric axis.
9. Click on the small vertical lines to make them symmetric.
10. Click on the other vertical lines to make them symmetric.

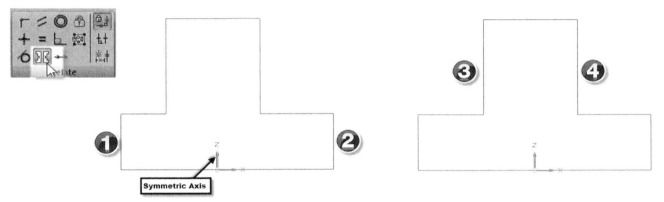

11. On the ribbon, click **Home > Relate > Collinear**. Click on the lower horizontal line and X-axis to make them collinear.
12. Activate the **Smart Dimension** command and apply dimensions in the sequence shown below.

Sketch Techniques

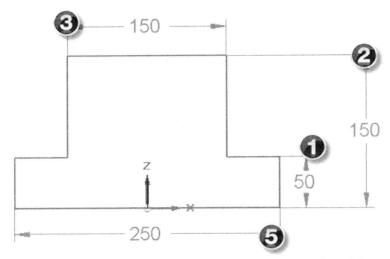

13. Click **Home > Draw > Rectangle by Center** on the ribbon. Click in the sketch region to define the center of the rectangle.
14. Move the mouse cursor toward top right and click to define the corner of the rectangle.

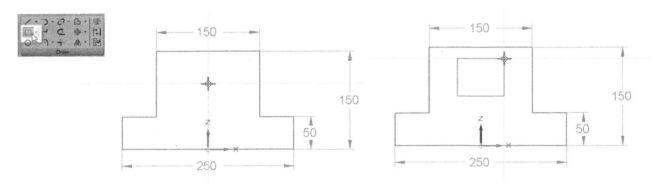

15. Activate the **Line** command and draw a horizontal line inside the loop.

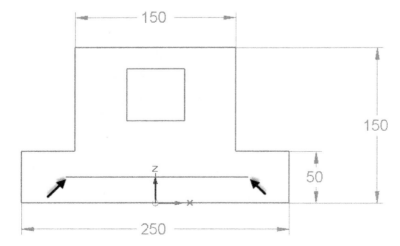

16. Activate the **Smart Dimension** command and apply dimensions in the sequence shown below.

Sketch Techniques

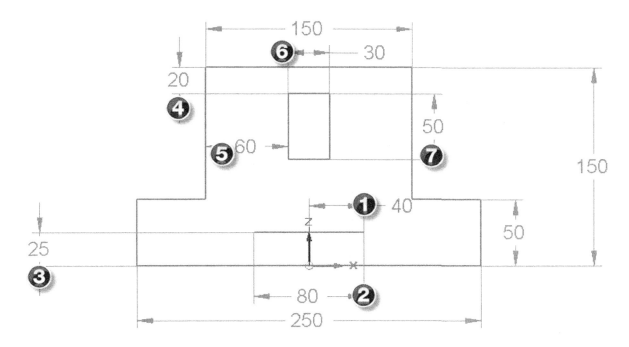

17. Click **Home > Draw > Offset > Symmetric Offset** on the ribbon; the **Symmetric Offset Options** dialog box pops up.

 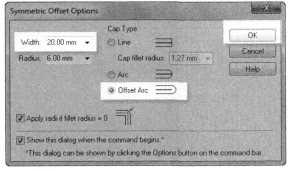

18. On this dialog box, type-in 20 in the **Width** box and select the **Offset Arc** option. Click **OK** to close the dialog box.
19. Select the horizontal line and click the green check on the command bar.

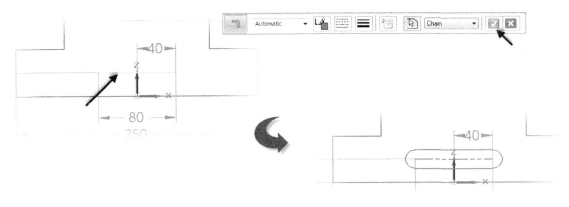

57

Sketch Techniques

20. Click **Home > Draw > Fillet** on the ribbon. Type-in 6 in the **Radius** box on the command bar.
21. Create fillets by clicking on lines of the sketch.

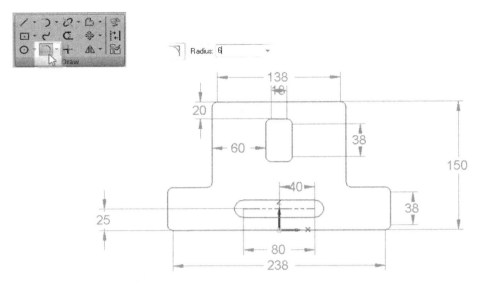

22. Save and close the file.

Questions

1. What is the procedure to create sketches in Synchronous mode?
2. List any two sketch *Relationships* in Solid Edge.
3. Which command orients the sketch normal to the screen?
4. What is the procedure to create sketches in Ordered mode?
5. Which command allows you to automatically apply dimensions to a sketch?
6. Describe the two methods to create ellipses.
7. How do you define the shape and size of a sketch?
8. How to create a tangent arc using the **Line** command?
9. Which command is used to apply different types of dimensions to a sketch?
10. List any two commands to the create circles?

Sketch Techniques

Exercises
Exercise 1

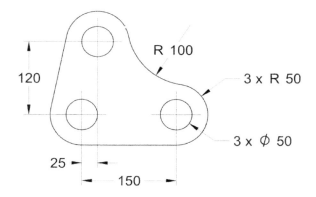

Exercise 2

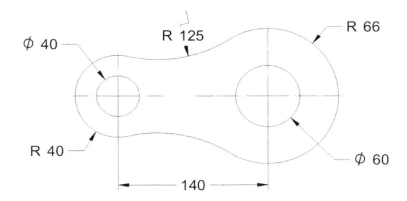

Exercise 3

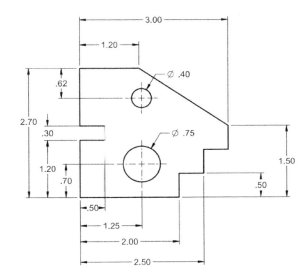

Sketch Techniques

Chapter 3: Extrude and Revolve Features

This chapter covers the methods and commands to create extrude and revolved features.

The topics covered in this chapter are:

- Constructing *Extrude* and *Revolve* features in the Part environment (Synchronous and Ordered mode)
- Creating Reference Planes
- Additional Options in the *Extrude* and *Revolve* commands

Extrude Features (Synchronous)

Extrude is the process of taking a two-dimensional profile and converting it into 3D by giving it some thickness. A simple example of this would be taking a circle and converting it into a cylinder. Once you have created a sketch profile or profiles you want to *Extrude*, click inside the sketch to display a two-sided arrow. Click the arrow and move the cursor. You will notice that a thickness is added to the sketch profile. Use the **Symmetric** option on the command bar, if you want to add thickness to both sides of the sketch. Next, type-in a value in the box that appears on the extrusion, and then press Enter to create the *Extrude* feature.

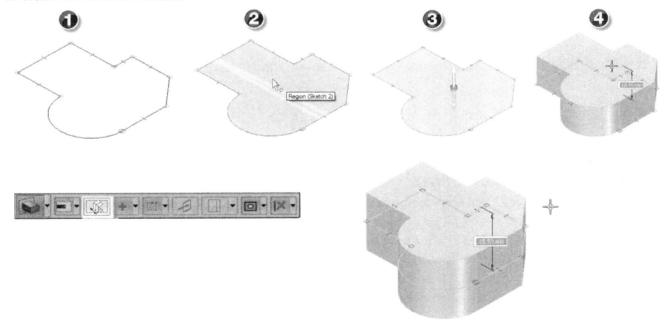

Extrude Features (Ordered)

The process of creating *Extrude* features in the **Ordered** mode is similar to **Synchronous**, but it includes few additional steps. Activate the **Extrude** command from the **Solids** panel on the ribbon. The **Extrude** command bar pops up on the screen. Select the **Select from Sketch** and **Chain** options on the command bar. Click on the sketch profile and click the green check on the command bar. Move the cursor upward or downward to add thickness to the sketch profile. Next, type-in a value in the **Distance** box on the command bar and press Enter to create the *Extrude* feature.

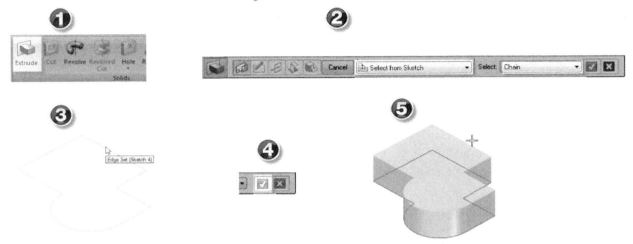

Use the **Symmetric Extent** option on the command bar to add equal thickness on both sides of the sketch. Use the **Non-Symmetric Extent** option to add separate thickness on either side of the sketch profile.

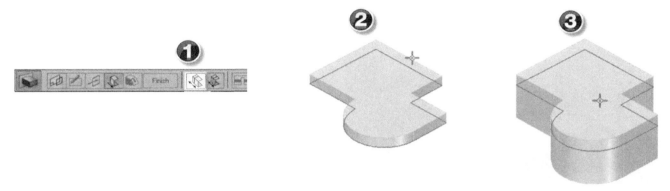

Revolve Features (Synchronous)

Revolve is the process of taking a two-dimensional profile and revolving it about a centerline to create a 3D geometry (shapes that are axially symmetric). While creating a sketch for the *Revolve* feature, it is important to think about the cross-sectional shape that will define the 3D geometry once it's revolved about an axis. For instance, the following geometry has a hole in the center. This could be created with a separate *Cut* or *Hole* feature. But in order to make that hole part of the *Revolve* feature, you need to sketch the axis of revolution so that it leaves a space between the profile and the axis.

Extrude and Revolve Features

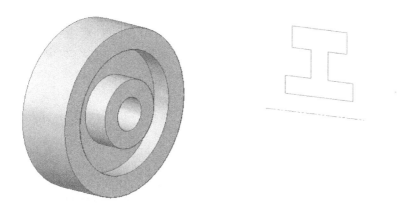

After completing the sketch, click inside the sketch region. The *Extrude Handle* appears on the sketch region. Activate the **Revolve** command from the command bar (click the down arrow next to the **Extrude** icon and select **Revolve**). You will notice that *Extrude Handle* is changed to *Revolve Handle* (a two-sided arrow with a torus and spear in the middle). Click the spear on the *Revolve Handle*, and drag and place it on the axis of revolution. Click the torus on the *Revolve Handle* and move the cursor to revolve the sketch. Type-in an angle value and press Enter to create the *Revolve* feature. Select **Finite > 360** on the command bar to revolve the sketch upto 360 degrees. You will notice that a live section is also created along with the *Revolve* feature. Uncheck the **Live Sections** option in the Pathfinder to hide it.

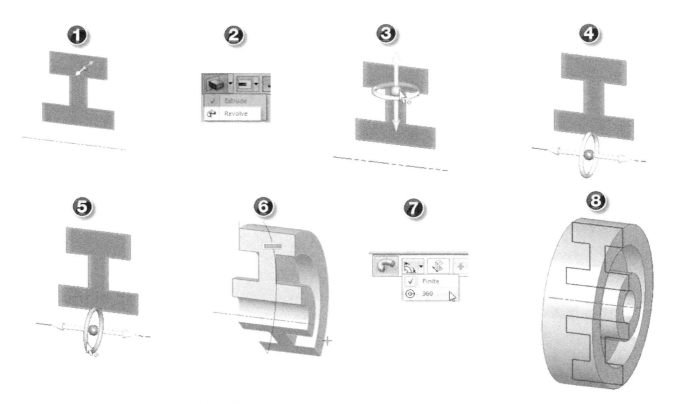

Revolve Features (Ordered)

The process of creating the *Revolve* feature in the **Ordered** mode is little bit different from **Synchronous**. First, you must activate the **Revolve** command (click **Home > Solids > Revolve** on the ribbon), and then select the sketching plane. Next, draw the cross-section and axis of revolution. Click **Home > Draw > Axis of Revolution** on the ribbon and select a line to define the axis of revolution. Close the sketch and type-in a value in the **Angle** field on the command bar (or) click the **Revolve 360** icon on the command bar to revolve upto 360 degrees. Next, click **Finish** to create the *Revolve* feature. Click **Cancel** to deactivate this command.

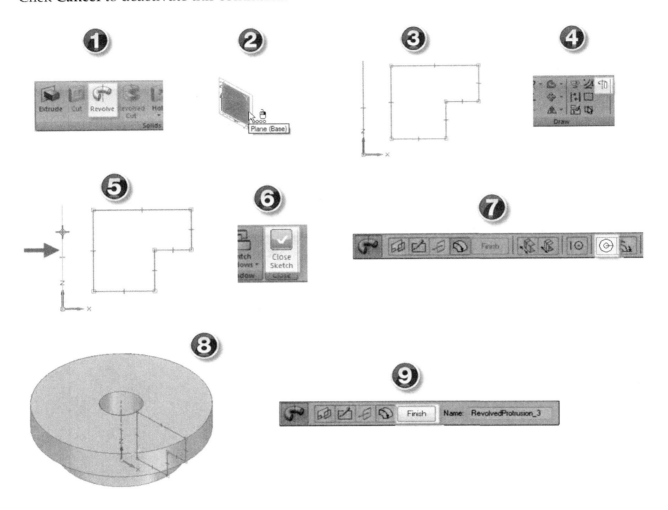

Creating Planes (Synchronous)

Each time you start a new part file, Solid Edge automatically creates default reference planes (Base Reference Planes) along with the default coordinate system. Planes and coordinate system make up a specific type of features in Solid Edge, known as Reference features. These features act as supports to your 3D geometry. In addition to the default reference features, you can create your own additional planes and coordinate systems too. Until now, you have known to create sketches on any of the default reference planes. If you want to create sketches and geometry at locations other than default reference planes, you can create new reference planes manually. You can do so by using the commands available in the **Planes** panel of the **Home** tab.

Extrude and Revolve Features

Coincident Plane

This command creates a reference plane, which is coincident with a selected face or plane. Activate this command (click **Home > Planes > Coincident Plane** on the ribbon) and click on a face. A plane coincident with the selected face will be placed. Also, the *Steering Wheel* tool appears on the plane.

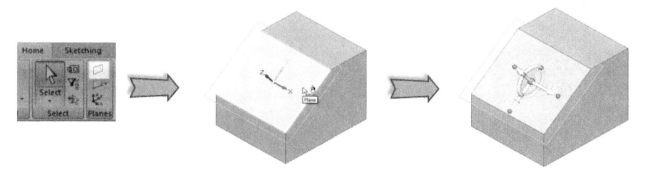

Click on any of the arrows of the *Steering Wheel* tool and drag the cursor to change the location of the plane.

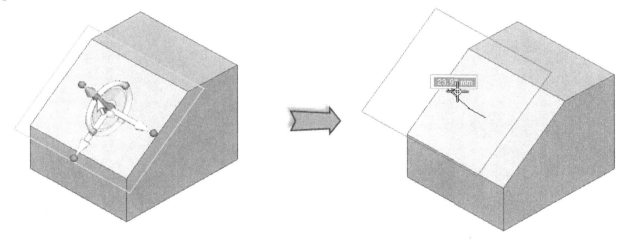

Click the torus of the *Steering Wheel* tool and drag the cursor to rotate the plane.

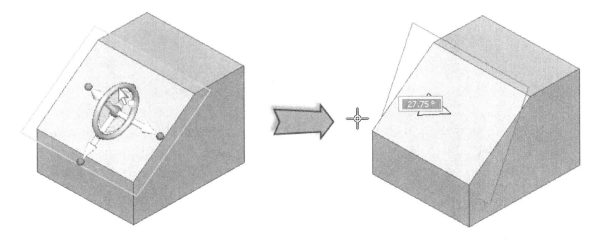

Normal to Curve

This command creates a reference plane which will be normal (perpendicular) to a line, curve, or edge. Activate this command (click **Home > Planes > More Planes > Normal to Curve** on the ribbon), and then select an edge, line, curve, arc, or circle. Drag the cursor and click on a point to define the location of the plane (or) type-in a value in the **Position** box (or) type-in a distance value in the **Distance** box and press Enter.

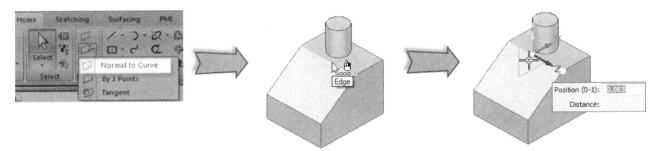

By 3 Points

This command creates a reference plane passing through three points. Activate this command (click **Home > Planes > More Planes > By 3 Points** on the ribbon), and then select three points from the model geometry. A plane will be placed passing through these points.

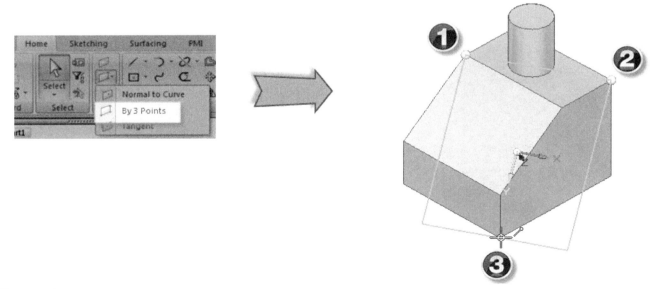

Tangent

This command creates a plane tangent to a curved face. Activate this command (click **Home > Planes > More Planes > Tangent** on the ribbon) and select a curved face. A plane tangent to the selected face appears. Drag the cursor and click to define the position of the tangent plane (or) type-in an angle value and press Enter.

Extrude and Revolve Features

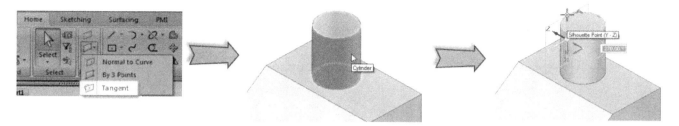

Coordinate System

This command creates a new coordinate system in addition to the default one. Activate this command (click **Home > Planes > Coordinate System** on the ribbon) and position the cursor on a point or face or line. Use the orientation keys, if you want to change the orientation of the coordinate system. For example, press F to flip the coordinate system about the z-axis. Press T to flip it about the x-axis. Press G to return to the default orientation. After orienting the coordinate system, click to define its location.

Creating Planes (Ordered)

The Ordered mode offers some additional methods to create reference planes.

Parallel

This command creates a reference plane, which will be parallel to a face or another plane. Activate this command (click **Home > Planes > More Planes > Parallel** on the ribbon) and select a flat face. Drag the cursor and click to define the location of the plane (or) type-in a value in the **Distance** box on the command bar and press Enter.

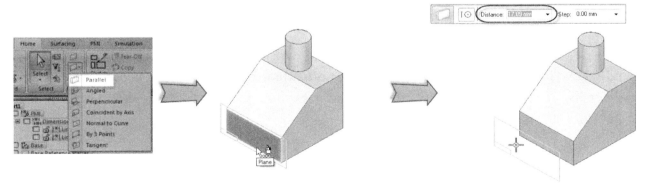

Angled

This command creates a plane, which will be positioned at an angle to a face or plane. Activate this command (click **Home > Planes > More Planes > Angled** on the ribbon) and select a flat face or plane. Next, select another face which acts as a base reference. Select a point to define the origin of the rotation axis, and then type-in a value in the **Angle** box on the command bar.

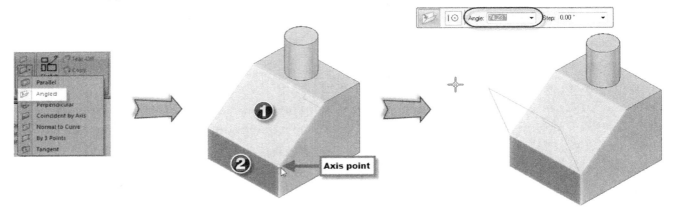

Perpendicular

This command creates a plane, which will be perpendicular to a face or plane. Activate this command (click **Home > Planes > More Planes > Perpendicular** on the ribbon) and select a flat face or plane. Next, select another face which acts as a base reference. Select a point to define the origin of the plane, and then click to specify the side of the plane.

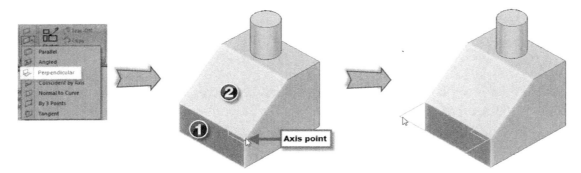

Coincident by Axis

This command creates a plane, which is coincident with a selected face or plane. Activate this command (click **Home > Planes > More Planes > Coincident by Axis** on the ribbon) and select a flat face or plane. Next, select a part edge to define the x-axis of the plane, and then select a point to define the x-axis origin.

Extrude and Revolve Features

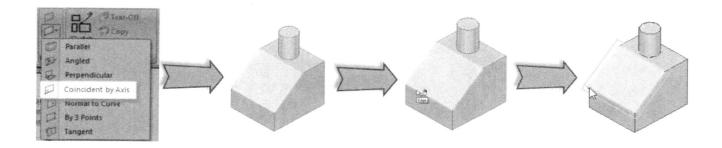

Additional options of the Extrude command

The **Extrude** command has some additional options to create a 3D geometry, complex features, and so on. These options are inactive by default and get active after you have created the first feature of the part.

Selection Type options

The **Selection Type** drop-down menu on the command bar has three options: **Single**, **Chain**, and **Face**. The **Single** option selects the individual elements of a sketch, whereas the **Chain** option selects the complete loop. The **Face** option selects the region enclosed by the sketch.

Include Internal Loops

This option is useful while working with a sketch having internal loops. If you select this option, the internal loops of the sketch will be detected while creating the *Extrude* feature.

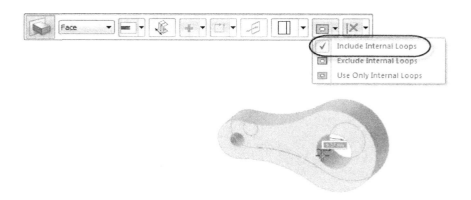

Exclude Internal Loops

This option ignores the internal loops of a sketch.

Extrude and Revolve Features

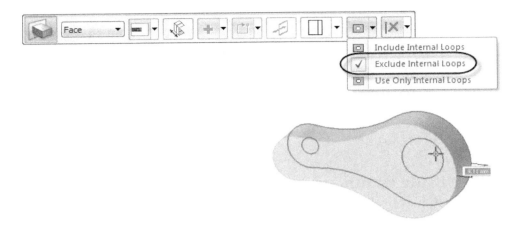

Use Only Internal Loops
This option considers only the internal loops of the sketch.

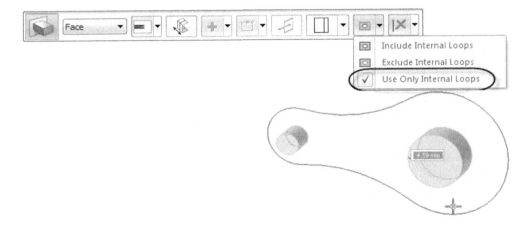

Add
This option adds material to the geometry.

Remove
This option removes material from the part geometry.

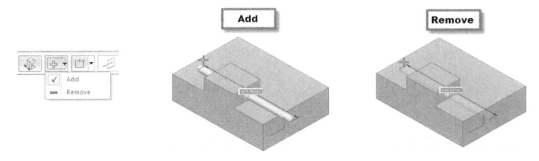

Extrude and Revolve Features

Open
This option extrudes an open sketch without using the adjacent edges.

Closed
Converts an open sketch into closed by using the adjacent edges.

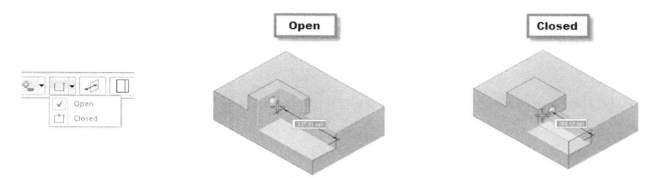

Side Step
This option defines the side of the sketch to extrude.

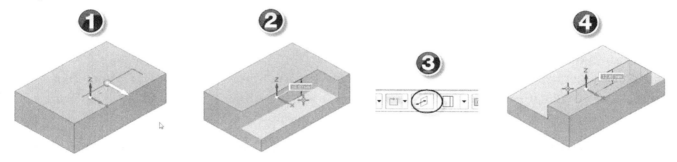

Extent Type options
The **Extent Type** drop-down menu on the command bar has four options: **Finite**, **Through All**, **Through Next**, and **From-To**. The **Finite** option extrudes the sketch upto the distance that you specify. The **Through All** option extrudes the sketch throughout the 3D geometry.

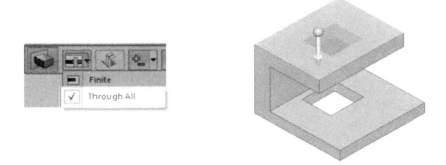

The **Through Next** option extrudes the sketch through the face next to the sketch plane.

Extrude and Revolve Features

 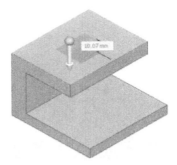

The **From-To** option extrudes the sketch from the sketch plane to a selected face.

 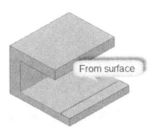 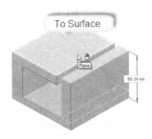

Treatments options

The **Treatments** drop-down menu on the command bar has three options: **No Treatment**, **Draft**, and **Crown**. The **No Treatment** option creates the *Extrude* feature without any treatment. The **Draft** option applies draft to the *Extrude* feature. Activate this option and type-in a draft angle value in the **Draft Parameters** dialog box. Click the **Flip** button next to the **Angle 1** box to flip the draft angle. Click **OK** on the **Draft Parameters** dialog box and define the *Extrude* distance. If you activate the **Symmetric** option on the command bar, you can define draft in the second direction as well.

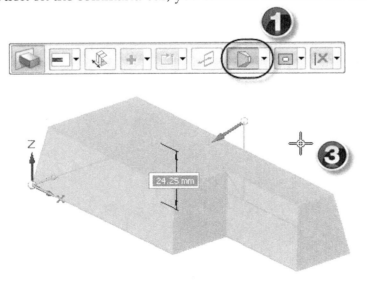 

Extrude and Revolve Features

The **Crown** option in the **Treatments** drop-down menu adds a crown to the *Extrude* feature. As you activate this option, the **Crown Parameters** dialog box appears. Type-in a value in the **Radius** box and click **OK**. Drag the cursor and click to define the thickness of the *Extrude* feature.

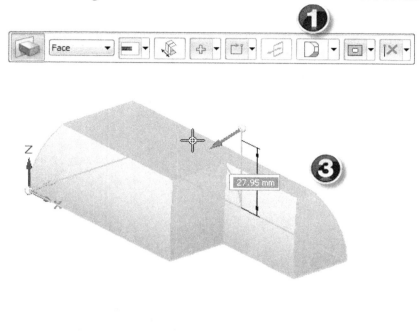

Examples
Example 1 (Millimetres)
In this example, you will create the part shown below.

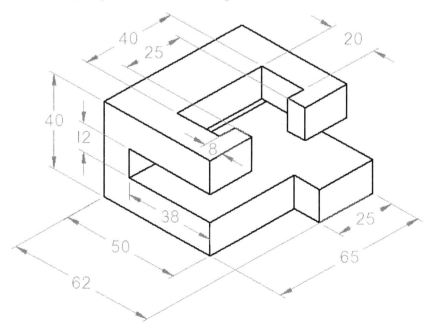

Extrude and Revolve Features

1. Start **Solid Edge ST6**.
2. On the initial screen, click **ISO Part**; a new part file is opened.
3. On the ribbon, click **Home > Draw > Rectangle by Center > Rectangle by 2 Points**.

4. Place the mouse cursor on the coordinate system; the XZ plane gets highlighted.
5. Click the lock icon on the XZ plane to lock the plane.
6. Click the origin point to define the first corner of the rectangle.
7. Move the mouse cursor toward right and click to define the second corner.
8. Use the **Smart Dimension** command and apply dimensions to rectangle.

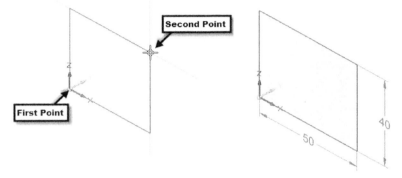

9. Click the lock icon on the screen to unlock the sketch plane. Press Esc to deactivate the **Smart Dimension** command.
10. Click inside the rectangle to display a two-sided arrow. Also, a command bar pops up.
11. On the command bar, click the **Symmetric** icon. Click the arrow on the sketch.

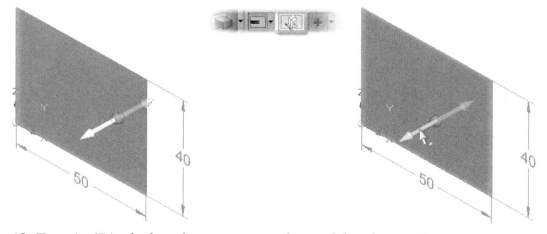

12. Type-in **65** in the box that appears on the model and press Enter.

Extrude and Revolve Features

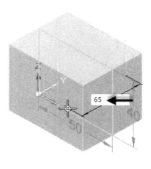 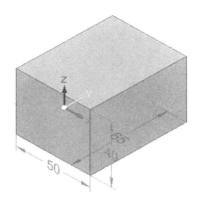

13. Activate the **Line** command and place the mouse cursor on the front face of the part geometry.
14. Click the lock icon to lock the sketching plane.
15. Click **Sketch View** on the status bar.
16. Draw the sketch and apply dimensions to it. Unlock the sketch plane.

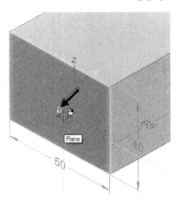 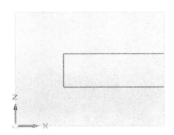 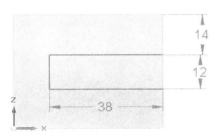

17. On the status bar, click **View Orientation > Dimetric View**; the model orientation is changed to dimetric.
18. On the ribbon, click **Home > Select > Select** and click inside the region enclosed by the sketch.
19. On the command bar, click **Extent Type > Through All**.
20. Click on the arrow pointing toward the part geometry.
21. Move the mouse cursor toward the part geometry and click to create the extruded cut.

   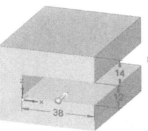

22. Click **Home > Draw > Line** on the ribbon. Place the cursor on the top face of the part geometry and click the lock icon.
23. Draw the sketch on the top face.
24. Click **Home > Relate > Symmetric** on the ribbon. Click on the X-axis to define the symmetric axis.

25. Click on the horizontal lines in the sequence shown in figure.
26. Use the **Smart Dimension** command and apply dimension to the sketch.

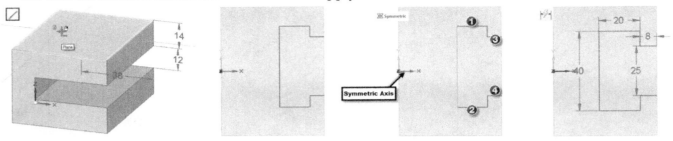

27. Unlock the sketch plane and change the view orientation to Dimetric.
28. On the ribbon, click **Home > Select > Select** and click inside the region enclosed by the sketch.
29. On the command bar, click **Extent Type > Through Next**.
30. Click on the arrow and move the mouse cursor downward.
31. Click to create the extruded cut.

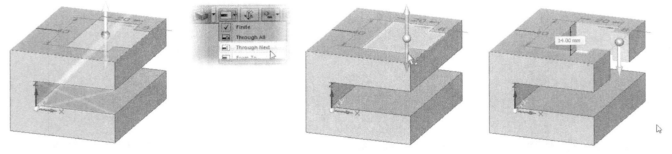

32. Activate the **Line** command and place the cursor on the horizontal face, as shown in figure.
33. Lock the face and draw the sketch. Apply dimensions and unlock the sketch plane.

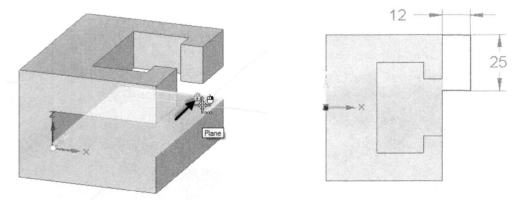

34. On the status bar, click **View Orientation > ISO View**; the view orientation changes to isometric.
35. Click **Home > Solids > Extrude** on the ribbon and click on the sketch region. Right-click to accept.
36. On the command bar, click **Extent Type > From-To**.
37. Place the mouse cursor on the side face of the geometry and right-click when the mouse icon appears. The **QuickPick** box appears.

Extrude and Revolve Features

38. From the **QuickPick** box, select the bottom face of the geometry to define the face upto which the sketch is extruded.

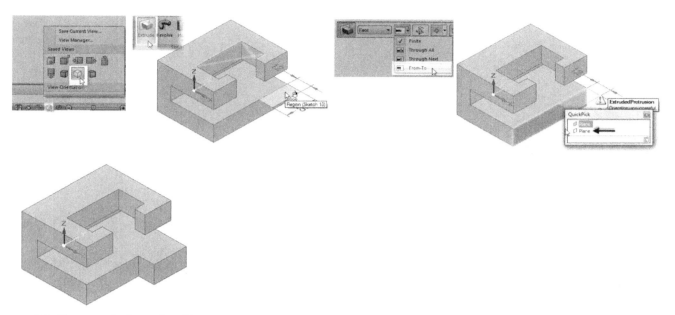

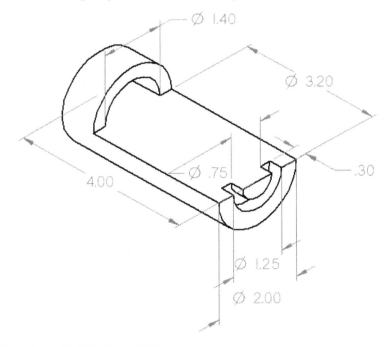

39. Save and close the file.

Example 2 (Inches)

In this example, you will create the part shown below.

1. Start **Solid Edge ST6**.
2. On the **Quick Access Toolbar**, click **New**; the **New** dialog box is appears.

Extrude and Revolve Features

3. On the **New** dialog box, click the **More** tab and select the **ansi part.par** template. Click **OK** to close the dialog box.
4. Draw a sketch on the XZ plane, as shown below.

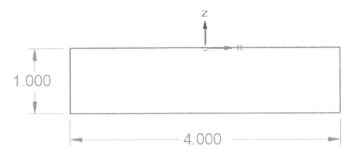

5. Unlock the sketch plane and change the model orientation to ISO.
6. Activate the **Select** command and click inside the region enclosed by the sketch.
7. On the command bar, click **Extrude > Revolve**; the *Extrude* handle is replaced by the *Revolve* handle.
8. Click the spear of the *Revolve* handle, and then drag and align it with the top horizontal line.
9. Click the torus of the *Revolve* handle. Activate the **Symmetric** icon on the command bar.

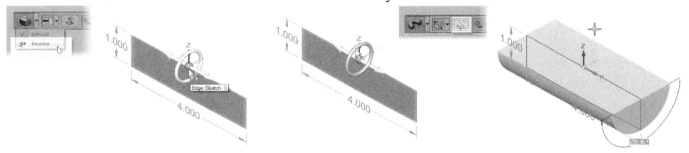

10. Type-in **180** in the box displayed on the model. Press **Enter** and click to create the *Revolve* feature. You will notice that a live section is also created.
11. Under the **Pathfinder**, uncheck the **Live Sections** and **PMI** options to hide the live section and dimensions.

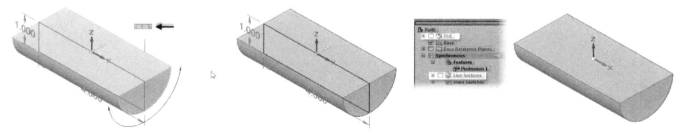

12. Activate the **Line** command and lock the top face of the part geometry.
13. Draw the sketch on top face and apply dimensions.

Extrude and Revolve Features

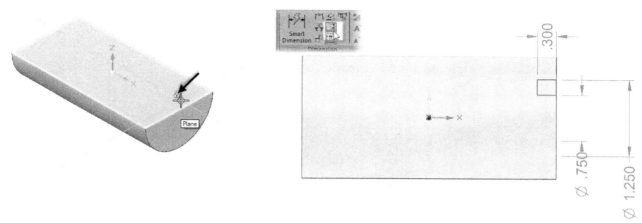

14. Unlock the sketch plane and change the model orientation to ISO.
15. Click **Home > Solids > Revolve** on the ribbon. Click inside the region enclosed by the sketch, and right-click to accept the selection.
16. Click on the X-axis to define the axis of the revolution.
17. On the command bar, deactivate the **Symmetric** icon.
18. Move the cursor and type-in **180** in the box displayed on the model.
19. Move the cursor downward and click to create the revolved cut.

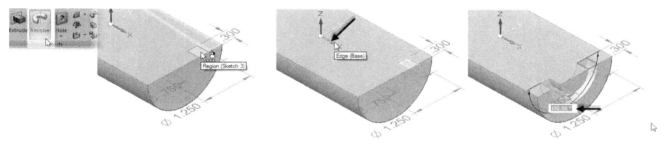

20. Draw a sketch on the top face of the part geometry.
21. Revolve the sketch to create the third feature.

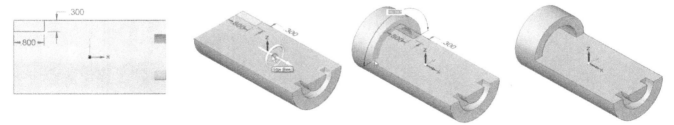

22. Save and close the file.

Questions

1. List the two methods two create *Extrude* features in Synchronous mode.
2. List the two methods two create *Revolve* features in Synchronous mode.
3. How to create parallel planes in Synchronous mode?

4. List three options to extrude sketches containing internal loops.
5. What are the treatment options available on the **Extrude** command bar.
6. List four extent types available on the **Extrude** command bar.

Exercises
Exercise 1 (Millimetres)

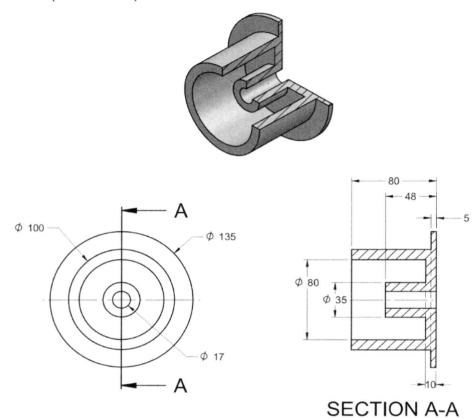

Exercise 2 (Inches)

Extrude and Revolve Features

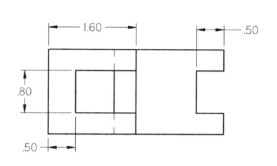
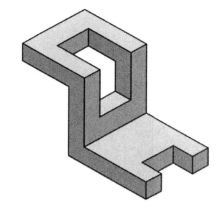
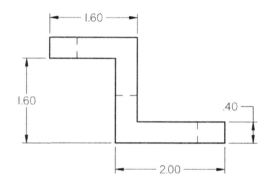
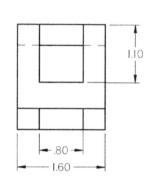

Exercise 3 (Millimetres)

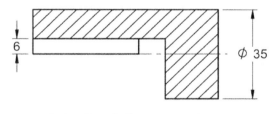
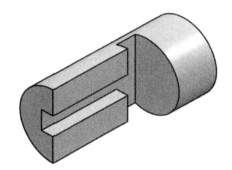
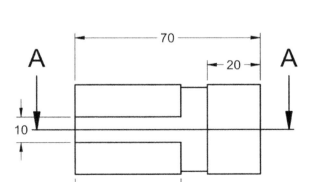

Chapter 4: Placed Features

So for, all of the features that were covered in previous chapters were based on two-dimensional sketches. However, there are certain features in Solid Edge that do not require a sketch at all. Features that don't require a sketch are called placed features. You can simply place them on your models. You must have some existing geometry to create placed features. Unlike a sketch based feature, you cannot use a placed feature as a first feature a model. For example, in order to create a *Fillet* feature, you must have an already existing edge. In this chapter, you will learn how to add placed features to your design.

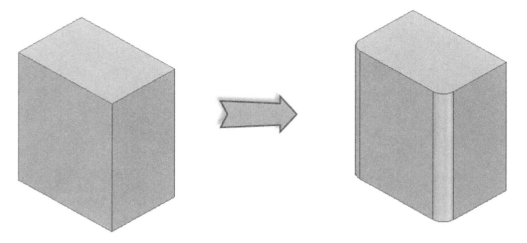

The topics covered in this chapter are:

- *Holes*
- *Threads*
- *Slots*
- *Rounds* and *Blends*
- *Chamfers*
- *Drafts*
- *Shells*

Hole

You know it is possible to use the *Extrude* command to create cuts and remove material. But, if you want to drill holes that are of standard sizes, the **Hole** command is a better way to do this. The reason for this is it has many hole types already predefined for you. All you have to do is choose the correct hole type and size. The other benefit is when you are going to create a 2D drawing, Solid Edge can automatically place the correct hole annotation. Activate this command (Click **Home > Solids > Hole** on the ribbon) and you will notice that a command bar pops up. Click the **Hole Options** icon on the command bar to open the **Hole Options** dialog box. There are quite a few options on this dialog box that make it easy to create different types of holes.

Placed Features

Create a Simple Hole feature

To create a simple hole feature, set the **Type** to **Simple** and select the **Unit** type. Set the **Diameter** of the hole and **Extents** type. If you have selected **Finite Extent**, type-in a value in the **Hole depth** box. If you want a V-bottom hole, check the **V-bottom angle** option and type-in a value in the angle box. Click **OK** to close the dialog box.

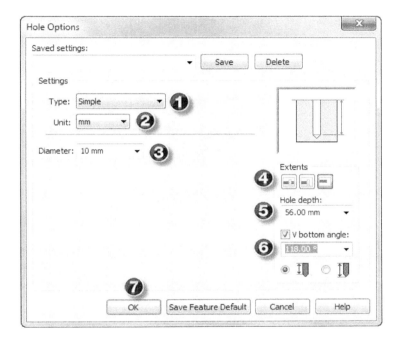

Set the **Keypoints** option on the command bar to **All** and start selecting points from the model. You can select an endpoint of a line, edge or curve (or) center point of an arc or circular edge by placing the cursor on the edge. After placing three holes continuously on a same face, you will notice that the face will be locked and all the future holes will be placed on the locked plane. Click the lock icon on the screen, if you want to unlock the face. After placing the holes, you can use the **Smart Dimension** command to position the hole.

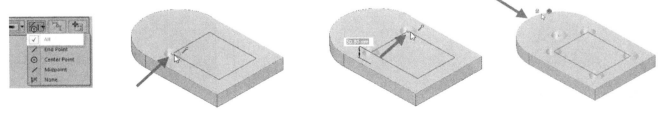

If you want to place a hole on cylindrical or curve surface, there is an easy technique to do this. Position the cursor on the cylindrical face and press F3 to lock the face. A plane tangent to the face will appear.

83

Placed Features

Drag the cursor and type-in an angle value (or) select a key point to define the plane orientation. Now, place holes on the locked plane.

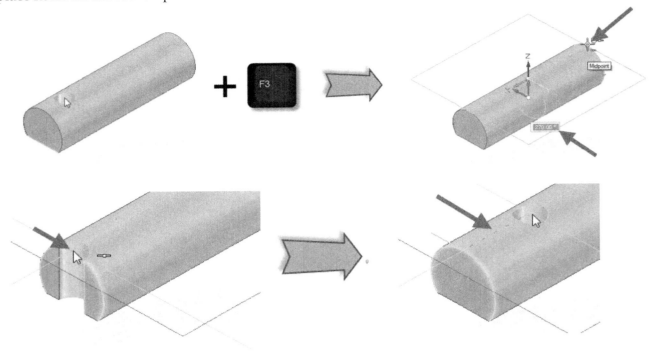

Create a Threaded Hole feature

To create a threaded hole feature, set the hole **Type** to **Threaded**, and then set the thread type, units, and diameter. Next, set the thread parameters such as thread size, thread extent, and taper angle (if applicable). After defining the hole and thread parameters, define the length and end condition of the hole in the **Extents** section. Click **OK** on the dialog box and place the hole.

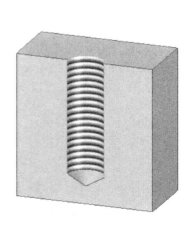
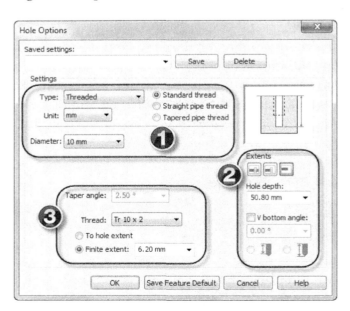

Placed Features

Create a Tapered Hole feature

Tapering is the process of decreasing the hole diameter toward one end. A tapered hole has a smaller diameter at the bottom. To create a tapered hole, set the hole **Type** to **Tapered**. Next, select the option to define the bottom diameter or top diameter. Type-in a value in the **Diameter** box, and then define the taper ratio. The taper ratio is the rate of decrease in the diameter for a specific length. You can define the taper by using the **Decimal (R/L)**, **Ratio (R:L),** or simply enter the taper angle in the **Angle** box. After defining the taper, specify the hole length and end condition in the **Extents** section. Click **OK** and place the hole feature.

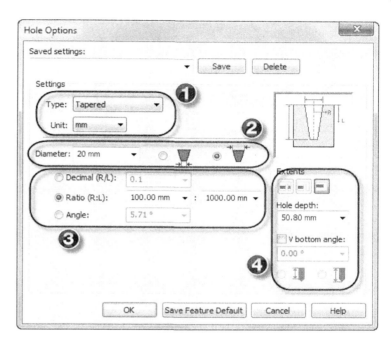

Create a Counterbore Hole feature

A counterbore hole is a large diameter hole added at the opening of another hole. This counterbore hole is used to accommodate a fastener below the level of workpiece surface. The three types counterbore holes that can be created in Solid Edge are shown in figure.

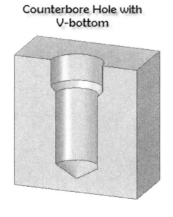
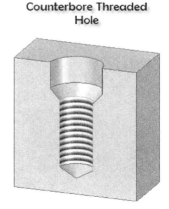

Counterbore Hole — Counterbore Hole with V-bottom — Counterbore Threaded Hole

Placed Features

To create a counterbore hole, set the hole **Type** to **Counterbore**. Next, define the diameter, counterbore diameter, and counterbore depth. Check the **V-bottom angle** option, if you want a V-bottomed counterbore hole. Check the **Thread** option and define the thread parameters, if you want to add thread to the hole.

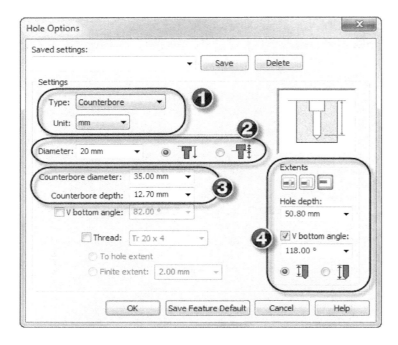

Create a Countersink Hole feature

A countersink hole has an enlarged V-shaped opening to accommodate fastener below the level of workpiece surface. To create a counterbore hole, set the hole **Type** to **Countersink**. Type-in values in the **Diameter**, **Countersink diameter**, and **Countersink angle** boxes. Set the hole depth and end condition in the **Extents** section. Click **OK** and place the hole.

 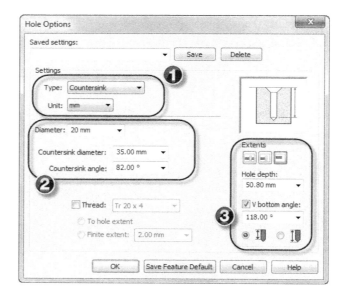

Placed Features

Modify Holes

After placing holes, you may be required to modify them or add more holes to the set. To modify a hole, you must select it and click on the hole diameter. A box appears with the hole parameters. Change the hole parameters by entering new values in the box. You can use the command bar options to change the hole type. Click and drag the arrows displayed on the holes to change the location of the hole.

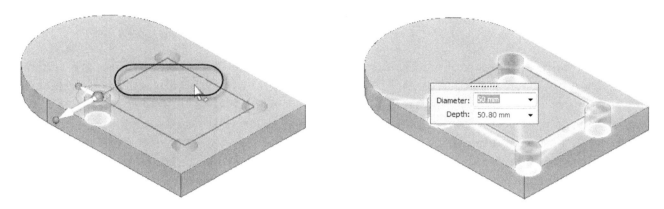

You will notice that, all the holes that are placed at a time are grouped under one set in the Pathfinder. If you modify one hole in the set, all the other holes will also be modified. Use the **More holes** option on the command bar to add more holes to the hole set. If you want to remove a hole from the set, click the right mouse button on it in the Pathfinder and select **Separate**. The hole will be separated.

Recognize Holes

This command converts the cylindrical features created by using the cutting operation into Hole features. This command is also helpful to convert the cylindrical cut features in the imported geometry in to holes. Activate this command (click **Home > Solids > Hole > Recognize Holes** on the ribbon). The **Hole Recognition** dialog box pops up and displays all the cylindrical cut features that are recognized as holes. As you place the cursor over the holes in the dialog box, they will be highlighted in the model. Click the **Hole Options** buttons on the dialog box to open the **Hole Options** dialog box of individual holes. Change the hole type and diameter (if required) in this dialog box and click **OK**. Uncheck the **Recognize** options, if you do not want to recognize the holes. Click **OK** on the **Hole Recognition** dialog box to convert the cut features into holes.

Placed Features

Thread

This command adds a reference thread feature to a cylindrical face. The thread features are added to a 3D geometry so that when you create a 2D drawing, Solid Edge can automatically place the correct thread annotation. Activate this command (click **Home > Solids > Hole > Thread** on the ribbon) and click the **Options** icon on the command bar. The **Thread Options** dialog box pops up. Set the thread parameters such as type, unit, diameter, thread size, and so on, and then click the **OK** button. Set the **Extent Type** on the command bar and select a cylindrical face. The **Change Diameter** message appears. Click **OK** to change the diameter of the cylindrical face to suit the selected thread size. Type-in the thread length and press Enter, if you have set the **Extent Type** to **Finite Value**.

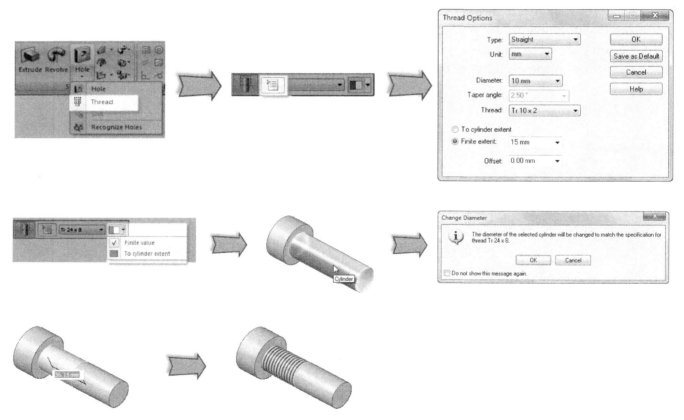

Round

This command breaks the sharp edges of a model and rounds them. It does not need a sketch to create a round. All you need to have is model edges. Activate this command (click **Home > Solids > Round** on the ribbon) and select edges. As you start selecting edges, you will see a preview of the geometry. You can select the edges which are located at the back of the model without rotating it. By mistake, if you have selected a wrong edge you can deselect it by holding the CTRL key and selecting the edge again. You can change the radius by typing a value in the box displayed on selected edge. As you change the radius, all the selected edges will be updated. This is because they are all part of one instance. If you want the edges to have different radii, you must create rounds in separate instances. Select the required number of edges and right-click to finish this feature. The *Round* feature will be listed in the Pathfinder.

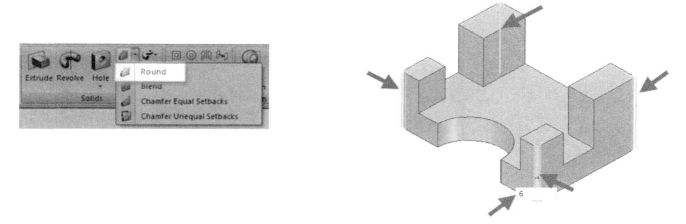

After creating the *Round* feature, the command will be still active so that you can create more *Round* features. Now, if you select the **Loop** option on the command bar, the cursor will be able to select a loop of edges on a face. Select a loop and change the radius. As you press Enter, all of the edges will be rounded.

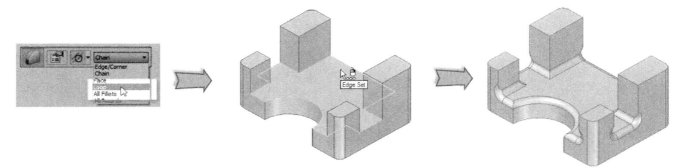

If you select the **All Fillets** option on the command bar, all fillets (concave corners) will be created on the model.

Placed Features

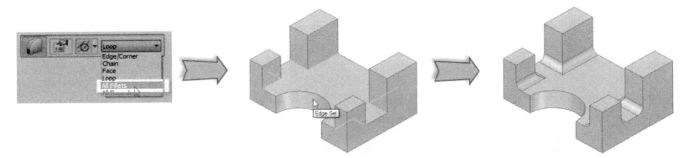

If you select the **All Rounds** option on the command bar, all rounds (convex corners) will be created on the model.

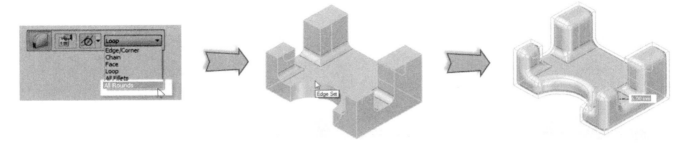

If you ever needed to change the radius of a *Round* feature, select it from the Pathfinder or from model, and then click the diameter value appearing on the feature. Next, type-in a new value in the box that pops up on the *Round* feature and press Enter. To remove a *Round* feature, right-click on it, and then select **Delete**.

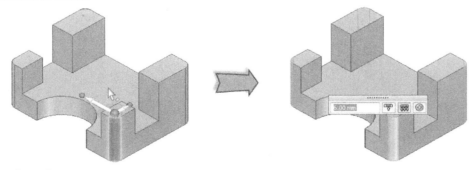

Blend

This command creates a variable radius blend, blend between two faces or surfaces. These three types of blends are explained next.

Variable Radius Blend
The process to create a variable radius blend is illustrated below.

Placed Features

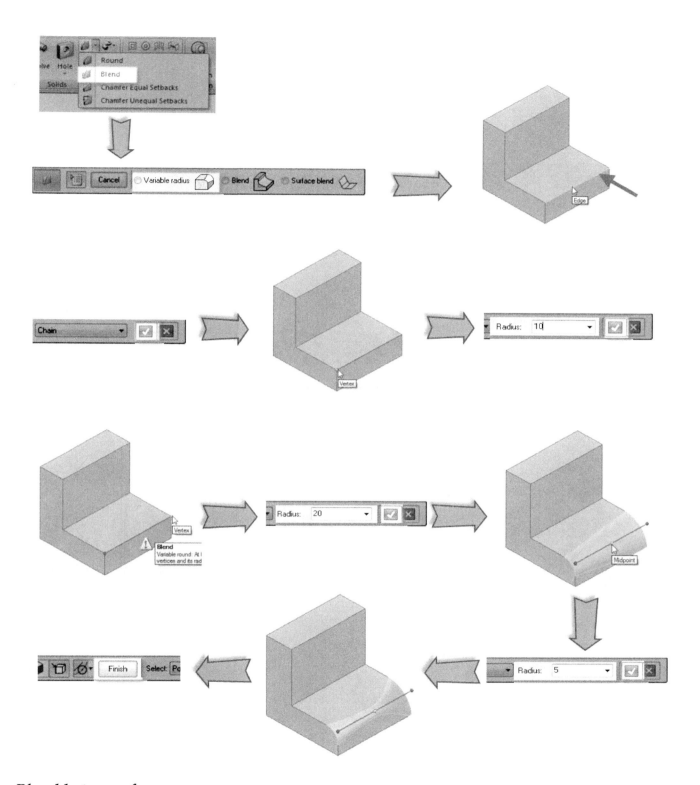

Blend between faces
The process to create a blend between two faces is illustrated in the figure.

Placed Features

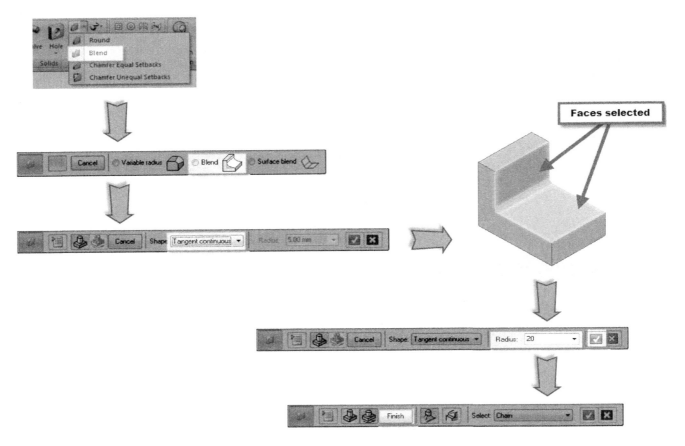

If you want the blend to be tangent to an edge, select the **Tangent Hold Line** option on the command bar and follow the steps given next.

Chamfer Equal Setbacks

The **Chamfer** and **Round** commands are commonly used to break sharp edges. The difference is that the **Chamfer Equal Setbacks** command adds 45-degree bevel face to the model. A chamfer is also a placed feature. Activate this command (click **Home > Round > Chamfer Equal Setbacks** on ribbon) and select an edge to chamfer. Type-in the distance value in the box attached to the chamfer and press Enter to create the chamfer.

Placed Features

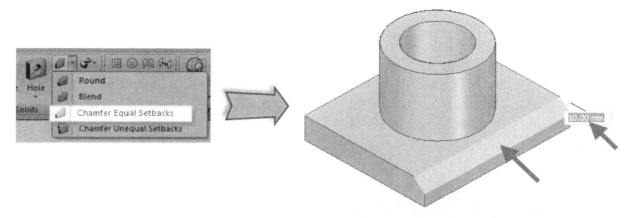

Chamfer Unequal Setbacks

This command will be useful, if you want a chamfer to have different setbacks on both sides of the edge. As you activate this command, you need to select both a face and an edge. First, you need to select a face which acts as the reference. Click the green check on the command bar, and then type-in the **Setback** and **Angle** value. Solid Edge measures the setback distance and angle with reference to the selected face. Again, click the green check, and then click **Finish**.

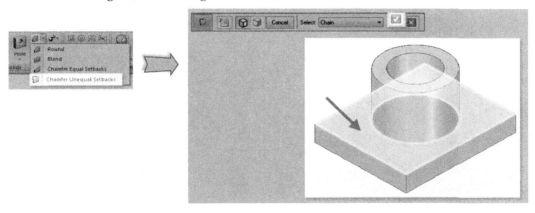

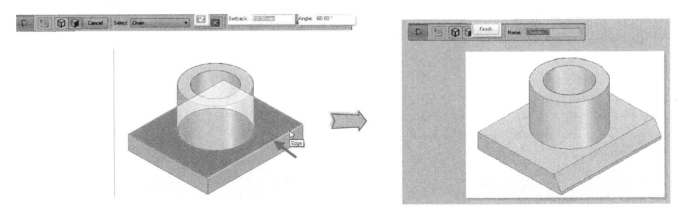

Draft

When creating cast or plastic parts, you are often required to add draft on them so that they can be molded. A draft is an angle or taper applied to the faces of parts to make it easier to remove them from

Placed Features

a mold. When creating *Extrude* features, you can predefine the draft angle. But most of the time, it is easier to apply the draft after the features are created. Activate the **Draft** command from the **Solids** panel. Select a face which will act a reference plane for the draft. The draft angle will be measured with reference to this face. After selecting the reference plane, select the faces to draft. There are four options on the command bar which will help you select the faces to draft. As you select the faces to draft, a two-sided arrow will appear along with a box. Use this two-sided arrow to define the direction of pull, and then type-in a value (angle) in the box. Press Enter to create the *Draft* feature.

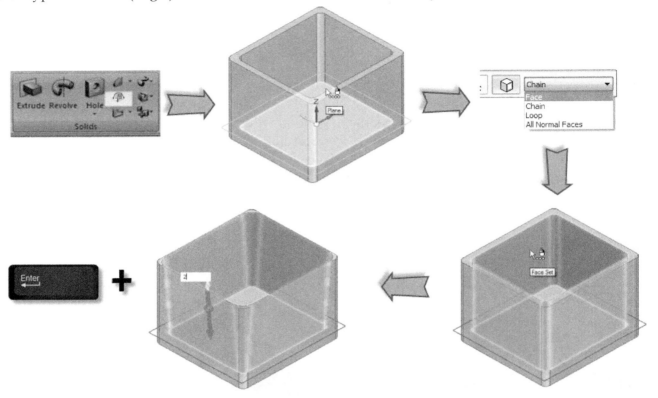

Thin Wall

The **Thin Wall** is another useful command that can be applied directly to a solid model. It allows you to take a solid geometry and make it hollow. This can be a powerful and timesaving technique, when designing parts that call for thin walls such as bottles, tanks, and containers. This command is easy to use. You should have solid part, and then activate this command from the **Solids** panel. Now, select the faces to remove, and then type-in the wall thickness in the box that appears on the model. Click the arrow on the model to specify whether the thickness is added inside or outside the model. Right-click to finish the feature.

Examples
Example 1 (Millimetres)
In this example, you will create the part shown below.

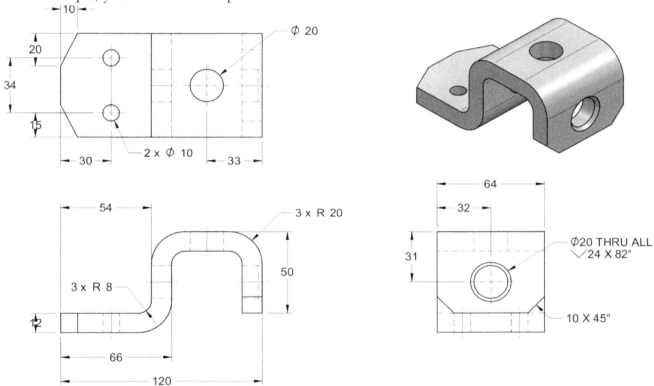

1. Start **Solid Edge ST6**.
2. On the initial screen, click **ISO Part**; a new part file is opened.
3. On the ribbon, click **Home > Draw > Line**.
4. Lock the XZ plane and draw the sketch, as shown below.
5. Create the *Extrude* feature of 64 mm thickness.

Placed Features

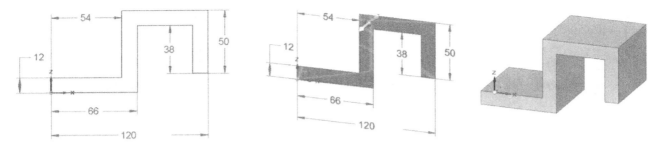

6. On the ribbon, click **Home > Solids > Hole**.
7. Place the mouse cursor on the side face and click the lock icon.
8. On the command bar, click the **Hole Options** icon; the **Hole Options** dialog box pops up.
9. On this dialog box, set the **Type** to **Countersink**.
10. Set the **Diameter** value to **20** mm.
11. Set the **Countersink diameter** and **Countersink angle** to **24** and **82**, respectively.
12. Set the **Extents** type to **Through All**. Click **OK** to close the dialog box.

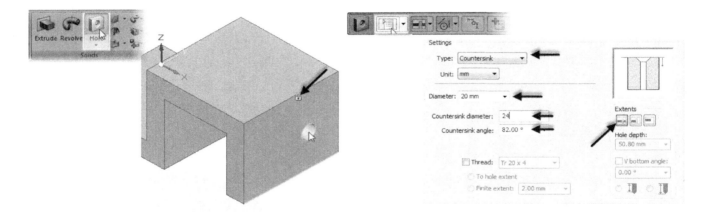

13. Place the mouse cursor on the top edge of the locked face and press E on the keyboard; a dimension appears between the edge and the hole.
14. Place the mouse cursor on the side edge of the locked face and press E on the keyboard; a dimension appears between the edge and the hole.
15. Set the dimension between the hole and top edge to 31 and press Tab on the keyboard.
16. Set the dimension between the hole and side edge to 32 and press Enter on the keyboard.

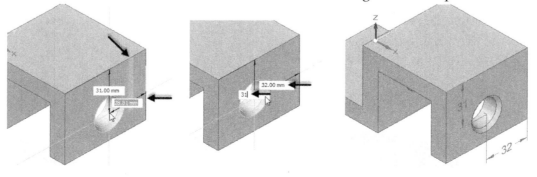

Placed Features

17. Unlock the plane by clicking the lock icon on the screen. Press Esc to deactivate the **Hole** command.
18. Activate the **Hole** command and place the mouse cursor on the top face of the part geometry. Lock the face.
19. Click the **Hole Options** icon the command bar; the **Hole Options** dialog box pops up.
20. On this dialog box, set the **Type** to **Simple**.
21. Set the **Diameter** to 20 mm.
22. Set the **Extents** type to **Through All**. Click **OK** to close the dialog box.
23. Place the mouse cursor on the front edge of the locked face and press E on the keyboard; a dimension appears between the edge and the hole.
24. Place the mouse cursor on the side edge of the locked face and press E on the keyboard; a dimension appears between the edge and the hole.
25. Set the dimension between the hole and front edge to 32 and press Tab on the keyboard.
26. Set the dimension between the hole and side edge to 33 and press Enter on the keyboard.

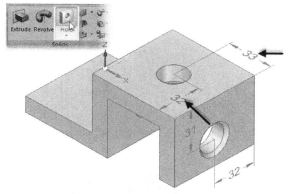

27. Unlock the face by clicking the lock icon. Press Esc to deactivate the **Hole** command.
28. Click **View > Orient > Common Views**; the **Common Views** dialog box pops up.
29. On the **Common Views** dialog box, click on the top left corner of the cube; the view orientation of the model changes.

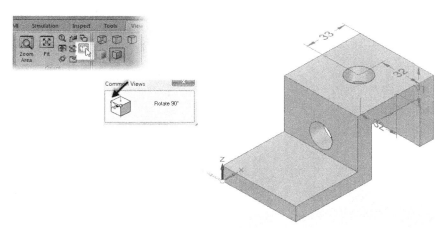

30. Close the **Common Views** dialog box and activate the **Hole** command.

Placed Features

31. On the command bar, click the **Hole Options** icon to open the **Hole Options** dialog box.
32. Set the hole **Type** to **Simple** and **Diameter** to 10 mm. Close the dialog box.
33. Place the mouse cursor on the lower top face, and then press F3.
34. Place the mouse cursor on the front edge of the locked face and press E on the keyboard; a dimension appears between the edge and the hole.
35. Place the mouse cursor on the side edge of the locked face and press E on the keyboard; a dimension appears between the edge and the hole.
36. Set the dimension between the hole and front edge to 30 and press Tab on the keyboard.
37. Set the dimension between the hole and side edge to 15 and press Enter on the keyboard; a hole is created and another hole is attached to the mouse cursor.

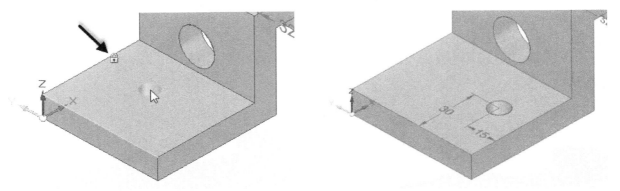

38. Likewise, place another hole on the other side. The positioning dimensions are same.

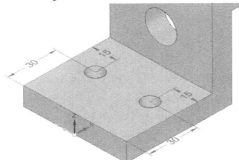

39. Click **Home > Solids > Round > Chamfer Unequal Setbacks** on the ribbon.
40. On the command bar, click the **Chamfer Options** icon; the **Chamfer Options** dialog box pops up.
41. On this dialog box, select **2 Setbacks** and click **OK**.
42. Click on the front face and click the green check on the command bar.

Placed Features

  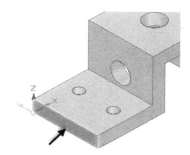

43. Set the **Setback 1** and **Setback 2** to **20** and **10**, respectively.
44. Click on the side edges of the selected face, as shown in figure.
45. Click the green check, and then **Finish** on the command bar.

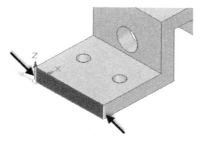 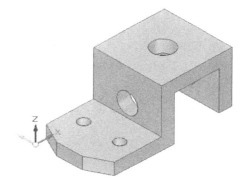

46. Click **Home > Solids > Round** on the ribbon.
47. Click on the horizontal edges of the geometry, as shown below.
48. Type-in **8** in the box that appears on the geometry, and then press Enter.

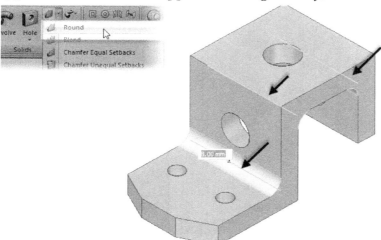

49. Click on the outer edges of the model, as shown below.
50. Type-in **20** in the box that appears on the geometry, and then press Enter.

Placed Features

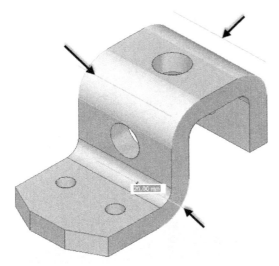

51. Change the orientation of the model view to ISO.
52. Click **Home > Solids > Round > Chamfer Equal Setbacks** on the ribbon.
53. Click on the lower corners of the part geometry.
54. Type-in **10** in the box that appears on the part geometry. Press Enter to chamfer the edges.

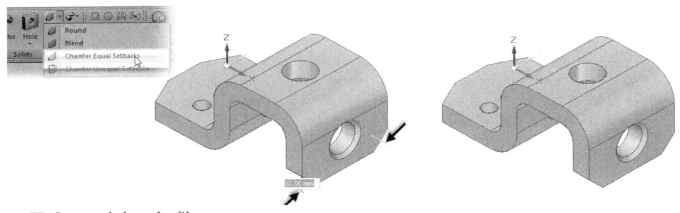

55. Save and close the file.

Questions

1. What are placed features?
2. How to create a hole on a cylindrical face?
3. Which command allows you to create chamfer with unequal setbacks?
4. Which command allows you create a variable radius blend?
5. When you create a thread on a cylindrical face, the diameter of the cylinder will remain the same or not?

Exercises
Exercise 1 (Millimetres)

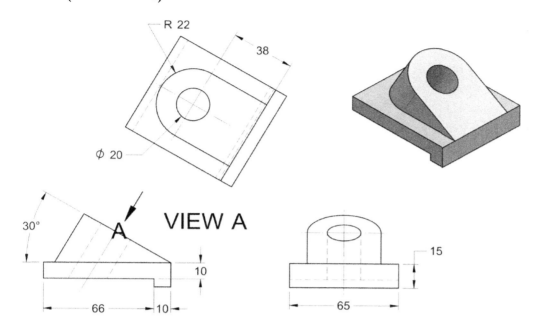

Exercise 2 (Inches)

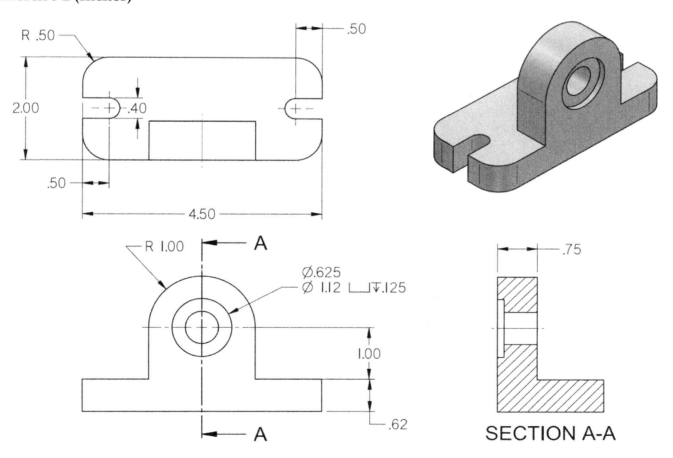

Placed Features

Chapter 5: Patterned Geometry

When designing a part geometry, oftentimes there are elements of symmetry in each part or there are at least a few features that are repeated multiple times. In these situations, Solid Edge offers you some commands that save your time. For example, you can use mirror features to design symmetric parts, which makes designing the part quicker. This is because you only have to design a portion of the part and use the mirror feature to create the remaining geometry.

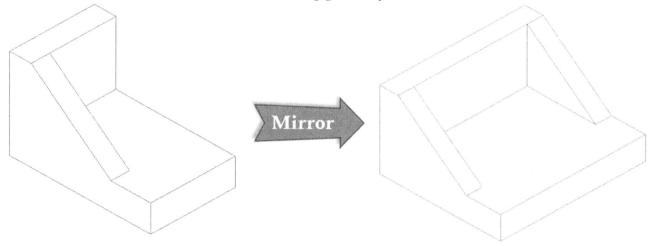

Also, there are some pattern commands to quickly replicate a feature throughout a part. They save you from creating additional features individually and help you modify the design easily. If the design changes, you only need to change the first feature and the rest of the pattern features will update, automatically. In this chapter, you will learn to create the mirrored and pattern geometries using the commands available in Solid Edge.

The topics covered in this chapter are:

- *Mirror* features
- *Rectangular Patterns*
- *Circular Patterns*
- *Along Curve Patterns*
- *Fill Patterns*
- *Recognize Hole Patterns*

Patterned Geometry

Mirror

If you are designing a part that is symmetric, you can save time by using the **Mirror** command. Using this command, you can replicate individual features of the entire body. To mirror features (3D geometry), you need to have a face or plane to use as a reference. You can use a model face, default plane, or create a new plane, if it does not exist where it is needed.

Click on the features to be mirrored in the Pathfinder, and then activate the **Mirror** command (click **Home > Pattern > Mirror** on the ribbon). Now, select the reference plane about which the features are to be mirrored.

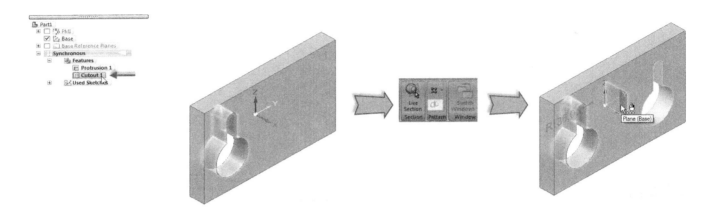

Now, if you make changes to original feature, the mirror feature will be updated automatically.

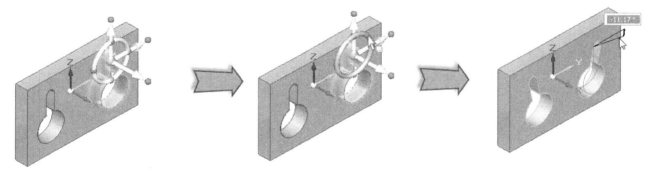

If you select the **Detach Faces** option on the command bar, the faces of the feature will be mirrored, but detached from rest of the model.

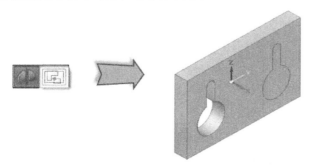

Patterned Geometry

Rectangular Pattern

This command creates a rectangular pattern of a feature. To create a rectangular pattern, you must first select the feature to pattern, and then activate the **Rectangular** command (click **Home > Pattern > Rectangular** on the command bar). Next, define the second corner of the rectangular pattern by clicking on the face of the model. You will notice that a pattern preview appears on the model. Now, select the **Fit** option on the command bar and set the parameters of the pattern (Total Spacing along X-axis and Y-axis, X Count, and Y Count). If you want to suppress some instances, click the **Suppress Instance** option on the command bar and select the green dots from the pattern preview. Next, click the green check on the command bar.

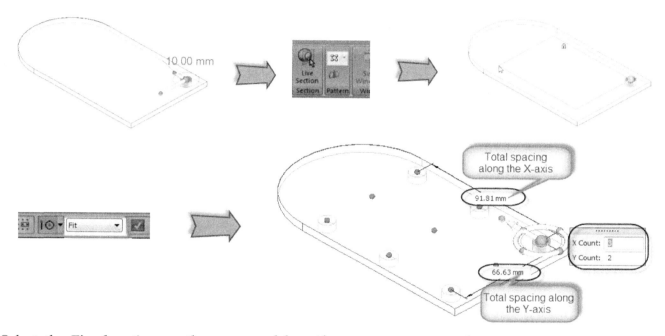

Select the **Fixed** option on the command bar, if you want to enter the spacing between individual instances of the pattern. Click the green check on the command bar to finish the rectangular pattern.

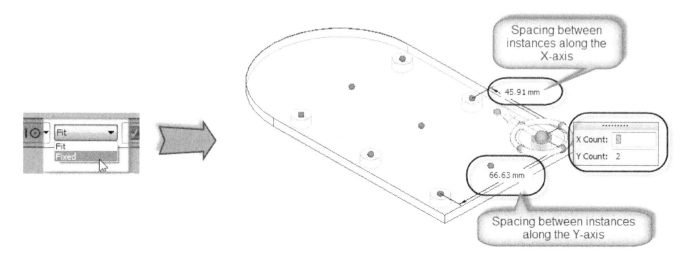

Patterned Geometry

If you want to modify the rectangular pattern, just select it from the model or Pathfinder. A pattern annotation appears on it. Select the annotation, and then modify the pattern parameters. You can use the **Add to Pattern** option on the command bar to add more features to the pattern.

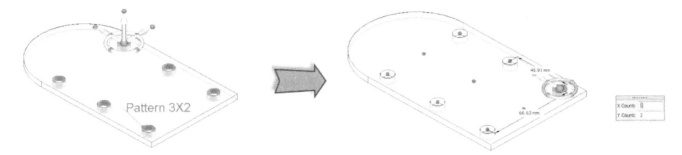

Circular Pattern

This command creates a pattern of selected features in a circular fashion. Select the feature to pattern and activate the **Circular** command (click **Home > Pattern > Rectangular > Circular** on the ribbon). Next, define the axis of the circular pattern by selecting a keypoint.

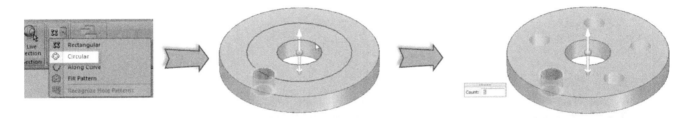

Use the **Circle/Arc Pattern** option on the command bar, if you want to create an arc pattern. Type-in values in the **Count** and **Angle** boxes, and click the green check to create the circular pattern.

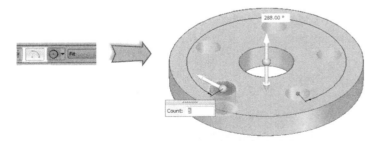

Along Curve Pattern

This command creates a pattern along a selected curve or edge. Activate this command (click **Home > Pattern > Rectangular > Along Curve** on the ribbon). Next, set the **Selection Type** on the command bar and click on a curve or edge. Click the green check on the command bar to accept the selection.

Patterned Geometry

Select a point on the selected curve/edge to define the anchor point of the pattern. Click to define the side of the pattern. On the command bar, click the **Advanced** icon to display a box.

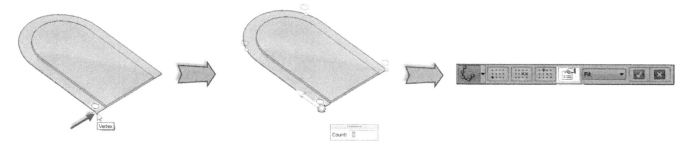

On this box, set the **Transformation Type** to **Full** and **Rotation Type** to **Curve Position**. Click the green check on the box and type-in a value in the **Count** box. On the command bar, set the **Fill Style** to **Fit** and click the green check to create the pattern along the curve.

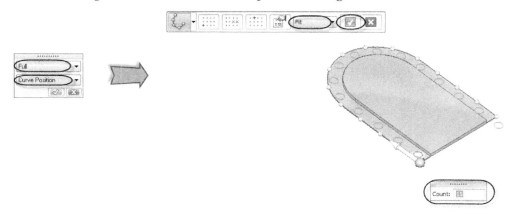

Fill Pattern
This command creates a pattern of a feature by filling it on a defined region. You can create three different types of fill patterns: **Rectangular**, **Staggered**, and **Radial**.

Rectangular Fill Pattern
Select the feature from the geometry and activate the **Fill Pattern** command (click **Home > Pattern > Rectangular > Fill Pattern** on the command bar). Select the face or region on which to create the fill pattern. Set the **Fill Style** to **Rectangular** and click the green check on the command bar. Type-in the spacing values between the pattern instances.

Patterned Geometry

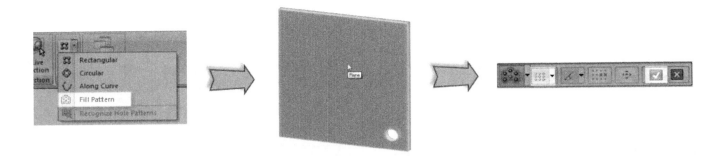

On the command bar, click the **Suppress Instance** icon to suppress the unwanted instances.

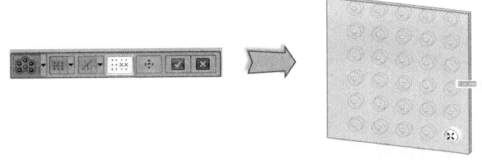

Click the **Use Occurrence Footprint** icon to include the instances lying on the boundary.

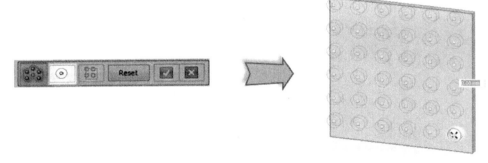

Click the **Allow Boundary Touching** icon to include the instances that are outside the region and touching the boundary. Click the green dots on the instances to suppress them. On the command bar, click the green check after suppressing the instances.

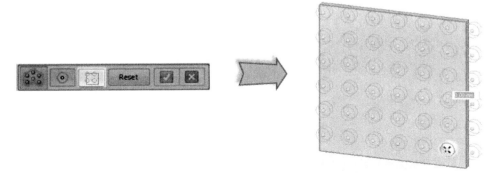

Click and drag the pattern boundaries to increase or decrease the fill pattern region. After defining the required settings, right-click to create the rectangular fill pattern.

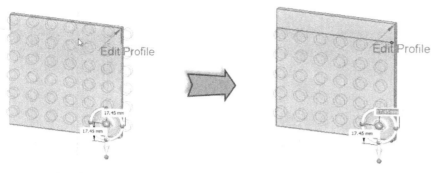

Staggered Fill Pattern

In this type of pattern, the features are arranged in a perforation fashion. To create a staggered fill pattern, set the **Fill Style** to **Stagger** on the command bar.

Next, define the spacing between the instances. This can be done by using the **Fill spacing** methods. There are three methods to define the spacing between the instances: **Polar**, **Linear Offset**, and **Complex Linear Offset**. The **Polar** method creates a pattern by using (a) rotation angle between two rows and (b) distance between the instances. The **Linear Offset** method creates a pattern by using (c) spacing between two rows and (d) stagger offset. The **Complex Linear Offset** method creates a pattern by using (e) spacing between two instances in a row, (f) spacing between rows, and (g) stagger offset.

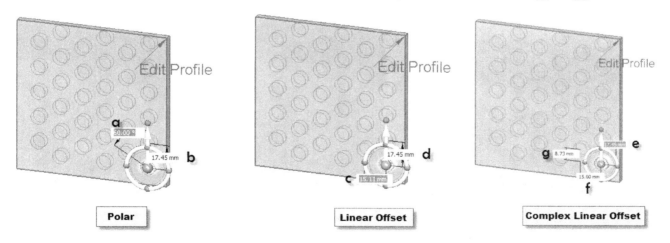

On the command bar, click the green check to create the staggered pattern.

Radial Fill Pattern

In this type of pattern, the features are filled in a radial fashion inside the selected region. To create a radial fill pattern, set the **Fill Style** to **Radial** on the command bar.

Patterned Geometry

Next, define the spacing between the instances. This can be done by using the Fill spacing methods. There are two methods to define the spacing between the instances: **Target Spacing** and **Instant Count**. The **Target Spacing** method creates a pattern by using (a) spacing between the rings and (b) spacing between the instances. The **Instant Count** method creates a pattern by using (a) number of instance per ring and (b) spacing between the rings.

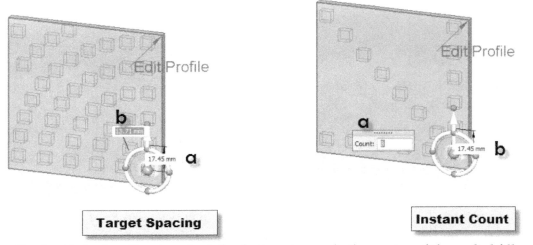

Use the **Center Orient** option to orient the feature towards the center of the radial fill pattern.

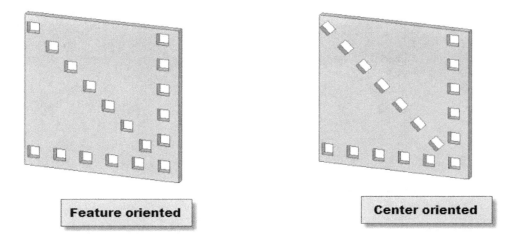

Recognize Hole Patterns

This command converts the holes arranged in a circular or rectangular fashion into patterns. It will be easier for you to modify patterns than individual features. Activate this command (click **Home > Pattern > Recognize Hole Patterns** on the ribbon) and select the holes that are arranged in a circular or rectangular fashion. Click the **Define Master Occurrence** button on the **Hole Pattern Recognition** dialog box and define the master occurrence of the pattern. Click **OK** to convert the group of holes into a pattern.

Patterned Geometry

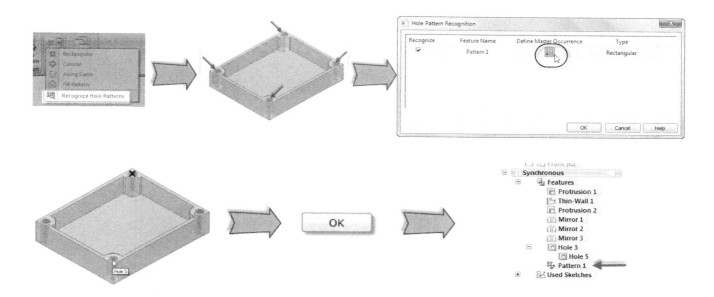

Examples
Example 1 (Millimetres)
In this example, you will create the part shown below.

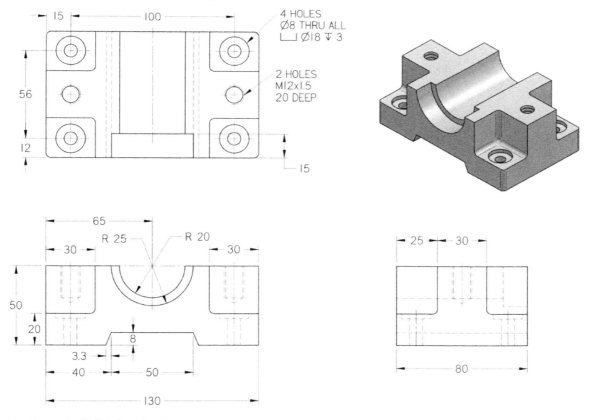

1. Start **Solid Edge ST6**.
2. On the initial screen, click **ISO Part**; a new part file is opened.

Patterned Geometry

3. To start a new sketch, click **Home > Draw > Rectangle by Center** on the ribbon.
4. Lock the XZ plane and draw the sketch, as shown below.

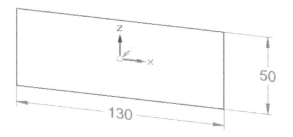
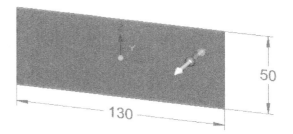

5. Create the *Extrude* feature of 80 mm thickness.

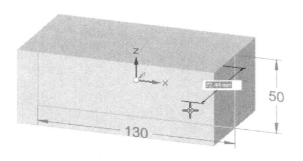
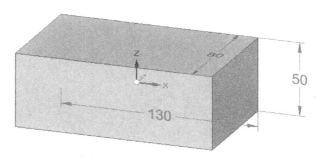

6. Click **Home > Draw > Rectangle by Center > Rectangle by 2 Points** on the ribbon.
7. Lock the top face of the part geometry and draw the sketch.
8. Create the *Cutout* feature of **30 mm** depth.

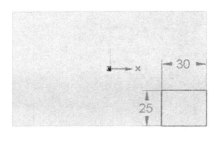
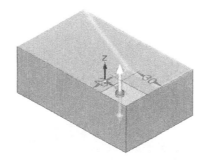
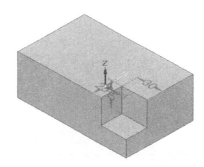

9. Click on the *Cutout* in the Pathfinder.
10. Click **Home > Pattern > Mirror** on the ribbon.
11. Check the **Base Reference Planes** option in the Pathfinder and click on the **Right (yz)** plane. The selected geometry is mirrored.

Patterned Geometry

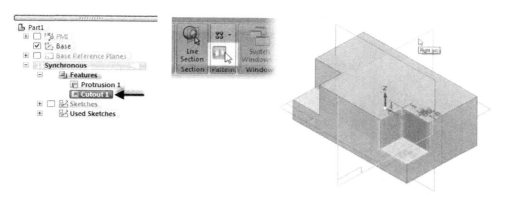

12. Press Shift on the keyboard and click on the *Cutout*, and *Mirror* in the Pathfinder.
13. Activate the **Mirror** command.
14. Click on the **Front (xz)** plane to mirror the selected geometry.

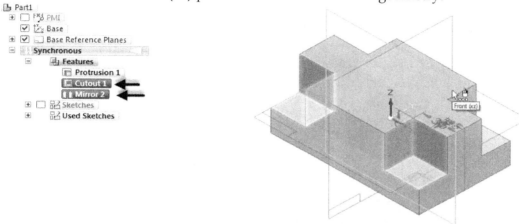

15. Activate the **Hole** command and place a counterbore hole on the *Cutout* feature.

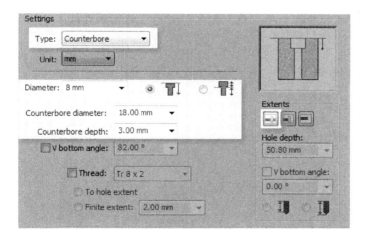

113

Patterned Geometry

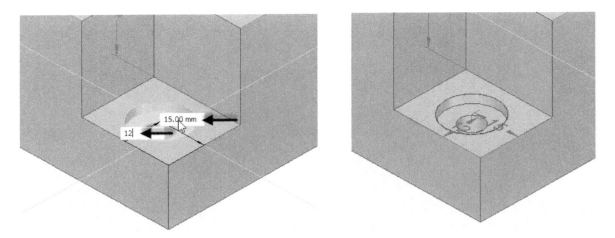

16. In the Pathfinder, click on the *Hole*, if not already selected.
17. Click **Home > Pattern > Rectangular** on the ribbon.
18. Click on the opposite corner of the part geometry to define the rectangular pattern.
19. On the command bar, set the **Fill Style** option to **Fit**.
20. Type-in **100** in the spacing box along the X-axis, and then press Tab.
21. Type-in **56** in the spacing box along the Y-axis.
22. Type **2** in the X and Y boxes, respectively.

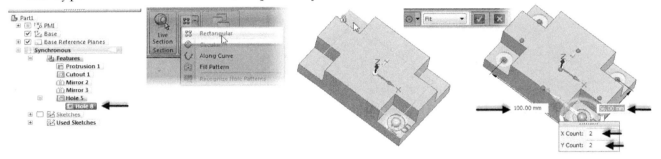

23. Click the green check on the command bar to create the rectangular pattern.
24. Activate the **Hole** command and lock the front face of the part geometry.
25. Activate the **Hole Options** dialog box and set the parameters of the counterbore hole, as shown in figure.
26. Click on the midpoint of the top of the model to place the hole.

Patterned Geometry

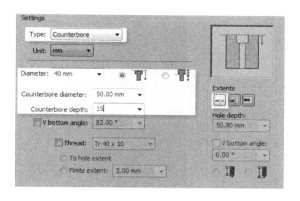 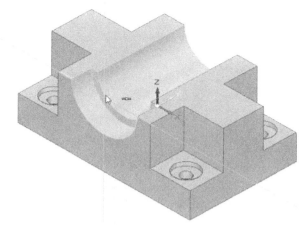

27. Unlock the front face. Press Esc to deactivate the **Hole** command.
28. Activate the **Hole** command and lock the top face of the part.
29. Activate the **Hole Options** dialog box and set the parameters of the threaded hole, as shown in figure. Click **OK** to close the dialog box.
30. Create the threaded hole and deactivate the **Hole** command.

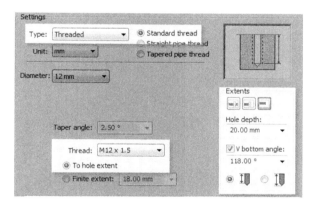 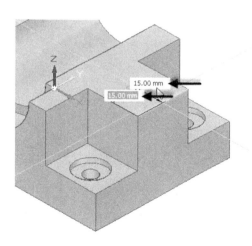

31. Mirror the threaded hole about the YZ plane.

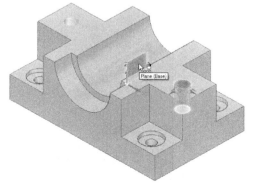

32. Draw a sketch on the front face of the pat geometry and create a *Cutout* throughout the geometry.

115

Patterned Geometry

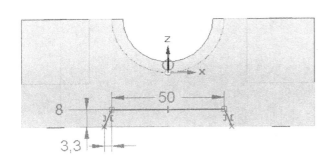

33. Round the sharp edges of the geometry.

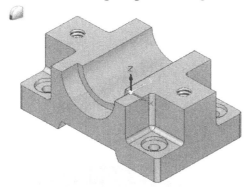

34. Save and close the part file.

Questions

1. Describe the procedure to create a mirror feature?
2. List any two commands to create patterns?
3. Why it is important to convert a set of holes into a pattern?
4. How to add more features to an existing pattern?
5. List the options that define the orientation of the feature in a fill pattern?

Exercises
Exercise 1 (Millimetres)

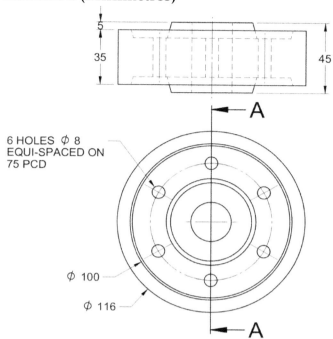
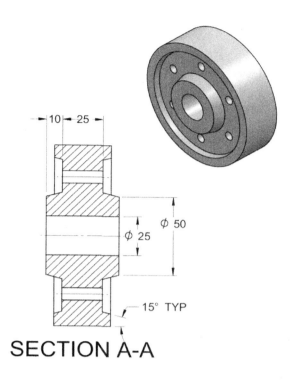

Exercise 2 (Inches)

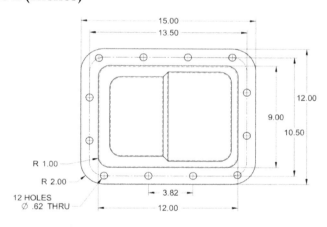
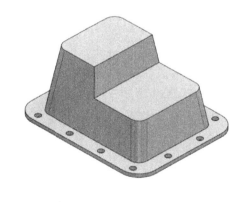
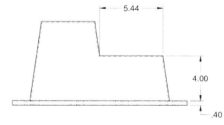
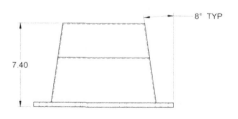

SHEET THICKNESS = 0.079 in

Chapter 6: Sweep Features

The **Sweep** command is one of the basic commands available in Solid Edge that allow you to generate solid geometry. It can be used to create simple geometry as well as complex shapes. A sweep is composed of two items: a cross-section and a path. The cross-section controls the shape of sweep while the path controls its direction. For example, take a look at the angled cylinder shown in figure. This is created using a simple sweep with the circle as the profile and an angled line as the path.

By the making the path a bit more complex, you can see that a sweep allows you to create shape you wouldn't be able to create using commands such as Extrude or Revolve.

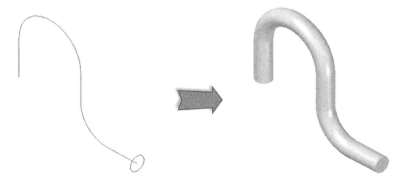

To take the sweep feature to the next level of complexity, you can add multiple paths and cross-sections. By doing so, the shape of the geometry is controlled by multiple cross-sections and paths. For example, the elliptical cross-section in figure varies in size along the path because it is controlled by an additional path.

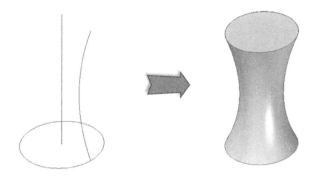

The topics covered in this chapter are:

- *Single Path and cross-section sweeps*
- *Multiple path and cross-section sweeps*

Sweep Features

- *Scaling and twisting the cross-section along the path*
- *Swept Cutouts*
- *Helical sweeps and cutouts*

Single path and cross-section sweeps

This type of sweep requires two elements: a path and cross-section. The cross-section defines the shape of the sweep along the path. A path is used to control the direction of the cross-section. A path can be a sketch or an edge. To create a sweep, you must first create a path and a cross-section. Create a path by drawing a sketch. It can be an open or closed sketch. Next, click **Home > Planes > More Planes > Normal to Curve** on the ribbon, and then create a plane normal to the path. Sketch the cross-section on the plane normal to the path.

Activate the **Sweep** command (click **Home > Solids > Sweep** on the ribbon). As you activate this command, a dialog box appears showing different options to create the sweep. Select the **Single path and cross-section** option on the dialog box and click **OK**.

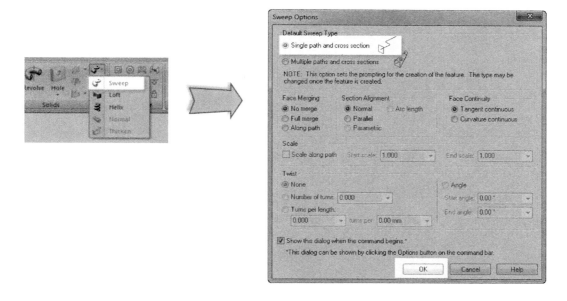

Select the path and click the green check on the command bar.

Sweep Features

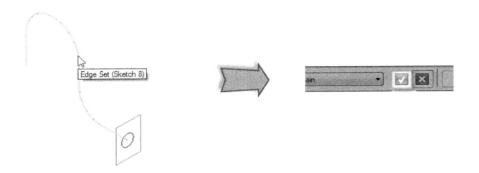

Select the cross-section and click **Finish** on the command bar. Click **Cancel** to deactivate the command.

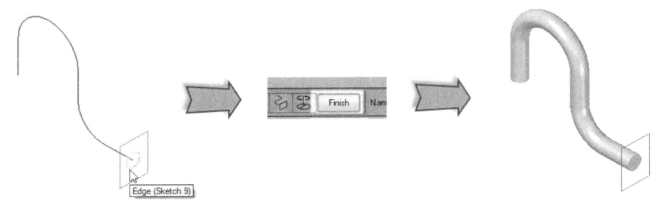

Solid Edge will not allow the sweep to result in a self-intersecting geometry. As the cross-section is swept along a path, it cannot comeback and cross itself. For example, if the cross-section of the sweep is larger than the curves on the path, the resulting geometry will intersect and the sweep will fail.

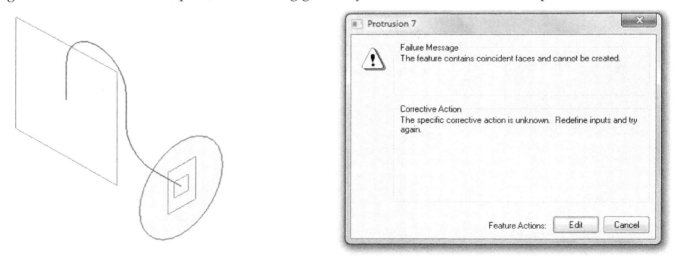

A sweep profile must be created as a sketch. However, a path can be a sketch, curve, or edge. The following illustrations show various types of paths and resultant sweep features.

Sweep Features

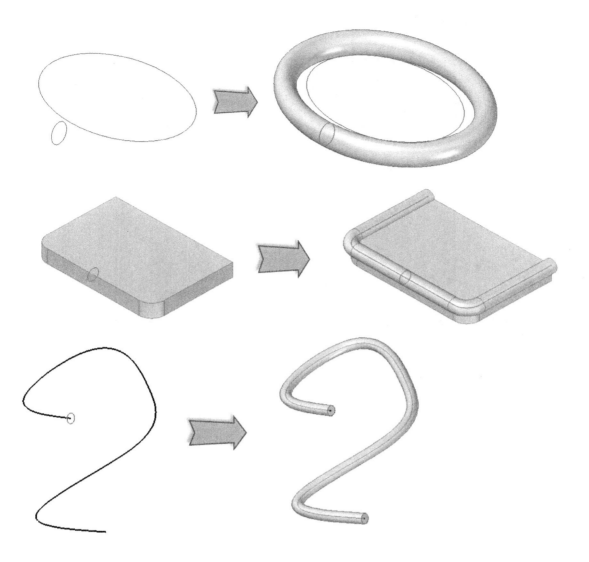

Face Merging

There are three options to merge faces of a sweep feature. These options are available on the **Sweep Options** dialog box. The **No Merge** option creates a sweep feature without merging its faces. The **Full Merge** option merges all the faces of a sweep feature. The **Along path** option merges the faces along the direction of the path.

Sweep Features

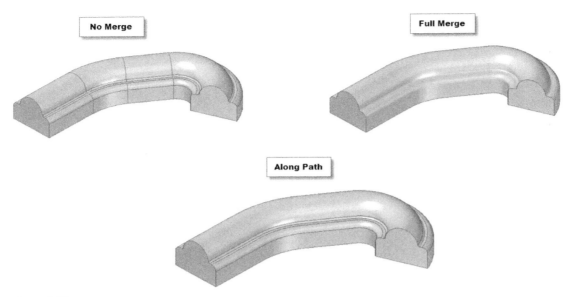

Section Alignment

The section alignment options define the orientation of the resulting geometry. The **Normal** option sweeps the cross-section in the direction normal to the path. The **Parallel** option sweeps the cross-section in the direction parallel to itself.

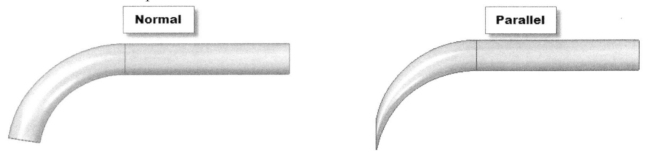

Face Continuity

The **Face Continuity** options define the tangency condition between the faces of a sweep feature. The **Tangent Continuous** option makes two faces tangent and continuous to each other. The **Curvature Continuous** option maintains the tangency as well as radius of curvature between two faces of a sweep feature.

Scale

Solid Edge allows you to scale the sweep along the path. Select the path and cross-section, and then click the **Options** icon on the command bar. Check the **Scale along** path option on the **Sweep Options** dialog box, and then type-in the start and end scale factors. Click **OK** and **Finish** creating a scaled sweep feature.

Sweep Features

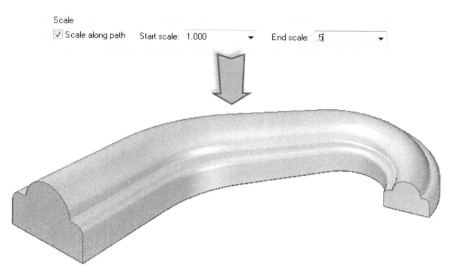

Twist

Solid Edge allows you to twist the cross-section along the path. Define the path and cross-section, and then click the **Options** icon on the command bar. The **Twist** options on the **Sweep Options** dialog box help you to apply a twist to the cross-section.

The **Number of Turns** option turns the cross-section by the value you enter in the box.

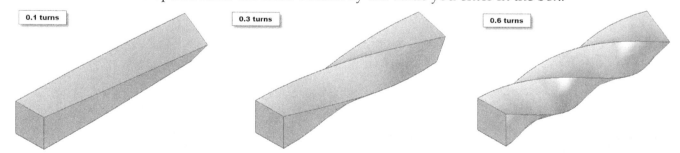

The **Turns per Length** option twists the cross-section by number of turns and length that you enter in the boxes.

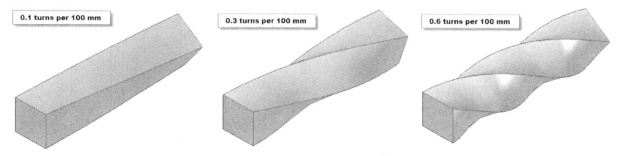

Sweep Features

The **Angle** option twists the cross-section by an angle. Select this option and type-in values in the **Start Angle** and **End Angle** boxes.

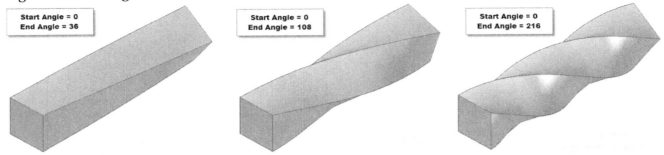

Axis Step

The **Axis Step** option on the command bar will be useful while sweeping a cross-section along a non-planar path. For example, define a path and cross-section similar to the one shown in figure and click the **Axis Step** option on the command bar. Select a line or axis from the Base coordinate system. The cross-section and the axis will be locked in the same plane. As a result, the orientation of the cross-section and axis become same and the cross-section will be swept maintaining the orientation of the axis.

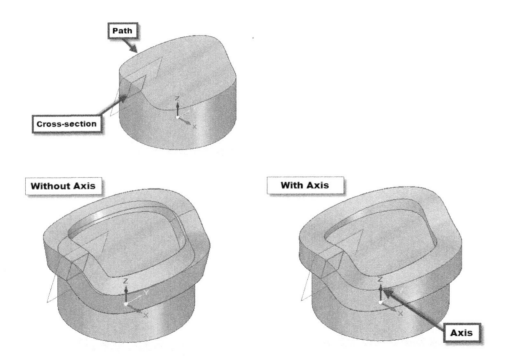

Multiple paths and cross-sections sweeps

Solid Edge allows you to create sweep features with multiple paths and cross-sections. This can be useful while creating complex geometry and shapes. To create this type of sweep feature, first create multiple paths and cross-sections as shown in figure. Activate the **Sweep** command and select **Multiple paths and cross-sections** on the **Sweep Options** dialog box. Click **OK** to close the dialog box.

Sweep Features

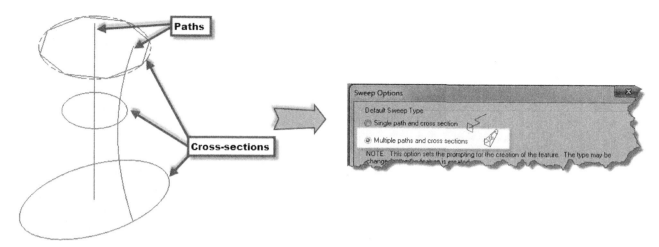

Select the first path and click the green check on the command bar. Select another path and click the green check on the command bar. Select the third path, if available. Otherwise, click **Next** on the command bar. Select the all the cross-sections one-by-one and click **Preview** on the command bar. The preview of the geometry will appear. Click **Finish** to complete the feature.

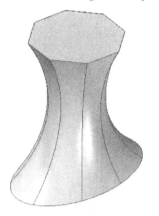

Swept Cutout

In addition to adding swept features, Solid Edge allows you to remove geometry using the **Swept Cutout** command. Activate this command (click **Home > Solids > Swept Cutout** on the ribbon) and select the sweep type from the **Sweep Options** dialog box. Click **OK** and select the path. Click the green check on the command bar to accept the path. Select the cross-section and click **Finish** to create the swept cutout.

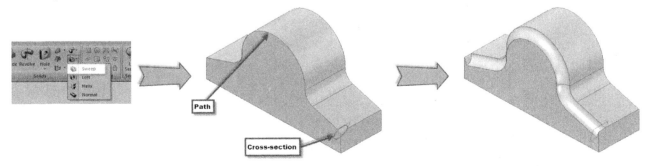

Sweep Features

You will notice that swept cutout is not created throughout the geometry. This is because the cross-section is swept only upto the endpoints of the path. In this case, you must define a new path which extends beyond the geometry. Delete the swept cutout from the Pathfinder and create two lines which are continuous and collinear with the path. Activate the **Derived** command (click **Surfacing > Curves > Derived** on the ribbon) and select the edges and lines. Click the green check on the command bar to create a new curve. Now, create a swept cutout by using the curve as path. The resultant swept cutout will be throughout the geometry.

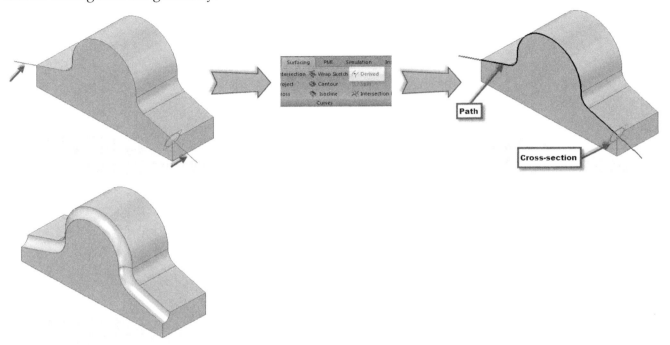

Helix

This command creates are spring shape feature. To create this type of feature, you must have a cross-section and a line (axis). They can be on a same plane or on different planes. Activate the **Helix** command (click **Home > Solids > Helix** on the ribbon), and then select the cross-section and line. Click the green check on the command bar. The preview of geometry appears on the screen.

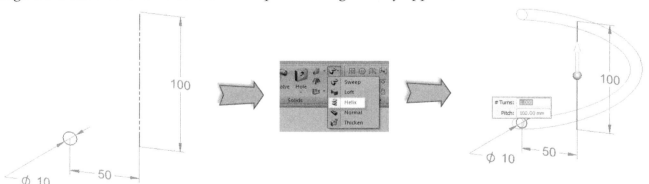

Now, define the **Helix Method** on the command bar. There are three helix methods: **Axis & Pitch**, **Axis & Turns**, **Pitch & Turns**. The **Axis & Pitch** method creates a helix by using the length of the axis and distance between the turns. The **Axis & Turns** method creates a helix by using the axis length and number of turns. The **Pitch & Turns** method uses the pitch and number of turns you specify to create the helix.

For more helix options, click the **Options** icon on the command bar. The **Helix Options** dialog box pops up on the screen. This dialog box has many options to define the parameters of the helix feature (such as helix direction, taper, and pitch). Define the helix direction by selecting the **Right-handed** or **Left-handed** option.

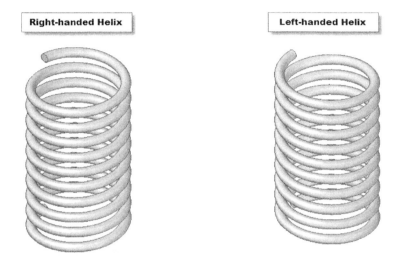

The **Taper** options on the **Helix Options** dialog box help you to apply taper to the helix. There are two methods to apply taper to a helix: **By Angle** and **By Radius**. The **By Angle** method applies a taper to the helix by using the taper angle that you enter in the **Angle** box. The **Inward** or **Outward** options define the taper direction. The **By Radius** method applies a taper to the helix by using the start and end radius that you specify.

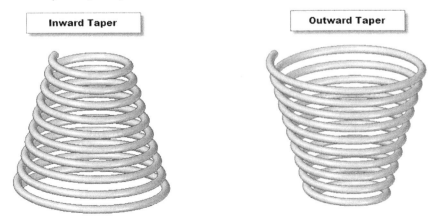

Sweep Features

The **Pitch** options on the **Helix Options** dialog box help you to create a variable pitch helix. Select the **Variable** option from the drop-down menu and type-in the **Pitch ratio** and **End Pitch** values. For example, if you specify the **Start Pitch** =10, **Turns** = 10, and **End Pitch** = 20, the pitch of the helix varies from 10 to 20. The rate of change in the pitch is calculated by the formula:

$$\text{Rate of change in pitch} = \frac{\text{End Pitch - Start Pitch}}{\text{No. of turns}} = \frac{20 - 10}{10} = 1$$

$$\text{The start pitch} = \text{Start Pitch} + \frac{\text{Rate of change in pitch}}{2}$$

$$\text{The end pitch} = \text{End Pitch} - \frac{\text{Rate of change in pitch}}{2}$$

Therefore, the pitch of the first turn = 10+.5 =10.5
                Second turn = 10.5+1 = 11.5
                Third turn = 11.5+1= 12.5…………………….tenth turn=19.5

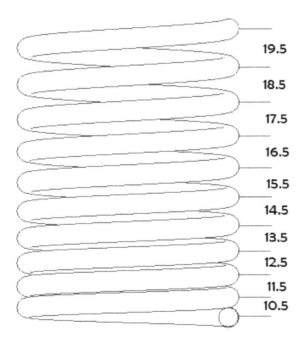

Helical Cutout

This command removes material from the part geometry by creating a helical feature. To create this feature, first you must have an existing geometry, and the sketches of the cross-section and axis. Activate this command (click **Home > Solids > Swept Cutout > Helical Cutout** on the ribbon) and select the cross-section and axis. Click the green check on the command bar to accept the selection. Define the number of turns and pitch, and then right-click to create the helical cutout.

Sweep Features

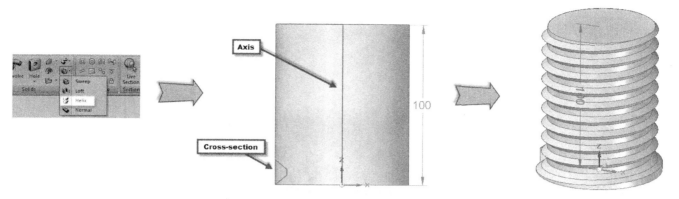

Examples
Example 1 (Inches)
In this example, you will create the part shown below.

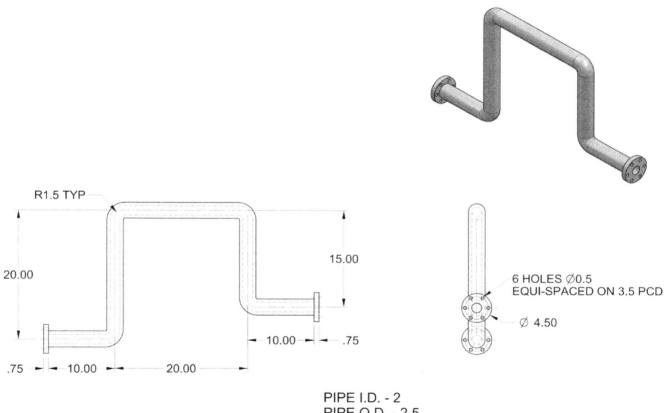

PIPE I.D. - 2
PIPE O.D. - 2.5

1. Start **Solid Edge ST6**.
2. On the **Quick Access Toolbar**, click **New**; the **New** dialog box pops up.
3. On this dialog box, click **More > ansi part.par**, and then click **OK**.
4. On the ribbon, click **Home > Draw > Line** and draw the sketch on the XZ plane, as shown below.

Sweep Features

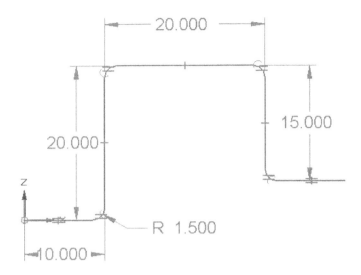

5. Unlock the sketch plane.
6. On the ribbon, click **Home > Planes > More Planes > Normal to Curve** and click on the lower horizontal line.
7. Click on the end point of the line to locate the plane.

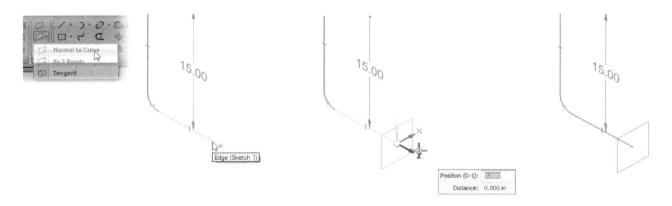

8. On the ribbon, click **Home > Draw > Circle by Center Point** and draw a circle of 2.5 inch diameter on the plane normal to curve.

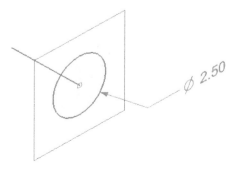

9. On the ribbon, click **Home > Solids > Sweep**; the **Sweep Options** dialog box pops up.

Sweep Features

10. On this dialog box, set the **Default Sweep Type** to **Single path and cross-section**.
11. Set the **Face Merging** option to **No Merge**.
12. Set the **Section Alignment** option to **Normal**. Click **OK** to close the dialog box.
13. Click on the first sketch to define the path of the *Sweep* feature. Click the green check on the command bar.
14. Click on the circle to define the cross section.

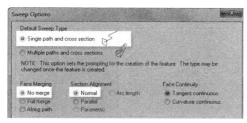
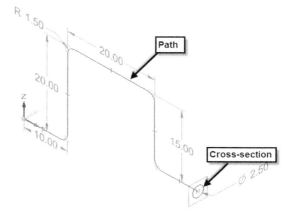

15. Click **Finish** to complete the *Sweep* feature.

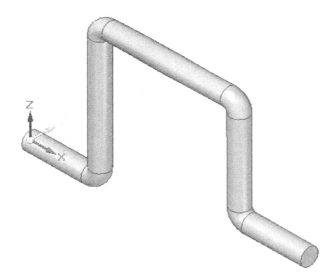

16. On the ribbon, click **Home > Solids > Thin Wall**. Click on the end face of the *Sweep* feature.
17. Rotate the part geometry and click the end face on the other side.
18. Type-in **0.5** in the box that appears on the geometry. Press Enter to shell the *Sweep* feature.

Sweep Features

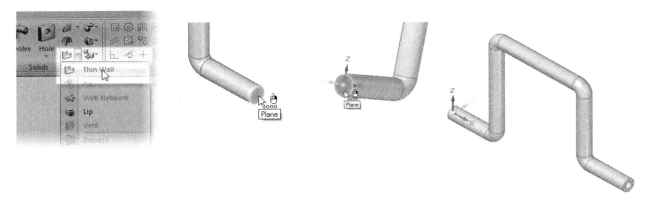

19. On ribbon, click **Home > Draw > Project to Sketch** and click on the end face.
20. Click on the inner edge of the end face to project it.
21. Draw another circle of 4.5 in diameter.

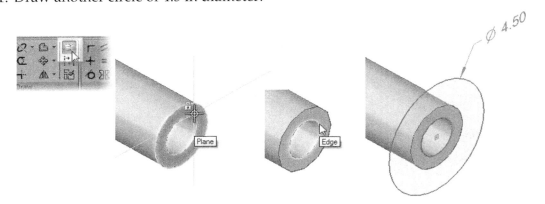

22. Activate the **Extrude** command and click inside the two sketch regions.
23. Right-click to accept the selection and move the mouse cursor. Type-in 0.75 in the box that appears on the geometry.
24. Press Enter to create the flange.

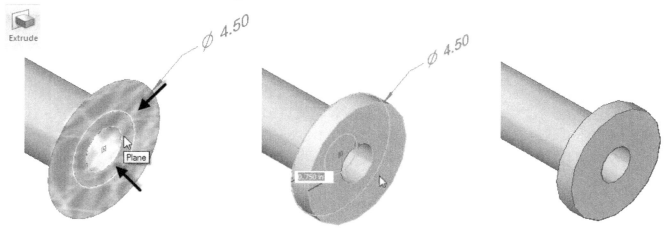

25. Draw a sketch on the flange face and create the *Cutout* feature.

Sweep Features

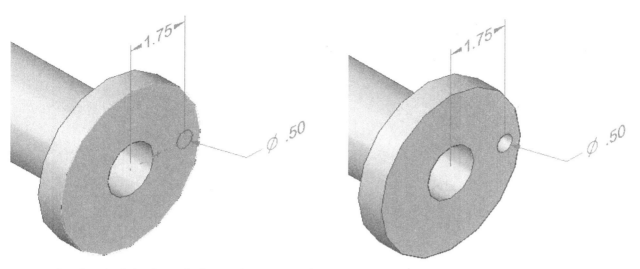

26. In the Pathfinder, click on the *Cutout* feature, and then click **Home > Pattern > Rectangular > Circular** on the ribbon. Now, you have to define the axis of the circular pattern.
27. Click on a circular edge of the flange to define the pattern axis.
28. Type-in **6** in the **Count** box and click the green check on the command bar. The cutouts are patterned in a circular fashion.

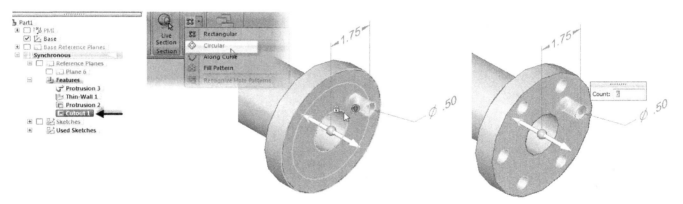

29. Change the model view orientation.

133

Sweep Features

30. Create another flange and circular pattern.

31. Save and close the part file.

Questions
1. List the methods to create *Sweep* features.
2. How to apply twist and turns to *Sweep* features?
3. Write the formula to calculate the variable pitch of a helical feature.
4. Why do we define the axis of a *Sweep* feature?
5. List any two methods to create helical features.

Exercises
Exercise1

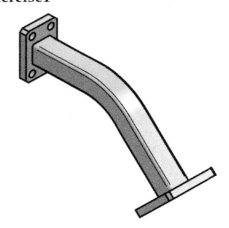

Sweep Features

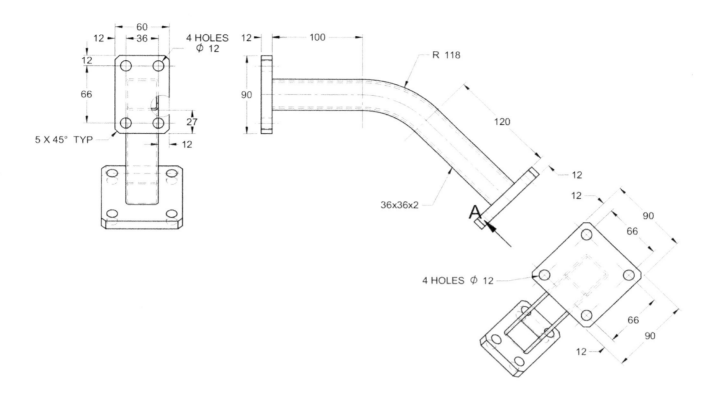

Sweep Features

Loft Features

Chapter 7: Loft Features

The **Loft** command is one of the advanced commands available in Solid Edge that allows you to create simple as well as complex shapes. A basic loft is created by defining two cross-sections and joining them together. For example, if you create a loft feature between a circle and a square, you can easily change the cross-sectional shape of the solid. This ability is what separates the loft feature from the sweep feature.

The topics covered in this chapter are:

- *Basic Lofts*
- *Loft options*
- *Loft Cutouts*

Loft

This command creates a loft feature between different cross-sections. To create a loft, first create two or more sections on different planes. The planes can be parallel or perpendicular to each other. Activate the **Loft** command (click **Home > Solids > Sweep > Loft** on the ribbon); the **Loft** command bar appears. The **Cross-Section Step** icon is active and ready for you to select the cross-sections that will define the loft. You need to select two or more cross-sections to define a loft. As with most features, you can either select the cross-sections from the **PathFinder** or from the graphics window. When creating a loft, you are recommended to select the cross-sections from the graphics window. The loft feature is sensitive to the location at which you will click to select the cross-section. For example, select the first cross-section by clicking near the right corner, and then select the second cross-section by clicking at corresponding location. Click **Preview** on the command bar; preview immediately updates, as shown below.

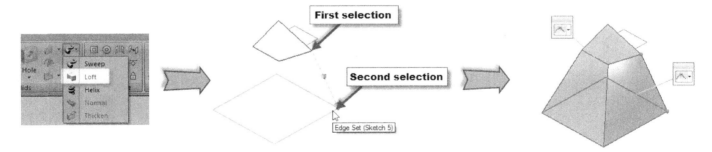

Now, click the **Cross-Section Step** icon on the command bar, and then click **Define Start Point**. Select the opposite corner on the first cross-section, and then click the **Preview** button; you will notice that a different result appears. For this reason, you have to be careful about where you click to select the cross-sections. However, if you do happen to make a mistake, you can use the **Define Start Point** icon to fix any unwanted twisting.

Loft Features

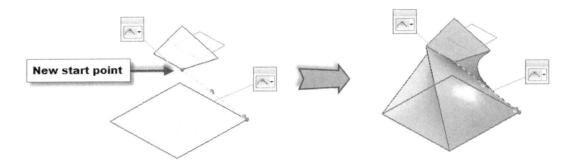

Tangency Controls

The shape of a simple loft is controlled by the cross-sections and the plane location. However, the behaviour of the side faces can be controlled by the **Tangency Controls** connected to the cross-sections. If you would like to change the appearance of the side faces, you can use the **Tangency Controls** either at the beginning of the loft, the end of the lofts or both. For instance, click on **Tangency Control** on the beginning of the loft and select **Normal to Section**; the preview of the loft updates. You can notice that the beginning of the loft starts in a direction normal to the cross-section. You can control how much influence the **Normal to Section** option will have by adjusting the parameter in the box attached to the cross-section. A lower value will have lesser effect on the feature. As you increase the value, the more noticeable the effect will be, eventually. If you increase the number high enough, the normal effect will lead to some weird results. You can also click and drag the handle attached to the cross-section to control the normal effect. If you want to change the direction of the Normal to Section effect, enter a negative value in the box attached to section. The same options can also be applied to the end of the lofts.

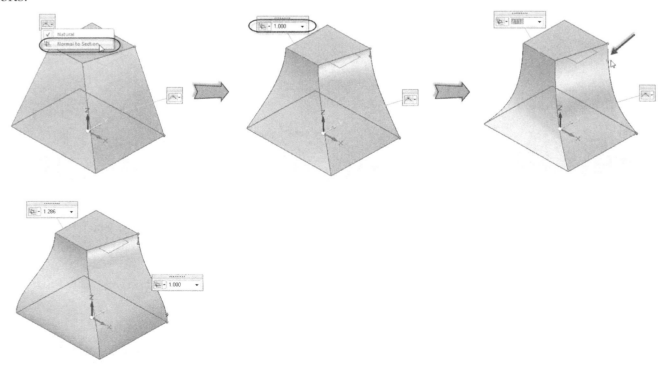

Loft Features

Loft Cross-sections

In addition to 2D sketches, you can also to define loft cross-sections by using different element types. For instance, you can use existing model faces, surfaces, curves, and points. The only restriction is that the points can be used at the beginning or end of a loft. Set the appropriate option in the **Select** drop-down menu to select different element types.

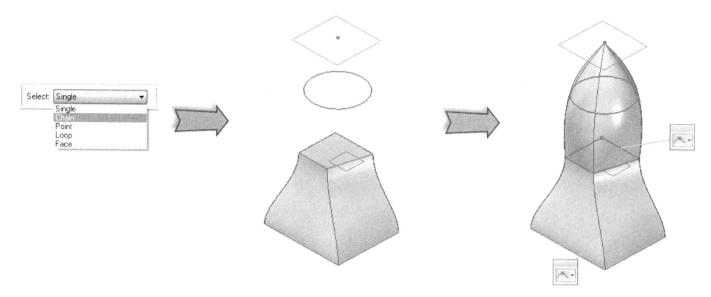

Closed Extent

Solid Edge allows you to create a loft that closes on itself. For example, to create a create a ring that lofts between each of the shapes, you must select four sketches as shown in figure, and then click the **Extent Step** icon on the command bar. Next, click the **Closed Extent** icon on the command bar, and click **Preview**; this will give you a closed loft.

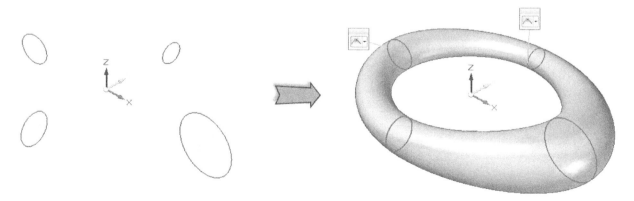

Guide Curves

Similar to **Tangency Controls**, guide curves allow you to control the behaviour of a loft between cross-sections. You can create guide curves by using 2D sketches. You can also use the **Keypoint Curve** command to create guided curves. Activate this command (click **Surfacing > Curves > Keypoint Curve** on the ribbon) and select points to create a curve, as illustrated below. Right-click and click **Finish** to complete the curve. Likewise, create the other curves.

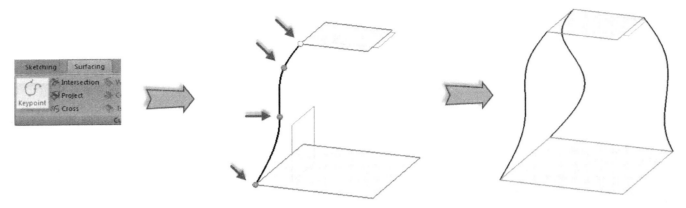

Now, activate the **Loft** command and select the cross-sections. To select guide curves, click the **Guide Curve Step** icon on the command bar and select the first guide curve, and then click the green check on the command bar. In the same way, select the other guide curves and click the **Preview** icon; you will see that the preview updates. Notice that the edges with guide curves are affected. The one without guide curve remains as it is.

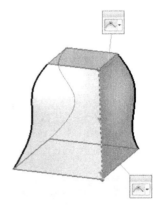

Section Geometry

Sections used for creating lofts should have a matching number of segments. For example, a three sided section will loft nicely to another three sided section despite the differences in the shape of the individual segments. The **Loft** command does a good job of generating smooth faces to join them.

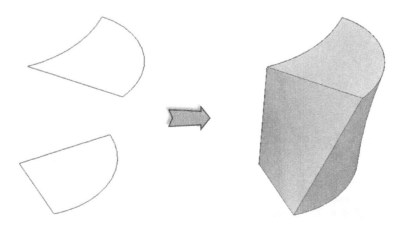

Loft Features

On the other hand, a four sided section will not loft nicely to a two-sided section. Although Solid Edge succeeds in generating a loft, it maps the end points incorrectly and you may not get the desired result.

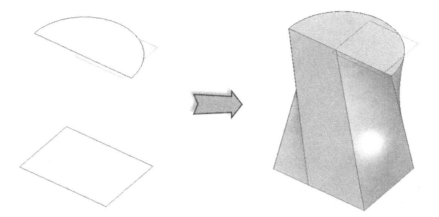

To get the desired result, you have to split one of the sections so that they have equal number of segments. Activate the **Split** command (click **Home > Draw > Split** on the ribbon) and split the arc into three segments. You can also use dimensions to define the exact location of the split points.

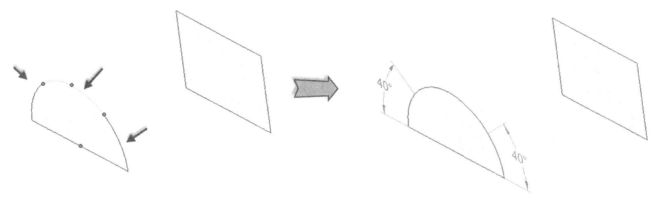

Now, create the loft feature by selecting the cross-sections.

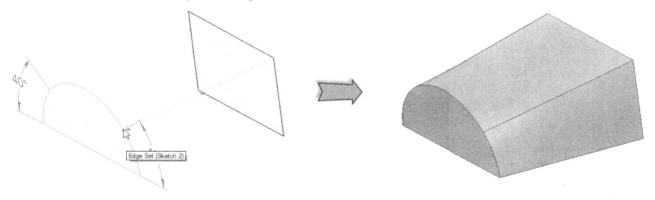

Let's take a look at another example for a loft with mismatching segments. Activate the **Loft** command and select the cross-sections. Click the **Extent Step** icon on the command bar, and then click the **Vertex Mapping** icon; the **Vertex Mapping** dialog box pops up. You can use this dialog box to map vertices of the cross-sections. Click **Set 1** on the dialog box and select two vertices. Click **Add** on the dialog box and select two vertices; another set of vertices is added to the loft. Similarly, add another set and close the dialog box. Click **Finish** to complete the loft.

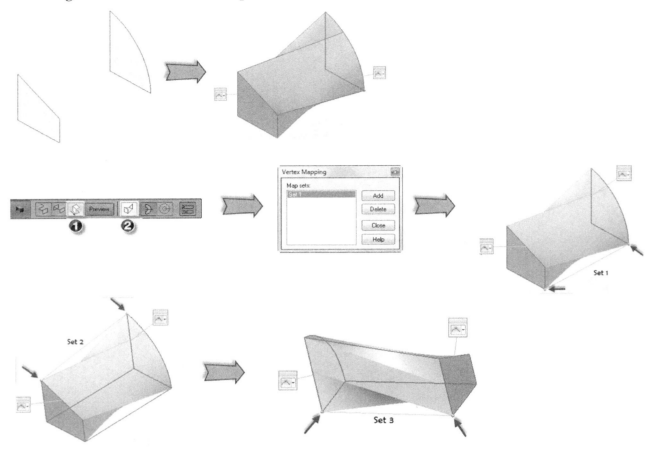

Loft Cutout

Like other standard features such as extrude, revolve and sweep, the loft feature can be used to add material. But, it can also be used to remove material. You can do this by using the **Loft Cutout** command. Activate this command (click **Home > Solids > Swept Cutout > Loft Cutout** on the ribbon) and select the cross-sections. Click **Preview** and **Finish** to create the loft cutout.

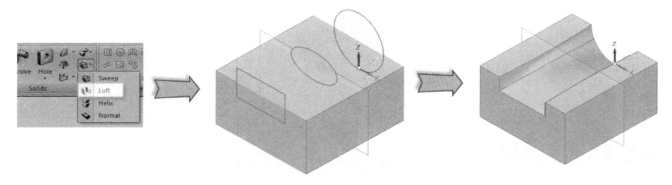

Loft Features

Examples
Example 1 (Millimetres)
In this example, you will create the part shown below.

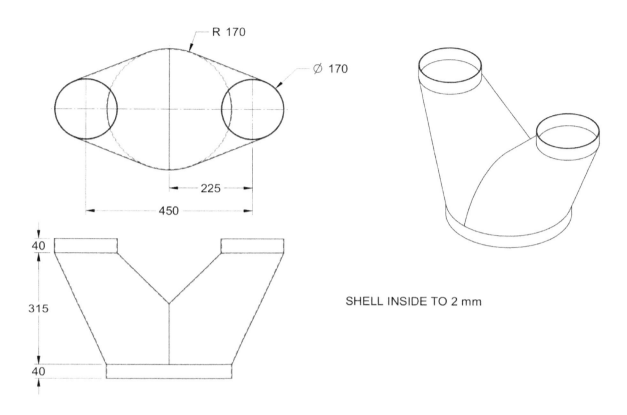

SHELL INSIDE TO 2 mm

1. Start **Solid Edge ST6**.
2. On the initial screen, click **ISO Part**; a new part file is opened.
3. To start a new sketch, click **Home > Draw > Circle by Center Point** on the ribbon.
4. Lock the XY plane and draw a circle of 340 mm diameter.
5. Create the *Extrude* feature with 40 mm thickness.

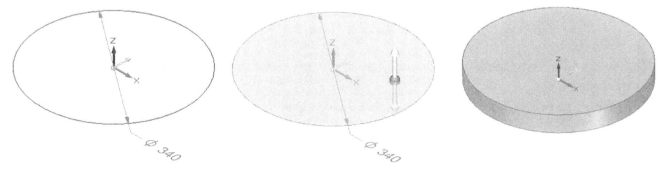

6. On the ribbon, click **Home > Planes > Coincident Plane**.
7. Click on the top face of the geometry to create a coincident plane.

Loft Features

8. Click on the Z-axis of the Steering Wheel tool and move the mouse cursor upward.
9. Type-in 315 mm in the dimension box and press Enter.
10. Activate the **Circle by Center Point** command and draw a circle of 170 mm diameter on the new plane.

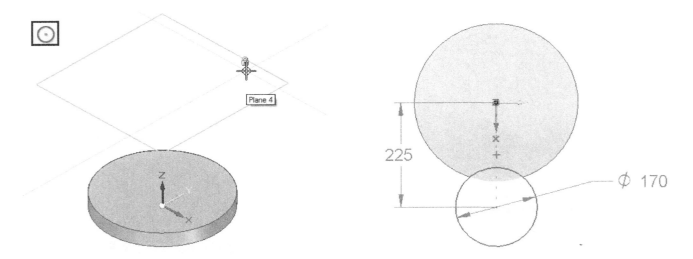

11. Change the model view orientation to ISO View.
12. On the ribbon, click **Home > Solids > Sweep > Loft**.
13. Click on the circle and the top circular edge of the *Extrude* feature.
14. Click **Preview** on the command bar to preview the loft protrusion.
15. Click **Finish** to complete the *Loft* feature.

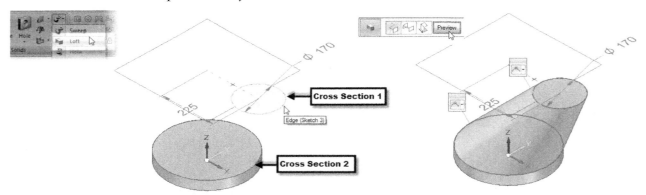

16. Activate the **Extrude** command and click on the top face of the *Loft* feature. Right-click to accept the selection.
17. Move the mouse cursor up and type 40 in the box that appears on the geometry. Press Enter.

Loft Features

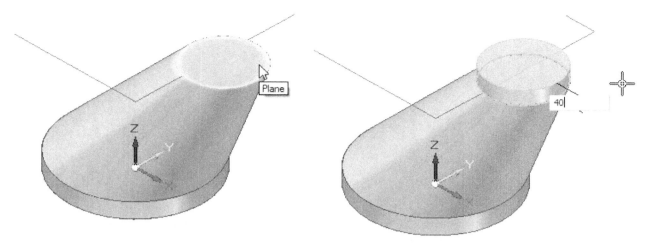

18. In the Pathfinder, press the Shift key and click on the *Loft Protrusion* and *Extrude Protusion*. Activate the **Mirror** command.
19. Click on the YZ plane of the coordinate system to mirror the selected features.

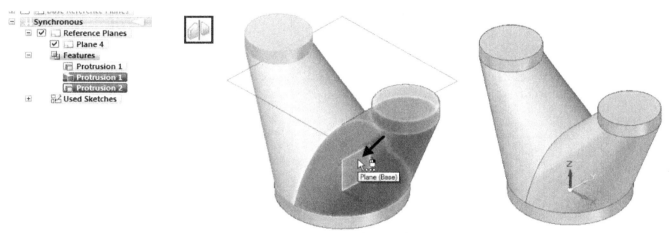

20. On the ribbon, click **Home > Solids > Thin Wall** and click on the flat faces of the part geometry.
21. Type 2 in the box that appears on the geometry and press Enter. The part geometry is shelled.

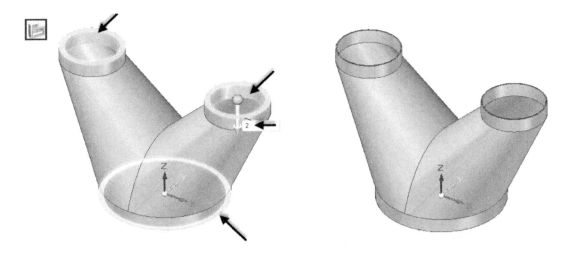

22. Save and close the part file.

Questions

1. Describe the procedure to create a *Loft* feature.
2. List any two **Tangency Control** options.
3. List the type of elements that can be selected to create a *Loft* feature.

Exercises
Exercise 1

Loft Features

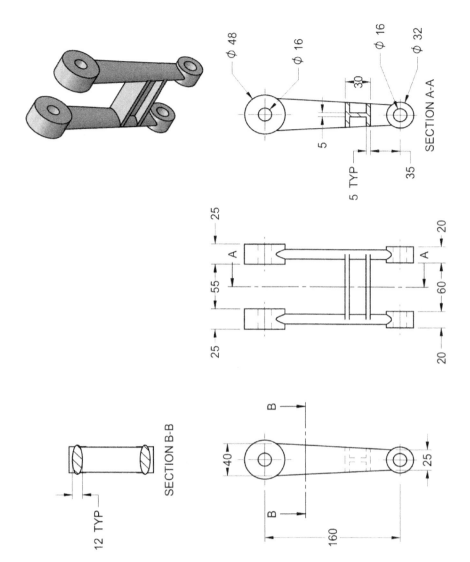

Additional Features and Multibody Parts

Chapter 8: Additional Features and Multibody Parts

Solid Edge offers you some additional commands and features which will help you to create complex models. These commands are explained in this chapter.

The topics covered in this chapter are:

- *Ribs*
- *Web Network*
- *Mounting bosses*
- *Lips*
- *Vents*
- *Slots*
- *Multi-body parts*
- *Split bodies*
- *Boolean Operations*
- *Emboss features*

Rib

This command creates a rib feature to add structural stability, strength and support to your designs. Just like any other sketch-based feature, a rib requires a two dimensional sketch. Create a sketch, as shown in figure and activate the **Rib** command (click **Home > Solids > Thin Wall > Rib** on the ribbon). Select the sketch and click the green check; the preview of the geometry appears. You can add the rib material to either sides of the sketch line or evenly to both sides. Set the **Alignment** type to **Centered** to add material to both sides of the sketch line. Type-in the thickness value of the rib feature in the box displayed on the model. You can use the steering wheel to change the direction of the rib.

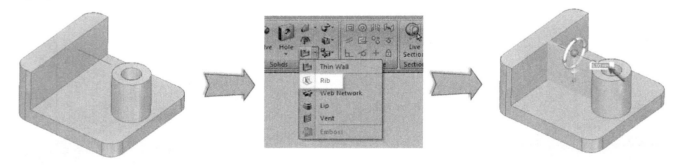

If you activate the **No Extend** option on the command bar, the material will not extend to meet the faces of the surrounding features.

Additional Features and Multibody Parts

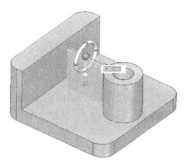

Activate the **Finite Depth** option, if you want to add material only upto to some distance. Click the green check to complete the rib feature.

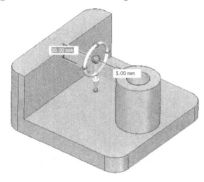

Web Network

This command is similar to the **Rib** command, but creates multiple ribs at a time forming a network. Create a two dimensional sketch as shown in figure and activate the **Web Network** command (Click **Home > Solids > Thin Wall** on the ribbon). Select the sketch elements one-by-one and click the green check; the preview of the geometry appears.

Use the **Draft** option on the command bar to add a draft to the web network feature. Click the green check to complete the feature.

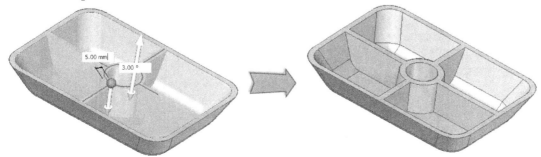

Additional Features and Multibody Parts

Mounting Boss

The process of creating mounting bosses can be automated using the **Mounting Boss** command. This command is available only in the Ordered mode. Switch to the Ordered mode and activate the **Mounting Boss** command (click **Home >Solids >Thin Wall > Mounting Boss** on the ribbon). On the command bar, select **Coincident Plane** from the **Create from Options** drop-down menu. Select the top face of the model and define the location of the mounting bosses. Click **Close Sketch** on the ribbon and define the side of the bosses.

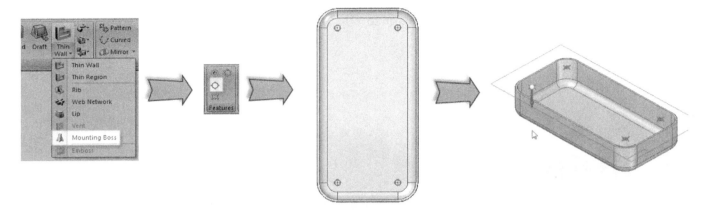

Click the **Options** icon on the command bar; the **Mounting Boss Options** dialog box pops up on the screen. Define the parameters of the mounting boss. The parameters are self explanatory. Click **OK** and then **Finish** to complete the feature.

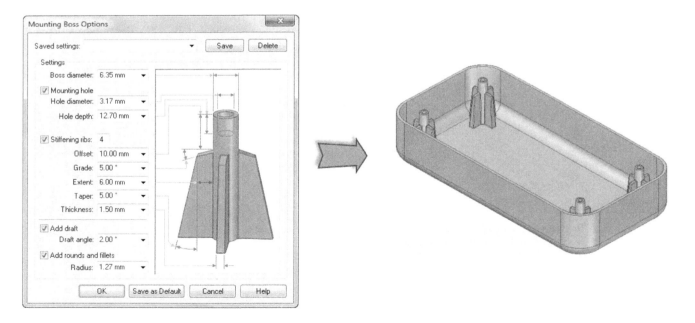

Lip

This command allows you to create lips and grooves on edges of parts, saving you time by not having to create a series of manual cuts. Activate this command (click **Home > Solids > Thin Wall > Lip** on

Additional Features and Multibody Parts

the ribbon) and select a chain of edges. Click the green check on the command bar and define the side of the lip. Click the left mouse button, and then click **Finish** to complete the feature.

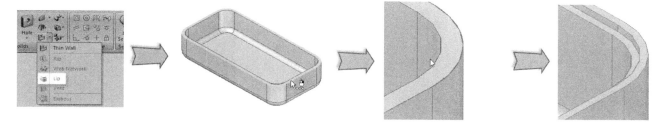

Vent

This command allows you to take a two dimensional sketch of a vent and convert it into a 3D cutout. To create a vent feature, first create a 2D sketch and activate the **Vent** command (click **Home > Solids > Thin Wall > Vent** on the ribbon). As you activate this command the **Vent Options** dialog box pops up on the screen.

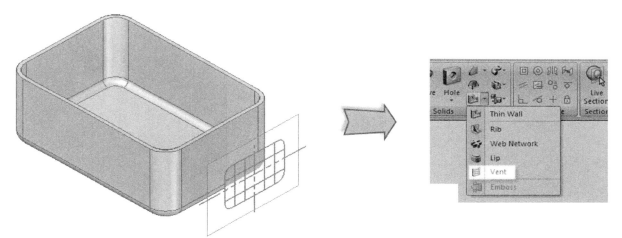

Define the thickness of **Ribs** and **Spars** to 4.

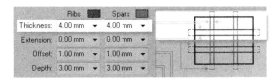

Set the **Offset** values to 1 and **Depth** to 3.

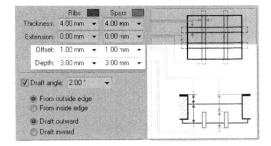

151

Additional Features and Multibody Parts

Check the **Draft angle** option and enter 5 in the box.
Check the **Round & fillet radius** option and enter 0.5 in the box. Click **OK** on the dialog box.

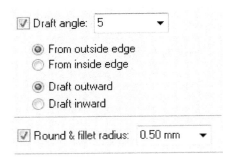

Select the boundary and click the green check on the command bar. Likewise, select the ribs and spars, and then click on the model to define the side of the vent. Next, click **Finish** to the complete the feature.

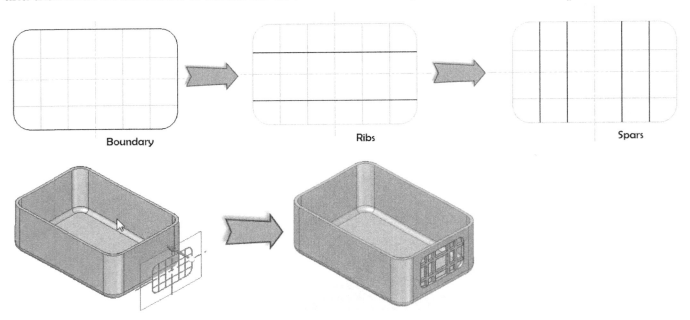

Slot

This command creates a slot by using a 2D sketch. The sketch can have a single or multiple elements. If the sketch is having multiple elements, they should be tangent and continuous to each other. To create a slot, create a 2D sketch and activate the **Slot** command (click **Home > Solids > Hole > Slot** on the command); the command bar pops up on the screen. Click the **Options** icon on the command bar to open the **Slot Options** dialog box. Type-in a value in the **Slot width** box and select the end type. Click **OK** and select the sketch. Next, define the extent of the slot feature. Click the right mouse button to complete the slot feature.

Additional Features and Multibody Parts

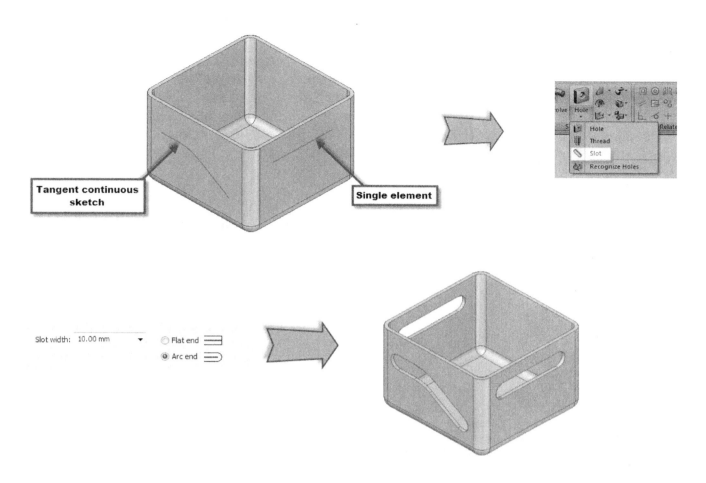

If you want to create a counterbore slot, check the **Counterbore** option on the **Slot Options** dialog box and define the **Path Offset** and **Depth Offset** values. You can create two types of the counterbore slots: **Recessed** and **Raised**.

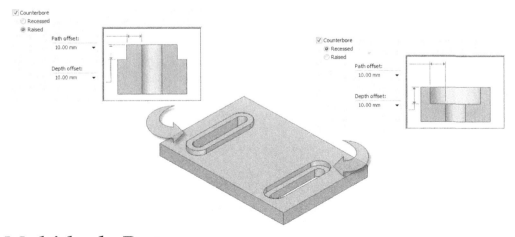

Multi-body Parts

Solid Edge allows the use of multiple bodies when designing parts. This opens the door to several design techniques that would otherwise not be possible. In this section, you will learn some of these techniques.

Additional Features and Multibody Parts

Creating Multibodies

The number of bodies in a part can change throughout the design process. Solid Edge makes it easy to create multiple bodies, and combine them into a single body. To create multiple bodies in a part, first create a solid body, and then activate the **Add Body** command (click **Home > Solids > Add Body** on the ribbon); the **Add Body** dialog box pops up on the screen. Select the **Add Part body** or **Add Sheet Metal body** option, enter the body name in the **New body name** field, and then click **OK**. Now, create a solid body using anyone of the solid modeling tools; the **Design Bodies** entry will be added to the **Pathfinder** tree.

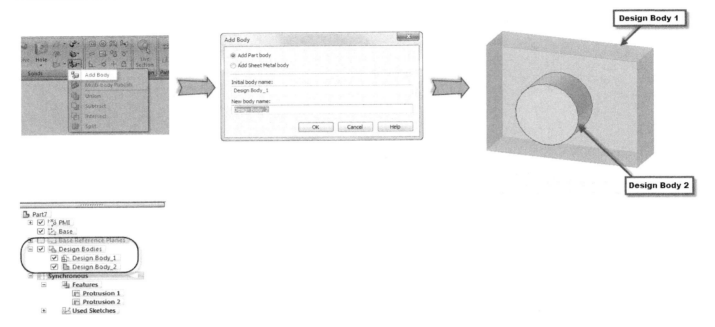

Split

The **Split** command can be used to separate single bodies into multiple bodies. This command can be used to perform local operations. For example, if you apply the shell feature to the front portion of the model shown in figure, the whole model will be shelled. To solve this problem, you must split the solid body into multiple bodies.

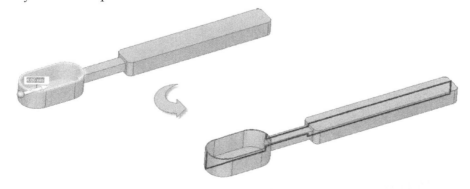

Additional Features and Multibody Parts

To split a body, you must have a splitting tool such as planes, sketch elements, surface, or bodies. In this case, a surface can be used as splitting tool. To create a surface, activate the **Bounded** command (click **Surfacing > Surfaces > Bounded** on the ribbon) and set the **Selection Type** on the command bar to **Single**. Now, select the edges, as shown in figure. Click the green check on the command bar and click **Finish** to create the bounded surface.

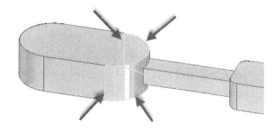

Activate the **Split** command (click **Home > Solids >Add Body** on the ribbon) and select the solid body from the graphics window. Next, select the bounded surface as the splitting tool and click the green check on the command bar. This results in two separate bodies.

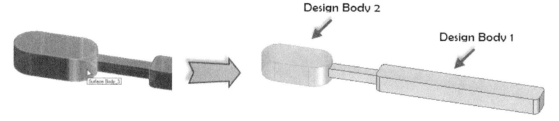

Now, double-click on **Design Body 2** in the **Pathfinder** tree to activate it, and then create the shell feature.

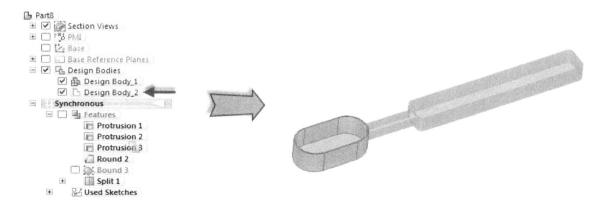

Additional Features and Multibody Parts

Union

If you apply rounds to edges between two bodies, it will result in a different outcome as shown in figure. To solve this problem, you must combine the two bodies using the **Union** command. Activate this command (click **Home > Solids > Add Body > Union** on the ribbon) and select the bodies. Click the green check on the command bar to combine the bodies. Now, apply rounds to the edges.

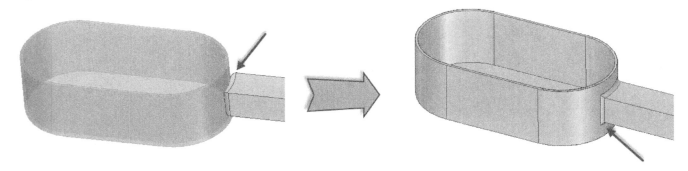

Intersect

By using the **Intersect** command, you can generate bodies defined by the intersecting volume of two bodies. Activate this command (click **Home > Solids > Add Body > Intersect** on the ribbon) and select two bodies. Click the green check to see the resultant single solid body.

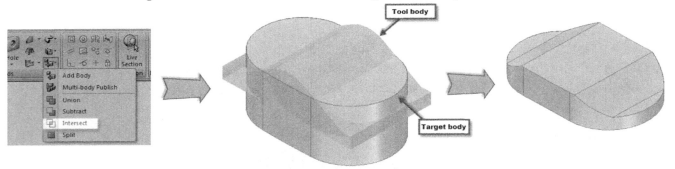

Subtract

This command performs the function of subtracting one solid body from another. Activate this command (click **Home > Solids > Add Body > Subtract** on the ribbon) and select target body. Click the green check, and then select the tool body. Again, click the green check to subtract the tool body from the target. Hide the tool body to see the result.

Multi Body Publish

In addition to creating multiple bodies, Solid Edge also offers an option to generate an assembly from the resulting bodies. For example, create the model shown in figure and split it into two separate bodies. Next, add lip/groove feature to the model.

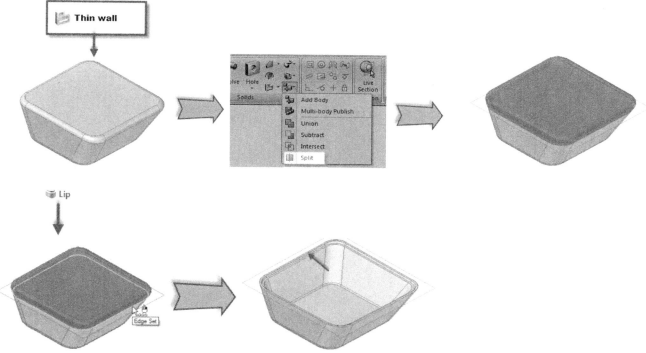

Activate the **Multi Body Publish** command (click **Home > Solids > Add Body > Multi Body Publish** on the ribbon); the **Multi-body Publish** dialog box pops up on the screen. Click **Save Files** on the dialog box to save the design bodies as individual files and create an assembly. Click the right mouse button on **Create Assembly path** and select **Open**. The newly created assembly is opened. Now, you can apply assembly relationships to the parts.

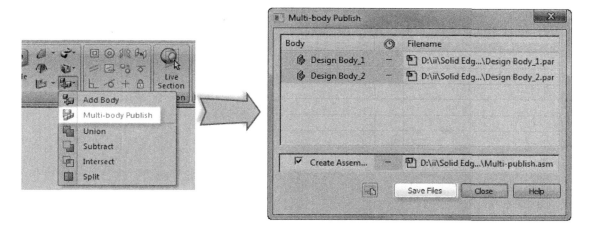

Emboss

This command allows you to change the shape of a solid body by using another solid body. The solid body that is changed is called the target body and the solid body that causes the changes is called the

Additional Features and Multibody Parts

tool body. To create an emboss feature, you must have two solid bodies in a part. Activate the **Emboss** command (click **Home > Solids > Thin Wall > Emboss** on the ribbon) and select the target and tool bodies. Type-in values in the **Clearance** and **Thickness** boxes. Use the **Direction** icon on the command bar to define the side on which the body is embossed. Click the green check on the command bar to complete the emboss feature.

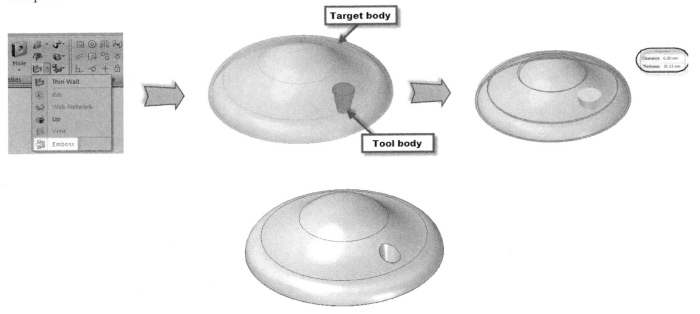

Examples

Example 1 (Millimetres)

In this example, you will create the part shown below.

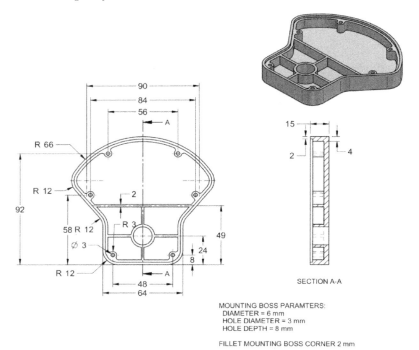

MOUNTING BOSS PARAMTERS:
DIAMETER = 6 mm
HOLE DIAMETER = 3 mm
HOLE DEPTH = 8 mm

FILLET MOUNTING BOSS CORNER 2 mm

Additional Features and Multibody Parts

1. Start **Solid Edge ST6**.
2. On the initial screen, click **ISO Part**; a new part file is opened.
3. On the ribbon, click **Home > Draw > Line** and draw the sketch on the XY plane, as shown below.

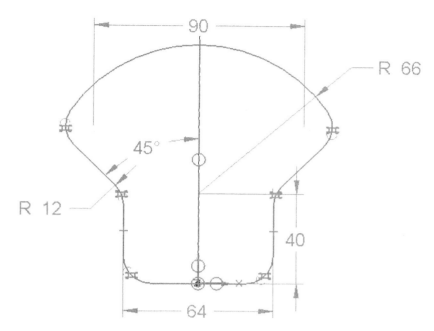

4. Create the *Extrude* feature of 15 mm depth.
5. Create the *Thin Wall* feature of 4 mm depth.

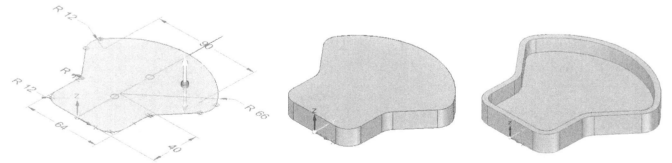

6. On the ribbon, click **Home > Solids > Thin Wall > Lip**.
7. Click on the inner edge of the *Thin Wall* feature and click the green check on the command bar.
8. Type **2** in the **Width** and **Height** boxes, respectively. Click inside the model to define the side of the lip. Click **Finish** and **Cancel** to complete the lip feature.

Additional Features and Multibody Parts

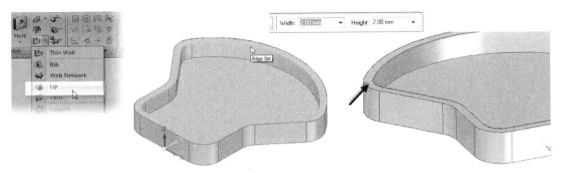

9. Click the right mouse button in the screen and select **Transition to Ordered**.
10. In the Ordered mode, click **Home > Solids > Thin Wall > Mounting Boss** on the ribbon.
11. On the command bar, select **Coincident Plane** from the **Create-From Options** menu.
12. Click on the top face on the lip feature.

13. Define mounting boss locations and add dimensions. Click **Close Sketch** on ribbon.
14. On the command bar, click **Mounting Boss Options** icon.
15. On the **Mounting Boss Options** dialog box, set the **Boss diameter** to 6, check the **Mounting hole** option, and then set the **Hole diameter** to 3 and **Hole depth** to 8. Click **OK** to close the dialog box.
16. Move the mouse cursor downward and click to define the side of the mounting boss.
17. Click **Finish** and **Cancel** to complete the mounting boss feature.

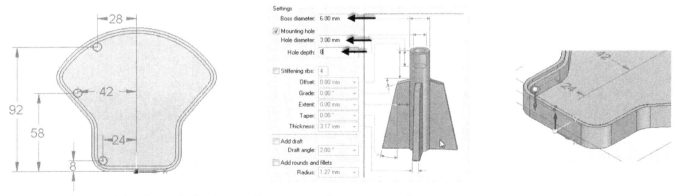

18. In the Pathfinder, click the right mouse button on the *Mounting Boss* and select **Move to Synchronous**.
19. Click the right mouse in the screen and select **Transition to Synchronous**.
20. Press and hold the Shift key and click on the *Lip* and *Mounting Bosses* in the Pathfinder.
21. On the ribbon, click **Home > Pattern > Mirror**.

22. Click on the YZ plane of the base coordinate system. The mounting bosses are mirrored.

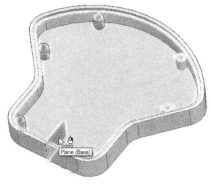

23. On the ribbon, click **Home > Solids > Round** and select the edges where the mounting bosses meet the walls of the geometry.
24. Type **2** in the box displayed on the geometry. Click the right mouse button to round the selected edges.

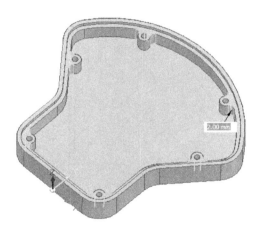

25. Activate the **Hole** command and create a hole on the flat face of the geometry. The hole diameter is 15 mm.

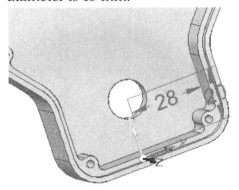

26. On the ribbon, click **Planes > Coincident Plane**. Click on the top face on the lip feature.
27. On the ribbon, click **Draw > Circle by Center Point**. Lock the new plane.
28. Draw the sketch on the locked plane, as shown below. Next, unlock the plane.

Additional Features and Multibody Parts

29. On the ribbon, click **Home > Solids > Thin Wall > Web Network**.
30. Click on the elements of the sketch, and then click the green check on the command bar.
31. Type **2** in the box that appears on the part geometry, and then click the green check.

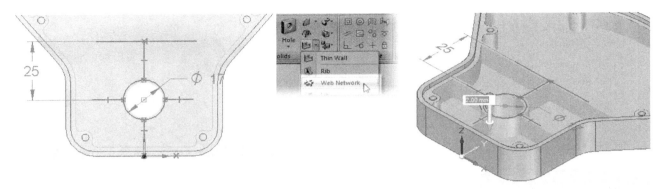

32. Save and close the file.

Questions

1. What is the use of the **Web Network** command?
2. How many types of can be created in Solid Edge?
3. Why do we create multi body parts?
4. Describe the terms 'Rib' and 'Spar' in *Vent* feature?
5. What is the use of the **Multi Body Publish** command?

Exercises

Exercise 1

Additional Features and Multibody Parts

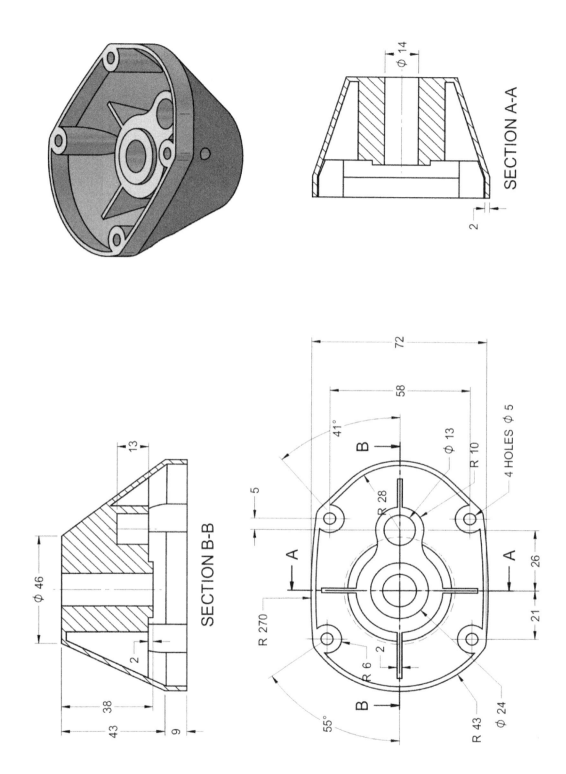

Additional Features and Multibody Parts

Exercise 2

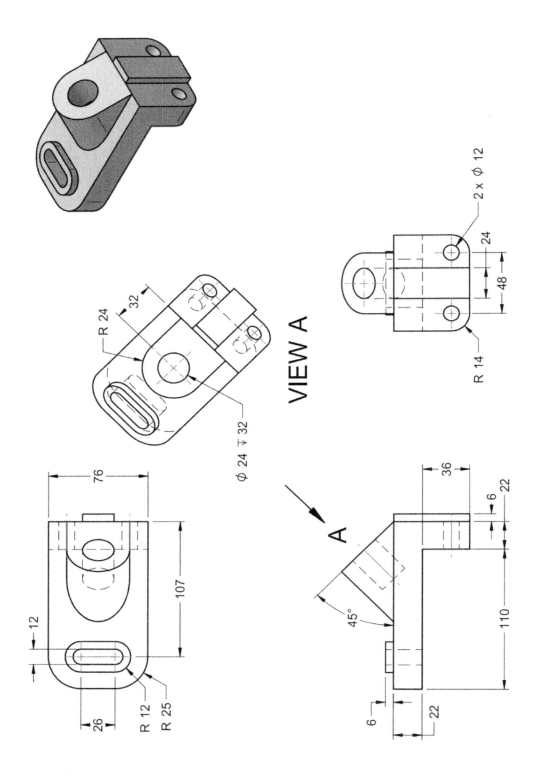

Exercise 3 (Inches)

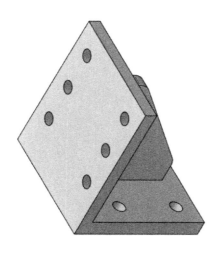
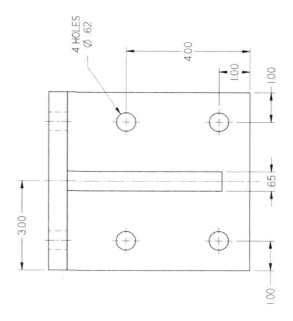
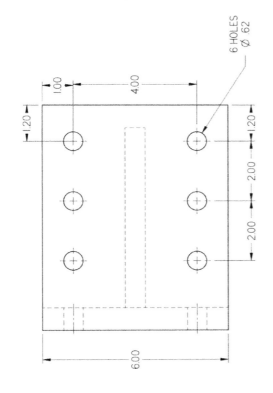
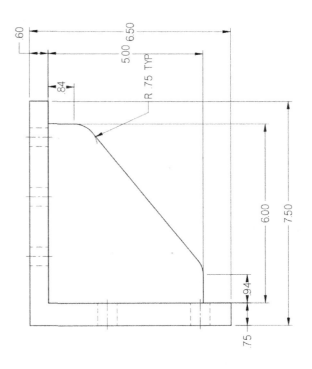

Chapter 9: Modifying Parts

In design process, it is not required to achieve the final model in the first attempt. There is always a need to modify the existing parts to get the desired part geometry. In this chapter, you will learn various commands and techniques to make changes to a part.

The topics covered in this chapter are:

- *Modify models using steering wheel*
- *Change model dimensions*
- *Live sections*
- *Face Relations*
- *Live Rules*

Face Relations

Solid Edge allows you to define relations between faces. This will help you to modify the part geometry to achieve the desired result. There are different relations that can be applied between faces. These are explained next.

Coplanar

This command brings the selected faces onto one plane. Activate this command (click **Home > Face Relate > Coplanar** on the ribbon) and select the first face. Right-click and select the second face. Again, right-click to make the two faces coplanar.

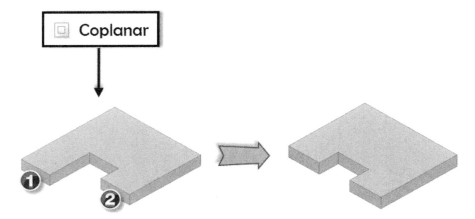

Concentric

This command makes two cylindrical faces share a same centerpoint. Activate this command (click **Home > Face Relate > Concentric** on the ribbon) and select the first cylindrical face. Click the right mouse button and select the second cylindrical face. Click the green check on the command bar to make the first face concentric to the second one.

Modifying Parts

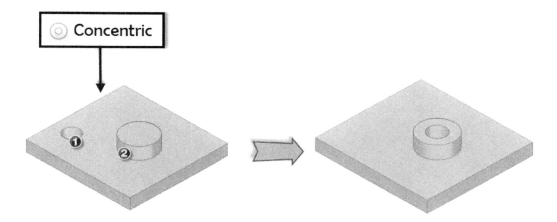

Symmetric

This command makes two faces symmetric about a plane. Activate this command (click **Home > Face Relate > Symmetric** on the ribbon), select the first face and click **Accept** on the command bar. Select the second face and click **Accept** on the command bar. Select the symmetric plane and click **Accept** to make the faces symmetric.

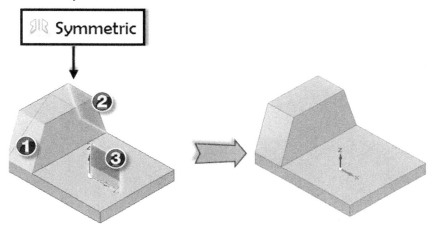

Offset

This command defines an offset distance between two faces. The selected faces should share a common face which is perpendicular to both of them. Activate this command (click **Home > Face Relate > Offset** on the ribbon), select the first face, and then click **Accept** on the command bar. Select the second face and click **Accept**. Type-in an offset value in the box displayed on the model. Click **Accept** on the command bar; the first face will be offset from the second face by the value you specified.

Modifying Parts

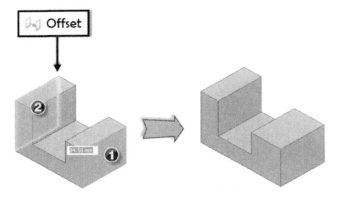

Parallel

This command makes two faces parallel to each other. The first face will be parallel to the second face.

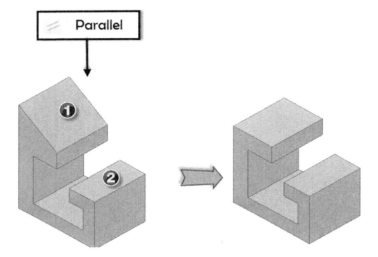

Coplanar Axis

This command makes the axes of selected cylindrical or conical faces lie on a same plane. Activate this command and select cylindrical faces from the part geometry. Click **Accept** on the command bar and select a plane. Click **Accept** on the command bar; you will notice that the axes of selected faces will be moved onto one plane.

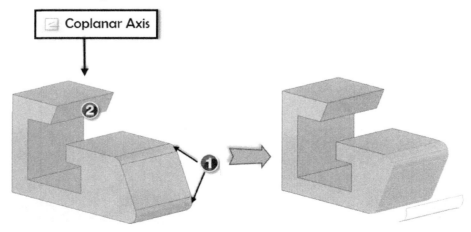

Modifying Parts

Equal Radius

This command makes the selected cylindrical faces equal in radius. The radius of the first face will be equal to that of the second face.

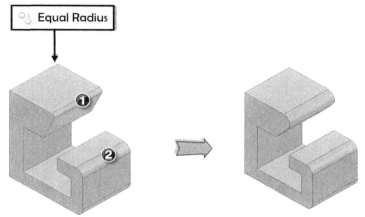

Tangent

This command makes two faces tangent to one another.

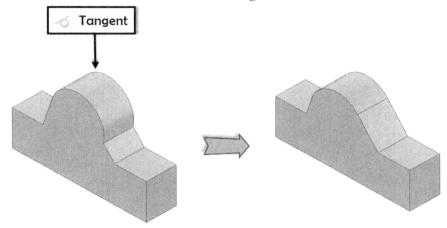

Horizontal/Vertical

This command aligns the selected faces or keypoints vertically/horizontally.

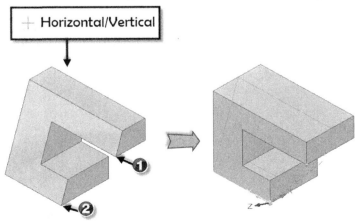

Modifying Parts

Using the Steering Wheel Tool to Modify Models

Solid Edge provides you with a special tool called Steering Wheel Tool to modify faces and planes of part geometry. You can perform two operations using this tool: **Move** and **Rotate** faces.

Move faces

To move a face, click on it and select the arrow displayed on it. Move the cursor and click to define the distance. You can also type-in a value in the box displayed on the model. The **Extend/ Trim** option on the command bar extends or trims the adjacent faces to match the new location of the selected face.

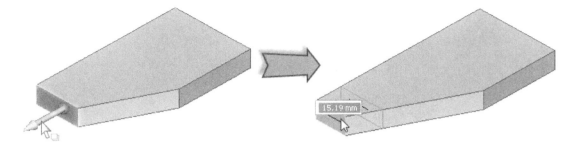

Use the **Tip** option, if you want to adjust the orientation of the faces connected to the selected face.

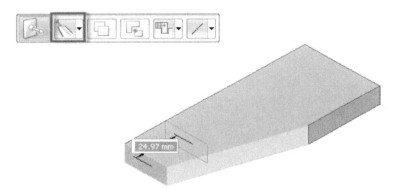

Use the **Lift** option, if you want to lift the selected face and add new faces to model.

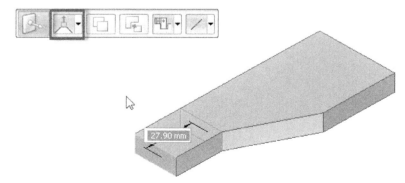

Use the **Detach** option, if you want to move and detach the selected face from the model.

Modifying Parts

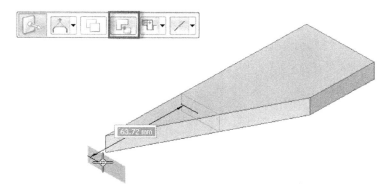

Use the **Copy** option, if you want to move and copy the selected face.

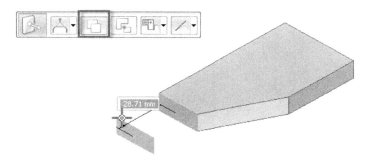

Use the **Model Priority** option, if you want to move the selected face only upto a particular face in the model.

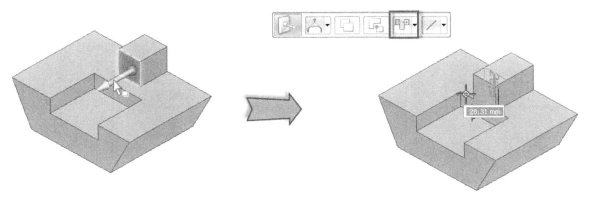

Use the **Select Set Priority** option, if you want to move the selected face beyond any faces in the model.

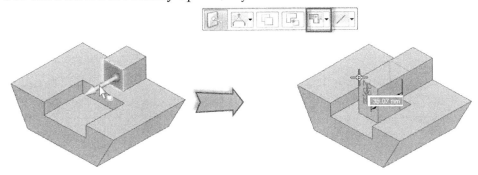

Modifying Parts

Rotate faces

To rotate a face, you must click on it to display the Steering Wheel arrow. Click and drag the spear attached to the arrow, and then align it to an edge. This defines the axis of rotation. Now, click on the torus of the steering wheel and rotate the face. You can type-in an angle value in the box displayed on the model.

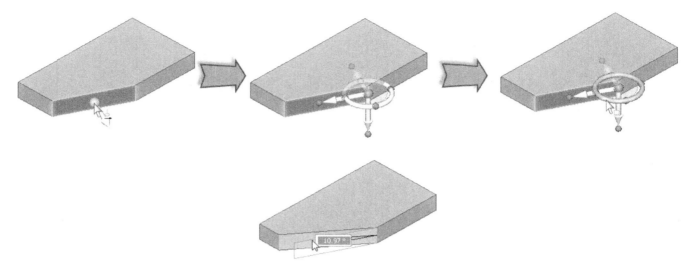

Dealing with Live Rules

Live Rules control the part geometry when you modify its faces. They appear automatically on selecting any model face. For example, if you move a hole which is concentric to another cylindrical face, the **Maintain Concentric Faces** option maintains the relationship between the two faces. As a result, the both the faces will be moved. If you turn off this option, only the hole will be moved. Similarly, other options maintain the corresponding relationships while modifying the faces.

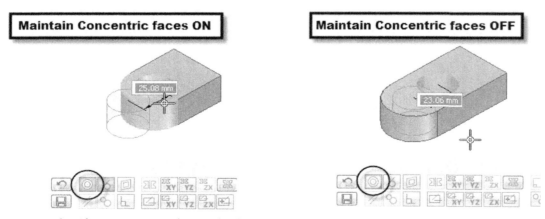

For example, if you move a face which is symmetric to another face about the YZ plane, the **Maintain Symmetry About Base Planes** option maintains the symmetric relationship. As a result, the other face will also be moved in the opposite direction. If you turn off this option, only the selected face will be moved.

Modifying Parts

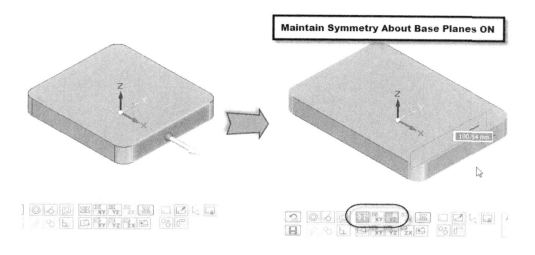

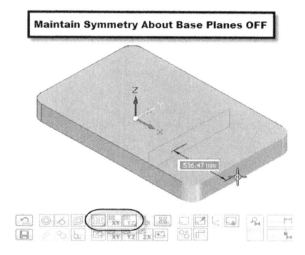

Click the **Suspend Live Rules** option, if you want to suspend all the live rules. Similarly, use the **Relax Dimensions** and **Relax Persistent Relationships** options to relax the dimensions and face relationships.

Use the **Solution Manager** option to solve the errors while moving or rotating faces of the part geometry. Click this option and you will notice that the model faces are highlighted in different colors. The selected face is highlighted in green color. The error path is highlighted in orange color and the faces which are being solved are highlighted in blue color. Click on the blue faces, if you want to suppress the relationship between the selected face (highlighted in green) and them. Click on the maroon faces, if you want to restore the relationship between them and the selected set (green faces). Move or rotate the green face to get the desired result. Click the right mouse button to accept the result.

Modifying Parts

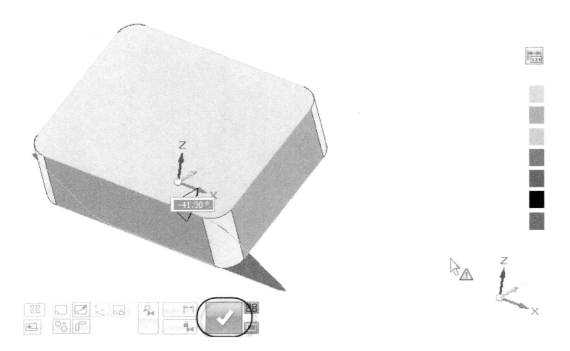

Modify the Part dimensions

Solid Edge allows you to add and modify dimensions between the faces of the part geometry. This will make the modification process much easy. To add a dimension, activate the **Smart Dimension** command and select an edge connecting two faces. Position the dimension and you will notice that a box pops up on the screen. Type-in a value in the box and click arrows displayed on the box to define the face to be affected. Click the double-arrow button, if you want to modify both the faces. Click the lock button on the box to lock the dimension. The locked dimension will act as a driving dimension.

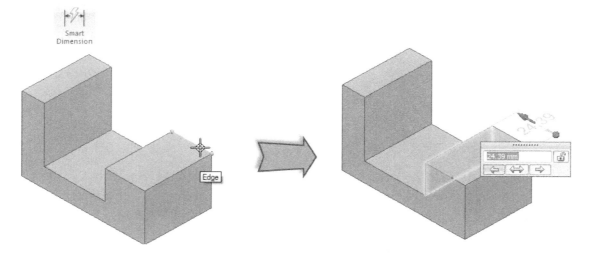

Live Sections

Live sections are created automatically when you create *Revolve* features. If you want to create live sections manually, activate the **Live Section** command (click **Home > Section > Live Section** on the ribbon) and select a flat face on the model. A live section will be created. Use the Steering Wheel Tool to

Modifying Parts

move the live section. You can click and drag the edge of a live section. The part geometry will be modified, automatically.

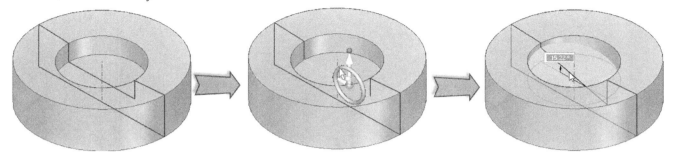

Examples

Example 1 (Millimetres)

In this example, you will create the part shown below, and then modify it using the Synchronous editing tools.

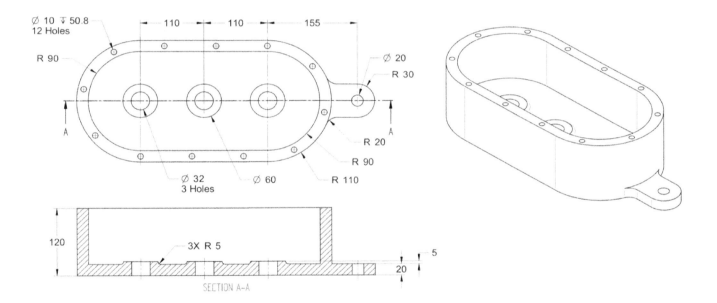

1. Start **Solid Edge ST6**.
2. On the initial screen, click **ISO Part**; a new part file is opened.
3. Create the part using the tools and commands in Solid Edge.
4. Click on the 20 diameter hole.
5. Click on the dimension value of the hole; the **Hole** command bar pops up on the screen.
6. On the command bar, click the **Hole Options** icon; the **Hole Options** dialog box pops up.
7. On the **Hole Options** dialog box, set the hole **Type** to **Counterbore**. Set the **Counterbore diameter** to 30 and **Counterbore depth** to 10. Click **OK** to close the dialog box.
8. Click the right mouse button to accept the changes.

Modifying Parts

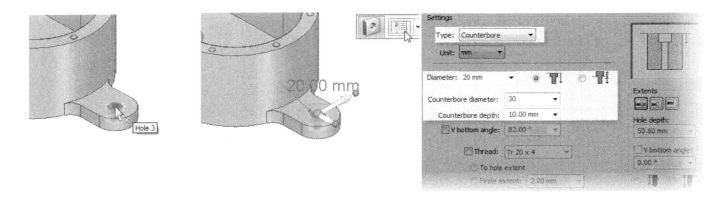

9. Again click on the counterbore hole and select the small arrow that appears on it.
10. Move the mouse cursor and type 20 in the box that appears on the part geometry. Press Enter to move the hole.

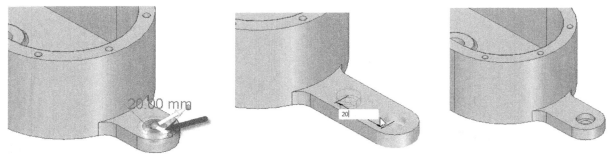

11. Click on the side face of the bottom feature. An arrow handle appears on the face.
12. Click the spear of the handle and drag it; the *Steering Wheel Tool* appears.
13. Align the Z-axis of the *Steering Wheel Tool* to the vertical edge, as shown in figure.

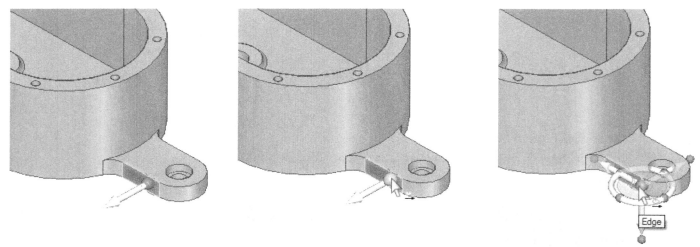

14. Click on the torus of the *Steering Wheel Tool* and move the mouse cursor outside.
15. Type -20 in the box that appears on the geometry. Press Enter to rotate the faces.

Modifying Parts

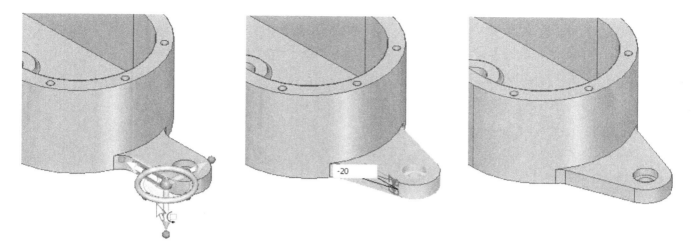

16. Click on anyone of the circle of the *Along Curve* pattern; the whole pattern is selected.
17. Click the *Pattern Handle* that appears on the geometry; the **Along Curve** command bar pops up along with the **Count** box.
18. Type 14 in the **Count** box and press Enter to update the pattern.

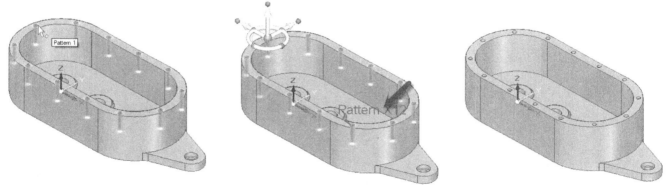

19. Click on the top face of the geometry to display an arrow.
20. Click on the arrow and drag the mouse cursor down. Type 40 in dimension box and press Enter to update the model.

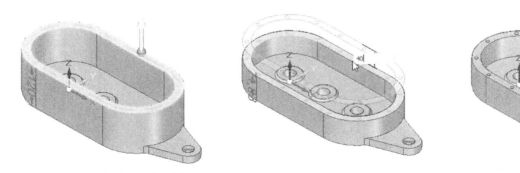

21. Save and close the file.

Questions

1. List any two face relationships.

2. How to activate the **Move** command?
3. List the three options on the **Move** command bar that help you in moving faces
4. List any two live rules.
5. How to modify revolved features using Live Sections?
6. What is **Select Set Priority**?

Exercises
Exercise 1

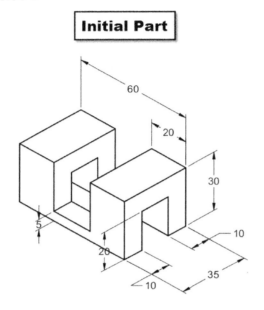

Initial Part

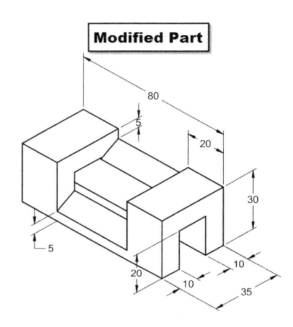

Modified Part

Modifying Parts

Chapter 10: Assemblies

After creating individual parts, you can bring them together into an assembly. By doing so, it's possible to identify incorrect design problems that may not have been noticeable at the part level. In this chapter, you will learn how to bring parts into the assembly environment and position them.

The topics covered in this chapter are:

- *Starting an assembly*
- *Inserting Parts*
- *Adding Relationships*
- *Dragging and Moving parts*
- *Check Interference*
- *Capture Fit*
- *Editing Assemblies*
- *Replace Parts*
- *Pattern and Mirror Parts*
- *Transfer Parts*
- *Create Subassemblies*
- *Disperse assemblies*
- *Assembly Features*
- *Top-down Assembly Design*
- *Assembly Relationship Assistant*
- *Create Exploded Views*

Starting an Assembly

To begin an assembly file, you can use the **ISO Assembly** option or use the **New** icon and select an assembly template.

OR

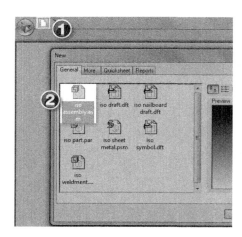

Assemblies

Now, you can insert parts into the assembly by using the **Parts Library** window. You can browse to the location of the parts by using the drop-down menu on the **Parts Library** window. As you select a component from the list, you can see a preview of the part in the **Preview** box. Now, double-click on the part to drop it into the graphics window.

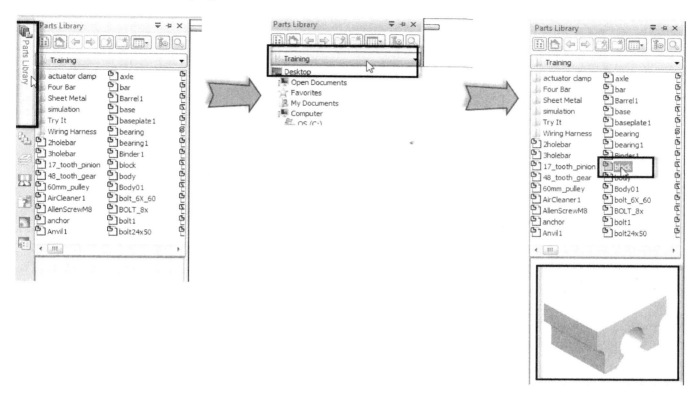

Another way to start an assembly is to create it while a part is open. On the Solid Edge **Application Menu**, click **New > Create Assembly**. The **Create Assembly** dialog box pops up on the screen. Click the **Browse** button and select an assembly template from the **New** dialog box. Click **OK** to start the assembly. You will notice that the part will be placed at the origin. By default, the first part will be grounded at the origin. Also, the ribbon displays the commands related to the assembly environment.

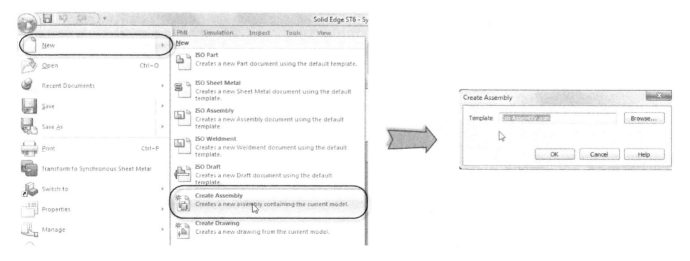

Assemblies

Inserting Parts

There are two different methods to insert an existing part into an assembly. The first one is to drag and place it into the graphics window. The second way is to drag it directly from Windows Explorer. In the second method, you are not required to open these parts in Solid Edge. You can simply drag-and-drop the part into the assembly.

Adding Relationships

After inserting parts into an assembly, you have to define relationships between them. By applying relationships, you can make parts to flush with each other or two cylindrical faces concentric with each other, and so on. As you add relationships between parts, the degrees of freedom will be removed from them. By default, there are six degrees of freedom for a part (three linear and three rotational). Eliminating degrees of freedom will make parts attached and interact with each other as in real life. Now, you will learn to add relationships between parts

Click and drag the first part from the **Parts Library** into the assembly window; it will be fixed at the origin. As a result, all degrees of freedom of the part will be eliminated. Now, drag the second part into the assembly window, the **Assemble** command bar pops up on the screen. Select a face on the newly inserted part, and then click on a face of the fixed part. The two selected faces will mate with each other.

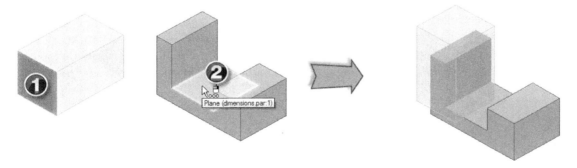

You can use the **Flip** icon on the command bar to flip the part.

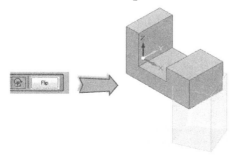

Assemblies

Select the second set of faces.

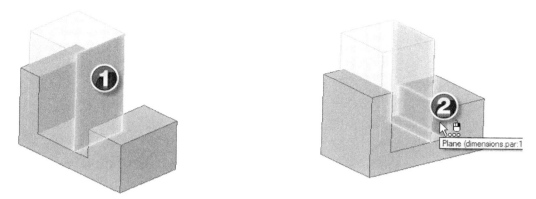

Select the third set of faces; the part will be fully positioned. To confirm this, place the cursor on the corresponding part in the Pathfinder; a message will appear showing that the part is fully positioned.

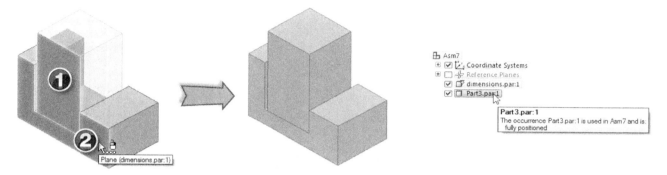

Drag Components

As you insert a part into an assembly, Solid Edge prompts you to define relationships between parts. If you choose not to define any relationships, press the **Esc** key. The part will be under-constrained and free to move and rotate. You can use the **Drag Components** command to the move or rotate the under-constrained parts in the assembly window. Activate this command by clicking **Home > Modify > Drag Components** on the ribbon. The **Analysis Options** dialog box pops up on the screen. The options on this dialog box are self-explanatory. Check the required options on this dialog box and click **OK**. Select a part from the assembly window drag it to a new location.

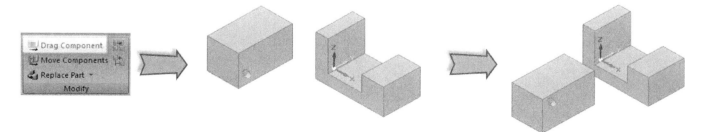

Use the **Move** option on the command bar to move the part in a particular direction. For example, to move the part in the X-direction, select the X-axis and move it (press and hold the left mouse button and drag the cursor).

Assemblies

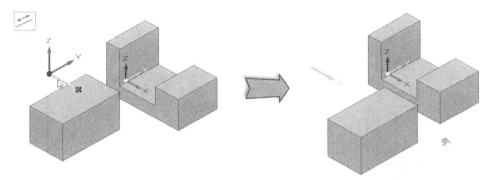

Use the **Rotate** option on the command bar to rotate the part about an axis. For example, to rotate the part about the X-axis, select the X-axis and rotate it (press and hold the left mouse button and drag the cursor)

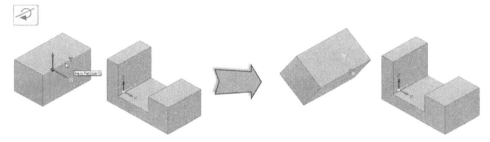

Use the **Detect Collisions** option on the command bar to detect collisions while moving or rotating the parts.

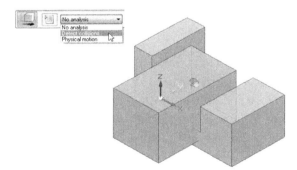

Use the **Physical Motion** option on the command bar to stop the part when it collides with another part.

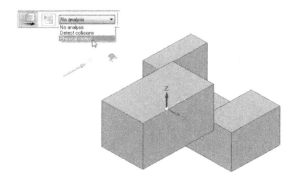

Assemblies

You can also move or rotate grounded parts using the **Drag Component** command. Click the **Options** icon on the command bar and check the **Locate grounded components** option on the **Analysis Options** dialog box. Click **OK** on the dialog box to close it. Now, select and move (or rotate) the grounded part.

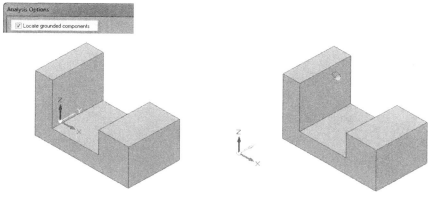

Mate Relationship

The **Mate** relationship makes two faces coincident and opposite to each other. You can define the **Mate** or any relationship between two parts immediately after you insert them. As you click and drag the part from Parts Library into the assembly window, the **Assemble** command bar pops up on the screen. On the command bar, click the **Relationship Types** icon and select **Mate**. Select a face of the inserted part, and then click on a face of the target part. The two selected faces will mate with each other.

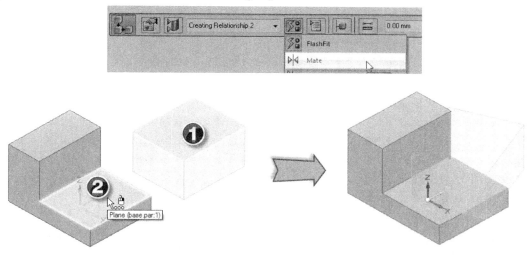

Similarly, select the second set of faces.

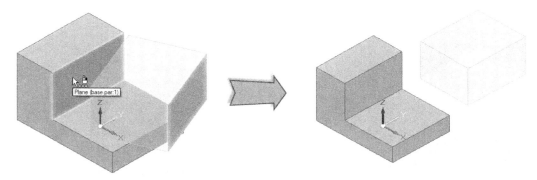

Assemblies

Planar Align Relationship

The **Planar Align** relationship makes two faces flush with each other. To define this relationship, click the **Relationship Types** icon and select **Planar Align** on the **Assembly** command bar. Select a face on the placement part, and then a face on the target part. The two faces will be levelled.

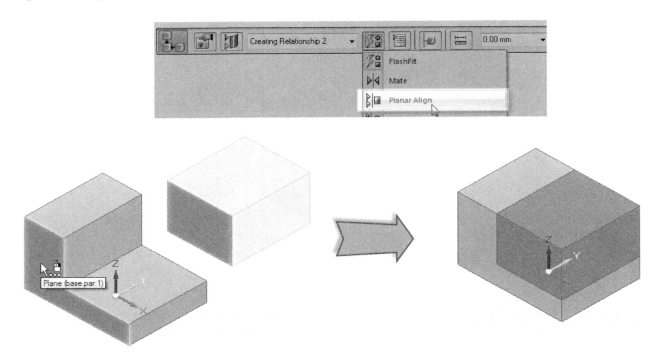

Axial Align Relationship

The **Axial Align** relationship makes the axes of two cylindrical faces coincide with each other. You can activate this command either from the **Assemble** command bar (click **Relationship Types > Axial Align**) or from the ribbon (click **Home > Relate > Axial Align**). After activating this command, click on a cylindrical face, linear edge, or axis of the placement part. Click the **Lock Rotation** icon on the command bar, if you want to lock the rotation of the part. Next, click on an element on the target part. The two cylindrical axes will be aligned together.

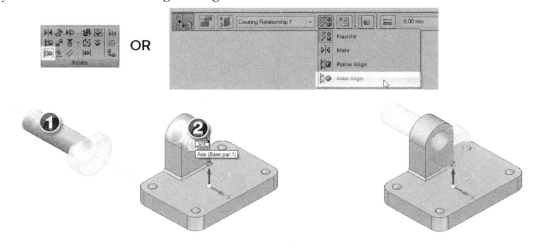

Assemblies

Insert Relationship

The **Insert** relationship helps you to position cylindrical parts into holes. This relationship is a combination of two relationships: the **Axial Align** and **Planar Align**. It aligns the cylindrical axes and the end faces of two parts. Activate this command either from the **Assemble** command bar (click **Relationship Types > Insert)** or from the ribbon (click **Home > Relate > Insert)**. After activating this command, click on a cylindrical face or axis to align. Next, click on a cylindrical face on the target part. Click on a face to mate on the first part, and then click on a face on the target part. The first part will be inserted into the second part.

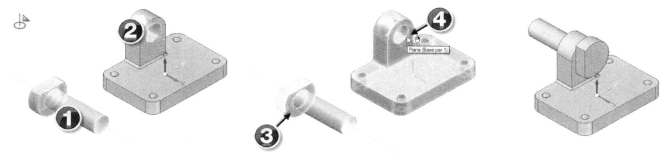

Angle Relationship

The **Angle** relationship is used to position faces at a specified angle. Activate this command either from the **Assemble** command bar (click **Relationship Types > Angle)** or from the ribbon (click **Home > Relate > Angle)**. After activating this command, type-in a value in the **Angle Value** box on the command bar and click on a plane or linear element of the first part. Next, click on a plane or linear element of the second part. Click on a plane on which the angle will lie. The first part will be positioned at the specified angle.

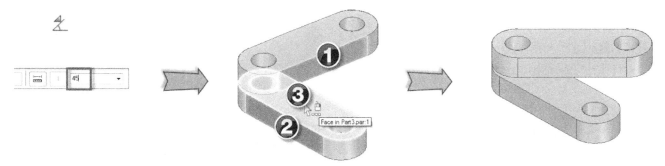

Tangent Relationship

The **Tangent** relationship is often used when working with cylinders and spears. It causes the geometry to maintain contact at a point of tangency. Activate this command either from the **Assemble** command bar (click **Relationship Types > Tangent)** or from the ribbon (click **Home > Relate > Tangent)**. After activating this command, click on the face to be made tangent. Next, click on the tangent face on the target part. The first part will be made tangent to the target part.

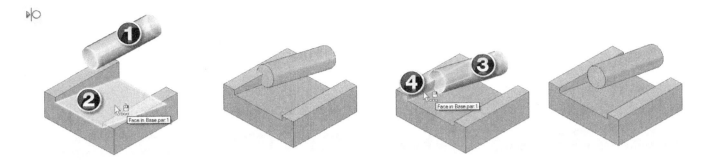

Connect Relationship

The **Connect** relationship connects a keypoint of one part to that of another part. Activate this command either from the **Assemble** command bar (click **Relationship Types > Connect)** or from the ribbon (click **Home > Relate > Connect**). After activating this command, click on a keypoint on the first part. Next, click on a keypoint, edge, or face to connect to. The first part will be connected to the second part.

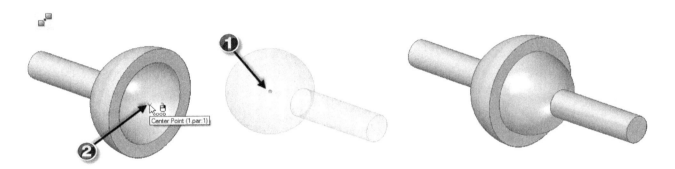

Parallel Relationship

The **Parallel** relationship makes an axis or edge of one part parallel to that of another part. Activate this command either from the **Assemble** command bar (click **Relationship Types > Parallel)** or from the ribbon (click **Home > Relate > Parallel**). After activating this command, type-in a value in the **Offset Value** box on the command bar and click on a cylindrical face, linear edge, or axis of the first part. Next, click on an element of the second part. The two selected edges or axes will be parallel to each other.

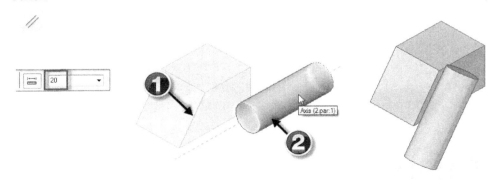

Assemblies

Center-Plane Relationship

The **Center-Plane** relationship allows you to center a part between two faces. Activate this command either from the **Assemble** command bar (click **Relationship Types > Parallel)** or from ribbon (click **Home > Relate > Parallel**). After activating this command, you must select the object to be positioned at the center of two planes. Click on a planar face, edge, axis, keypoint, or reference plane on the first part. Next, click on two faces or reference planes on the second part. The first part will be centered between the two planes.

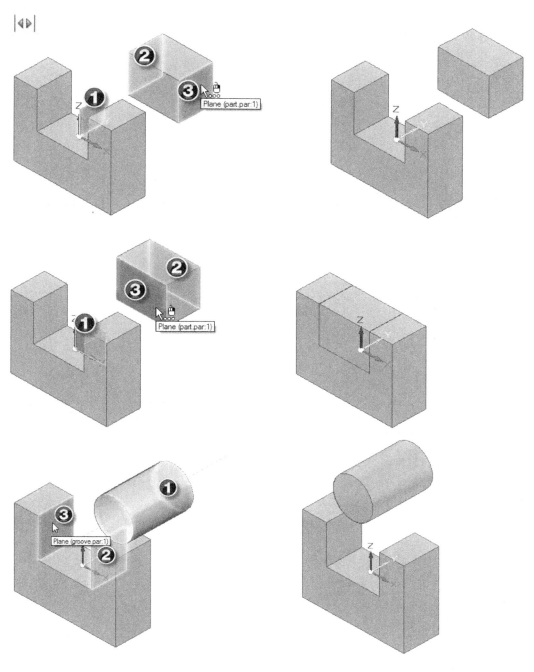

Assemblies

Match Coordinate Systems Relationship

The **Match Coordinate Systems** relationship matches the coordinate systems of two parts. This is the easiest way to constrain parts in an assembly. To apply this relationship, first you must display the coordinate systems of the parts. You can do so by clicking the **Construction Display** icon on the **Assembly** command bar and selecting the **Show Coordinate Systems** option (or) by right-clicking on the part and selecting **Show Hide Component**, and then turning on **Coordinate Systems**.

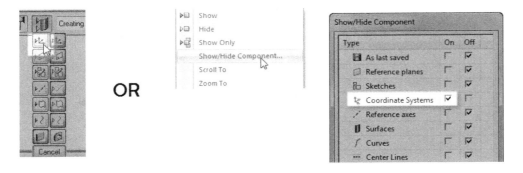

Activate this command either from the **Assemble** command bar (click **Relationship Types > Match Coordinate Systems)** or from the ribbon (click **Home > Relate > Match Coordinate Systems**). After activating this command, you have to select the coordinate systems of two parts. They will be positioned together.

Rigid Set Relationship

The **Rigid Set** relationship makes the selected parts to form a rigid set. As you move a single part of a rigid set, all the other parts will also be moved. Activate this command from the ribbon (click **Home > Relate > Rigid Set**); a command bar pops up on the screen. On the command bar, select an option from **Shared Relationships** menu. You can select to **Suppress**, **Delete**, or **Ignore** already existing relationships between the parts. Next, select parts from the assembly window and click the green check on the command bar. The selected parts will form a rigid set. Now, if you change the position or orientation of one part, all the other parts of the rigid set will also be affected.

Assemblies

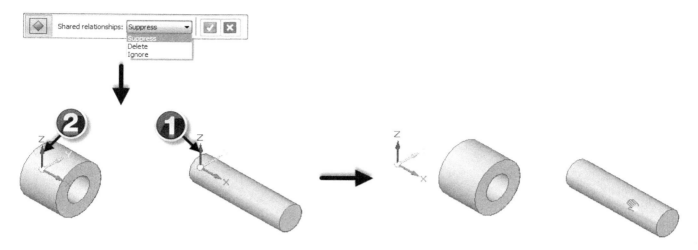

Ground Relationship

By default, the first inserted part in an assembly is grounded or fixed. As a result, all the degrees of freedom of the part are constrained. However, you can make any other part grounded by using the **Ground** command. Activate this command (click **Home > Relate > Ground** on the ribbon) and select the part to ground. A ground symbol appears on the selected part in the Pathfinder.

Path Relationship

The **Path** relationship is used to constrain a selected point or line along a path. Activate this command either from the **Assemble** command bar (click **Relationship Types > Path)** or from the ribbon (click **Home > Relate > Cam > Path**). After activating this command, click on a point or linear edge to define the follower. Next, click on an edge to define the path. Click the green check on the command bar to apply this relationship. Use the **Drag Component** command to drag the follower.

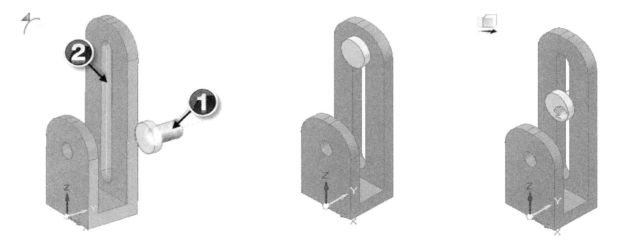

Cam Relationship

The **Cam** relationship is similar to a **Tangent** relationship except that it allows you to mate a cylinder, plane, or point to a series of tangent faces. Activate this command either from the **Assemble** command bar (click **Relationship Types > Cam)** or from the ribbon (click **Home > Relate > Cam**). After activating this command, click on a face or a point to define the follower. Next, click on a face chain to define the cam. Click the green check on the command bar to apply this relationship.

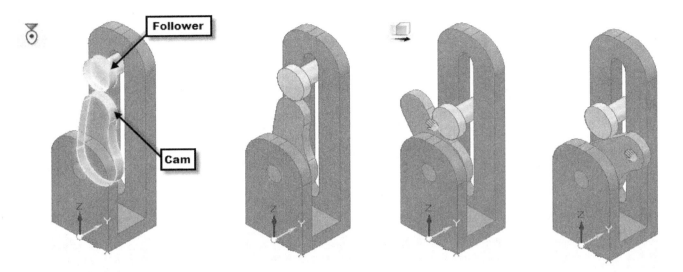

Check Interference

In an assembly, two or more parts can overlap or occupy the same space. However, this would be physically impossible in the real world. When you add relations between parts, Solid Edge develops real-world contacts and movements between them. But, sometimes interferences can occur. To check such errors, Solid Edge provides you with a command called **Check Interference**. Activate this command (click **Inspect > Evaluate > Check Interference** on the ribbon) and select the first set. Click the green check on the command bar and select the second set. Click the **Process** icon to show the interference. If there is no interference, a message box appears showing that there are no interferences in the assembly.

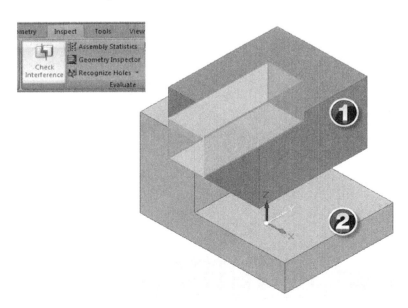

Assemblies

Capture Fit

If you have an assembly in which you need to assemble the same part multiple times, it would be a tedious process. In such cases, the **Capture Fit** command will drastically reduce or even eliminate the time used to assemble commonly used parts. To use this command, first you need to define a relation or set of relations between two parts. For example, define the **Insert** relationship between the screw and the hole.

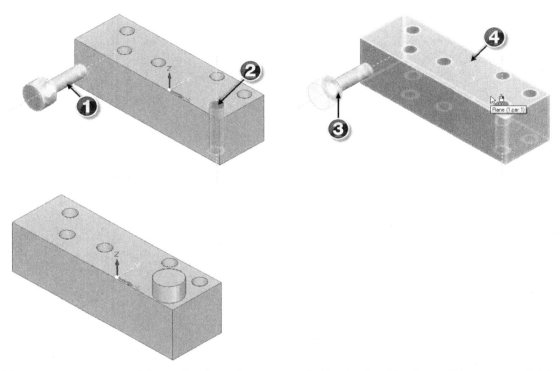

Next, save the assembly and select the screw. Activate the **Capture Fit** command (click **Home > Relate > Capture Fit** on the ribbon); the **Capture Fit** dialog box pops up on the screen. This dialog box shows the list of relations that can be captured. If you do not want to capture some relations, select them from the list and click **Remove**. Next, click **OK** on the dialog box to capture the relations.

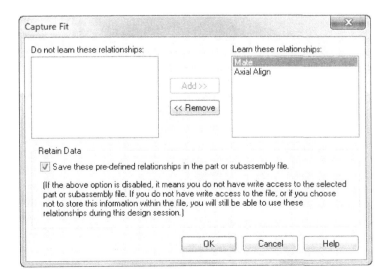

Now, click and drag the screw from the **Parts Library** and place it into the assembly window; you will notice that the flat face on the screw is selected, automatically. Select the top face of the block; the axis of the cylinder is selected, automatically. Select the axis of anyone of the holes on the block; the screw is inserted into the hole.

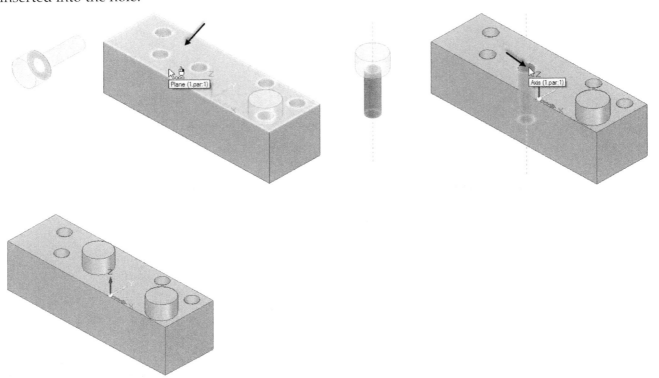

Editing and Updating Assemblies

During the design process, the correct design is not achieved on the first attempt. There is always a need to go back and make modifications. Solid Edge, allows you to accomplish this process very easily. To modify a part in an assembly, right-click on it and select **Open**; the part will be opened in a separate window. Make changes to the part and save it. Next, switch to the assembly window. The part will be automatically updated in the assembly. If it is not updated, click **Tools > Links > Update All Links** on the ribbon.

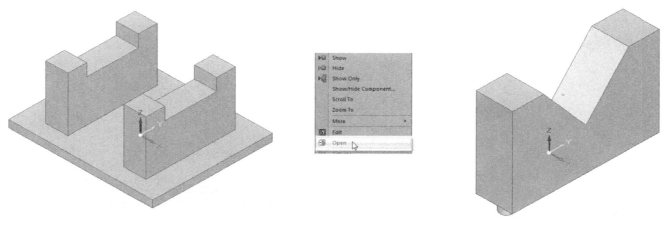

Assemblies

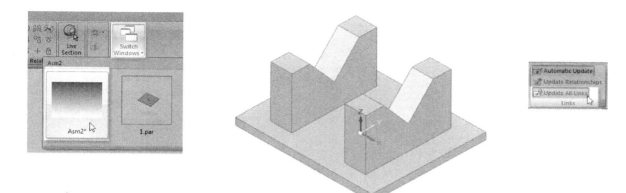

You can also edit relationships in an assembly. Select a part from the Pathfinder; the relationships applied to the part appear at the bottom of the Pathfinder. Click the right mouse button on a particular relationship to display a menu. You can use this menu to delete, suppress, flip, or edit relationship. If you select **Edit Definition**, the **Assemble** command bar pops up on the screen. You can redefine the faces or elements between which the relationship is applied. For example, if you want to edit the **Mate** relationship, right-click on it and select **Edit Definition**. On the **Assemble** command bar, click the **Placement Part –Element** icon, and then click on a face of the placement part. Next, click on a face of the target part, and then right-click to apply the relationship.

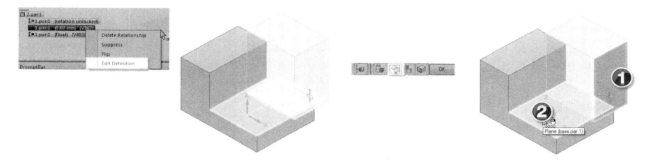

Replace Part

Solid Edge allows you to replace any part in an assembly. Activate the **Replace Part** command (click **Home > Modify > Replace Part** on the ribbon), and then click on parts to replace. Click the green check on the command bar to accept; the **Replacement Part** dialog box pops up on the screen. Browse to the location of the replacement part and double-click on it; the **Assembly** message box pops up on the screen. It shows, "The affected Assembly relationships must be either deleted or suppressed to complete the operation". Click **Delete** or **Suppress** on the message box to replace the part. It is a good practice to delete relationships and redefine them.

Assemblies

Pattern

The **Pattern** command allows you to replicate individual parts in an assembly. However, instead of defining layouts of rectangular or circular patterns, you can select an existing pattern as a reference. For example, in the assembly shown in figure, you can position one screw using relationships, and then use the **Pattern** command to place screws in the remaining holes.

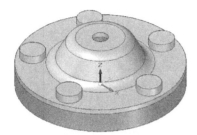

First, position the screw in one hole using the **Insert** relationship. Next, activate the **Pattern** command (click **Home > Pattern > Pattern** on the ribbon) and click on the part to include in the pattern. Click the green check on the command bar to accept the selection. Next, click on the part or sketch which contains the pattern.

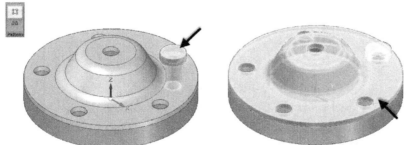

Click on the pattern, and then select the reference feature in the pattern. Click **Finish** on the command bar to create the pattern.

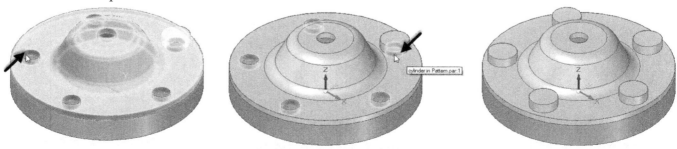

Assemblies

Mirror Components

When designing symmetric assemblies, the **Mirror Components** command will help you in saving time and capture the design intent. Activate this command (click **Home > Pattern > Mirror Components** on the ribbon) and click on the parts to be mirrored. Click the green check on the command bar, and then click on an assembly reference plane to mirror about; the **Mirror Components** dialog box pops up on the screen. On this dialog box, select the required action from the **Action** drop-down menu. Type-in the output file name in the **Output File** field and click **OK**. Next, click **Finish** to complete the mirroring.

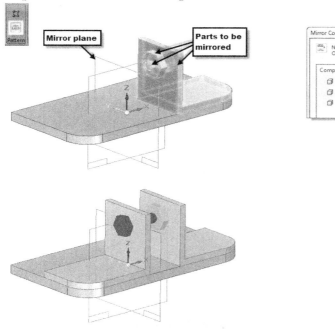
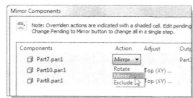

Sub-assemblies

The use of sub-assemblies has many advantages in Solid Edge. Sub-assemblies make large assemblies easier to manage. They make it easy for multiple users to collaborate on a single large assembly design. They can also affect the way you document a large assembly design in 2D drawings. For these reasons, it is important for you to create sub-assemblies in a variety of ways. The easiest way to create a sub-assembly is to insert an existing assembly into another assembly. You need to simply drag and place the assembly from the **Parts Library** window into an existing assembly. Next, apply relationships to constrain the assembly. The process of applying relationships is also simplified. You are required to apply relationships between only one part of a sub-assembly and a part of the main assembly. In addition, you can easily hide a group of parts with the help of sub-assemblies. Click the right mouse button on a sub-assembly and select **Hide**.

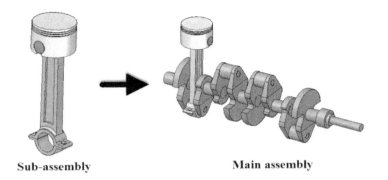

Sub-assembly   Main assembly

Rigid and Adjustable Sub-Assemblies

By default, Solid Edge makes a sub-assembly as a rigid body. When you move a single part of a sub-assembly, the entire sub-assembly will be moved. If you want the individual parts of a sub-assembly to be moved, you must define the sub-assembly as adjustable. Click the right mouse button on the sub-assembly in the **Pathfinder** and select **Simplified/Adjustable > Adjustable Assembly**. Now, you can move the individual parts of a sub-assembly. In case, if you have multiple occurrences of a sub-assembly, each occurrence can be defined as rigid or adjustable. To help you recognise the difference between the rigid and adjustable assemblies, Solid Edge displays a different icon for each of them in the Pathfinder.

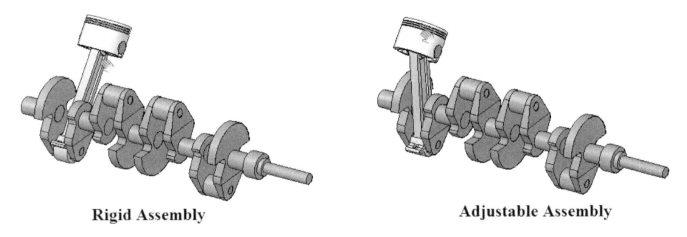

Rigid Assembly   Adjustable Assembly

Transfer

In addition to creating sub-assemblies and inserting them into another assembly, you can also take individual parts that already exist in an assembly and make them into a sub-assembly. For example, press and hold the **Shift** key and select the four parts from the assembly. Next, activate the **Transfer** command (click **Home > Modify > Transfer** on the ribbon); the **Transfer to Assembly Level** dialog box pops up on the screen.

Assemblies

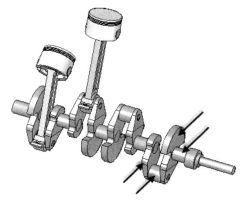

On this dialog box, click on the **Assem** option, and then click **New Subassembly**; the **Create New Subassembly** dialog box pops up on the screen. On this dialog box, select the assembly template, enter file name, specify location, and specify positioning method. Click **OK** twice; the subassembly is created and listed in the Pathfinder.

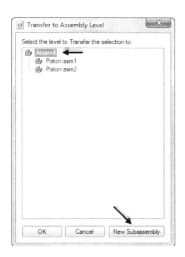
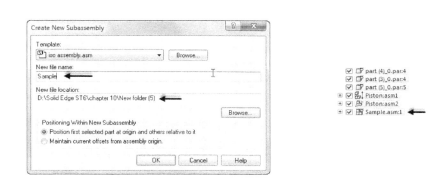

Disperse

After inserting subassemblies, you may require to disperse them into individual parts. Solid Edge provides you with the **Disperse** command to break a subassembly into individual parts. Activate this command (click **Home > Modify > Disperse** on the ribbon); the **Disperse Assembly** dialog box pops up on the screen. On this dialog box, click **Disperse Selected Assembly** to disperse the selected assembly (or) click **Disperse All Assemblies** to break down all subassemblies in to individual parts. After clicking the required option, a message box pops up showing, "Transfer the parts in the selected assembly to the next higher level, and delete the selected assembly occurrence". Click **Yes** to transfer the parts to the main assembly.

Assembly Features

Assembly features are the features that exist only in assemblies i.e. instead of creating them at the part level they are created at the assembly level. Most often the features created at the assembly level are cuts, revolved cuts, holes, and welds. These features are commonly created at the assembly level to represent post assembly machining. For example, to add a cut feature to the assembly shown in figure, activate the **Cut** command (click **Features > Assembly Features > Cut** on the ribbon); the **Assembly Feature Options** dialog box pops up on the screen. On this dialog box, select **Create Assembly Features** and click **OK**. Select the top face of the block and draw the sketch of the cut feature. Finish the sketch and extrude it using the **Through All** option.

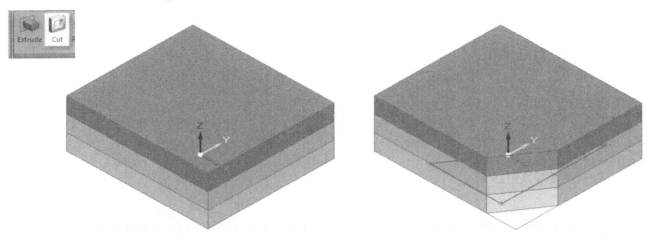

Now, open the individual part in another window. You will notice that part is not affected by the cut feature.

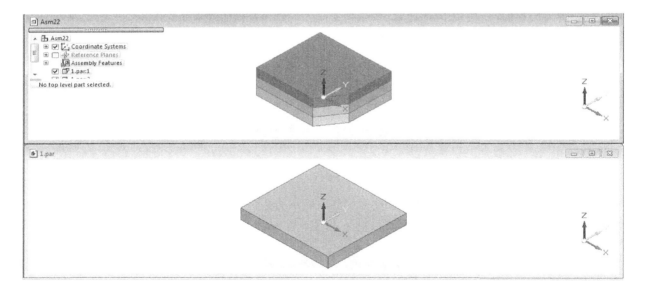

You will also notice that the Cut feature is added to the Pathfinder. You can edit the cut feature by clicking the right mouse button on the **Cut** feature and selecting **Edit Definition**. A command bar pops up on the screen. On the command bar, click the **Select Part Step** icon, and then press the Shift key and select the parts to be excluded from the cut feature. Click the green check on the command bar, and then click **Finish**; you can see that the cut feature no longer affects the selected components.

Assemblies

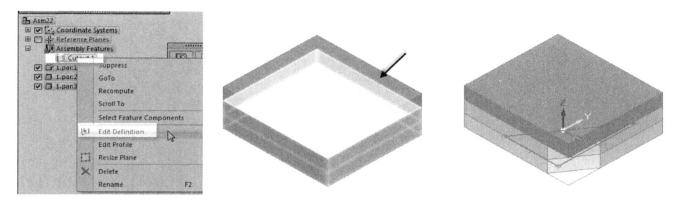

If add a new part to the assembly, the cut feature will not affect it. Again, you need to edit the cut feature and use the **Select Part Step** icon to include the part in the cut feature.

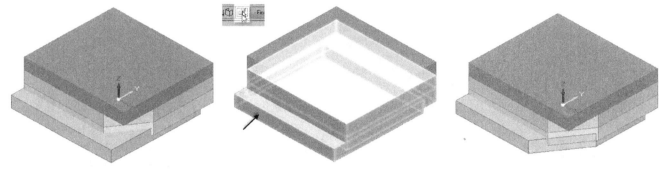

Assembly-Driven Part Features

Assembly-Driven Part features are features which are created in an assembly and are also reflected in the part documents. To create this type of feature, first save the assembly file, and then activate anyone of the commands available in the **Assembly Features** panel. Next click **Create Assembly-Driven Part Features** on the **Assembly Options** dialog box and click **OK**. Create the assembly driven feature and it is listed in the Pathfinder. Now, open the individual part in another window. You will notice that part is also affected by the feature. Also, the feature is listed in the **Ordered** environment of the part file. When you update the feature in the assembly file, it will be reflected in the part file as well.

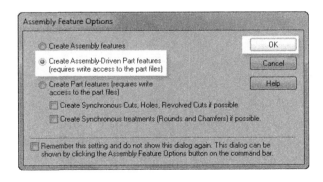
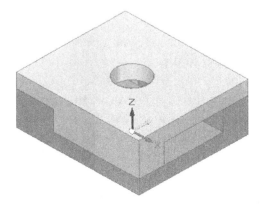

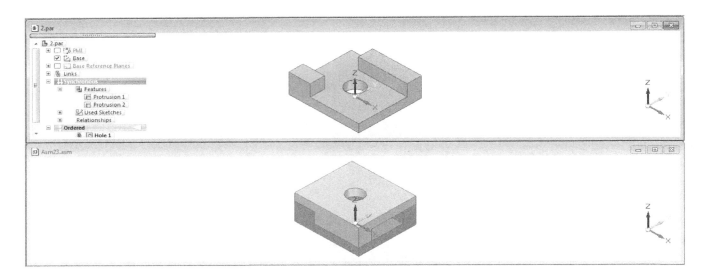

Part Features

Part features are features created in an assembly but are not associated to the assembly. Instead they are associated to the part file on which they are created. To create a part feature, activate anyone of the commands available in the **Assembly Features** panel and click **Create Part features** on the **Assembly Feature Options** dialog box. Click **OK** and create the part feature. Now, open the individual part in another window. You will notice that part is also affected by the feature. Also, the feature is listed in the **Synchronous** environment. If you want to edit a part feature, you must open the part file and make changes to it.

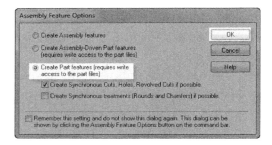

Top Down Assembly Design

In Solid Edge, there are two methods to create an assembly. The method you are probably familiar with is to create individual parts, and then insert them into an assembly. This method is known as Bottom-Up Assembly Design. The second method is called Top Down Assembly Design. In this method, you will create individual parts within the assembly environment. This allows you to design an individual part while taking into account how it will interact with other parts in an assembly. There are several advantages in Top-Down Assembly Design. As you design a part within the assembly, you can be sure that it will fit properly. You can also use reference geometry from the other parts.

Inserting a New Part

Top-down assembly design can be used to add new parts to an already existing assembly. You can also use it to create assemblies that are entirely new. To create a part at using the Top Down Design,

Assemblies

activate the **Create Part In-Place** command (click **Home > Assemble > Create Part In-Place** on the ribbon); the **Create Part In-Place** dialog box pops up on the screen. The options available on this dialog box are self explanatory. Set the options on this dialog box and click **OK** to close it.

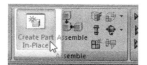
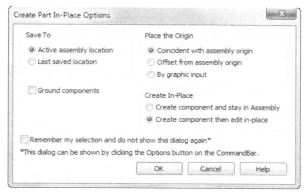

On the command bar, select a template from the **Template** drop-down menu. If you want to access more templates, click the **Browse for Template** icon to display the **New** dialog box. On this dialog box, click the **More** tab and select the template you need.

On the command bar, click the **Ground** icon to make the part grounded at the origin.

Use the **Origin** drop-down menu to specify the origin location.

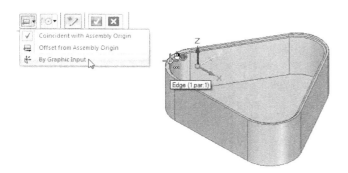

Activate the **Edit In Place** icon to directly switch to the part environment to create the part. Click the green check on the command bar; the **Save As** dialog box pops up on the screen. On this dialog box, specify the part name and location on the drive, and then click **Save** to create the part. Now, create the features of the part, and then close and return to the assembly.

Assemblies

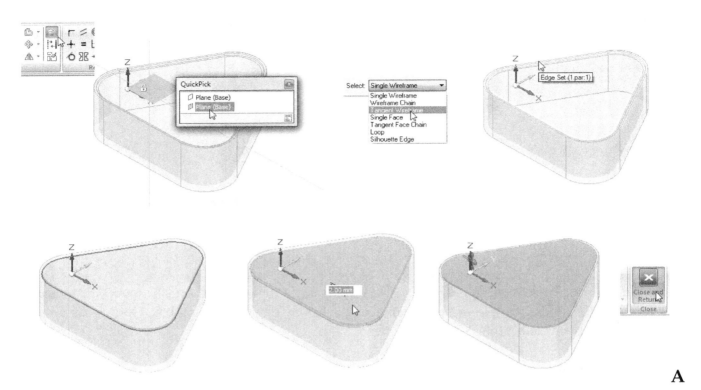

Assembly Relationship Assistant

Assembly Relationship Assistant is the command provided by Solid Edge intelligent technology. This command helps you to create relationships automatically based on the position and interaction between the parts. This command is very helpful while creating relationships in a top down assembly design. Activate this command (click **Home > Relate > Assembly Relationship Assistant** on the ribbon); the **Relationship Assistant Options** dialog box pops up on the screen. Set the options on this dialog box and click **OK**. Click on parts to define the first set, and then click the green check on the command bar. Click on parts to define the second set, and then click the green check on the command bar; the **Relationship Assistant Settings** dialog box pops up on the screen. On this dialog box, check the **Allowable Relationship Types**, and then click **Process**. This will analyze the position and interaction between the parts, and then apply relationships between them. The possible relationships are listed on the **Relationship Assistant Settings** dialog box. Check the required relationships, and click **Accept**. Close the dialog box and click **Finish** to apply the relationships.

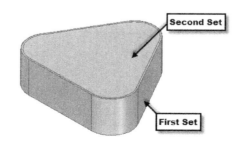

Assemblies

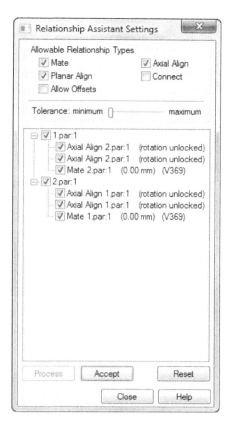

Exploding Assemblies

To properly document an assembly design, it is very common to create an exploded view. In an exploded view, the parts of an assembly are pulled apart to show how they were assembled. To create an exploded view, activate the **ERA** command (click **Tools > Environs > ERA** on the ribbon); the **Explode – Render – Animate** environment is activated.

Use the **Auto Explode** command to explode the assembly, automatically. On activating this command, the **Auto Explode** command bar pops up on the screen. On the command bar, select **Top-Level Assembly** if you want to explode the complete assembly. If you want to explode only selected subassemblies, then select the **Subassembly** option. Next, click the green check on the command bar.

Deactivate the **Automatic Spread Distance** icon on command bar and type-in the spread distance in the **Distance** box. Click **Explode** and **Finish** to explode the assembly.

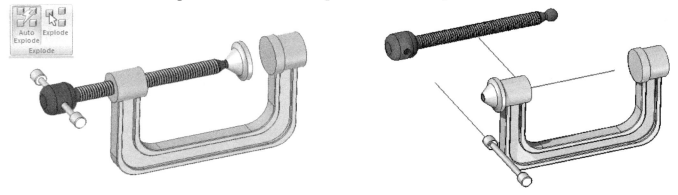

You will notice that the parts are not exploded properly. To get a desired explosion, you need to use the **Explode** command. First, unexplode this assembly using the **Unexplode** command. On clicking this button, the **Solid Edge** message box pops up showing, "This action will delete the current explosion". Click **Yes** to explode the assembly.

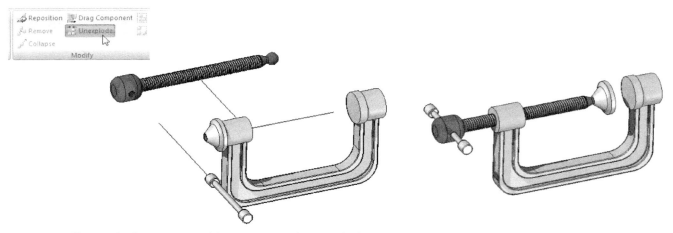

To manually explode an assembly, activate the **Explode** command; the **Explode** command bar pops up. Click on the parts to be exploded, and then click the green check on the command bar. Click on the part to be remained stationary in the explosion.

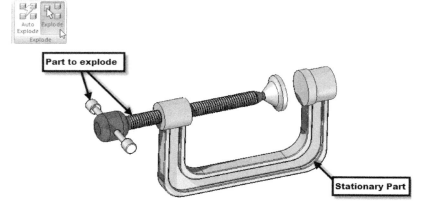

Assemblies

Click on the stationary part face from which you want to explode; an arrow appears on it. Move the cursor and click to define the direction of explosion; the **Explode Options** dialog box pops up.

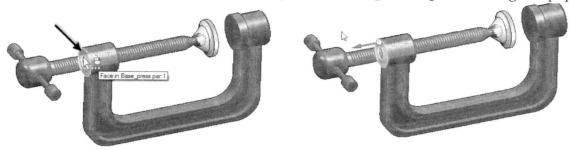

On this dialog box, select an option to specify the **Explode Technique**. You can select **Move components as a unit** or **Spread components evenly**. Next, specify the **Explode order** by selecting the parts listed and using the **Move Up** and **Move Down** buttons. Click **OK** to close this dialog box.

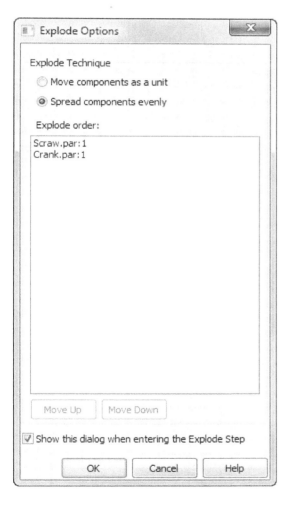

Type-in a value in the **Distance** box and click **Explode** to explode the parts. Click **Finish** to complete the explosion.

Assemblies

If the distance between the exploded parts is less or more, you can use the **Drag Component** command to adjust the spacing between them.

You can also select individual parts and type-in a new explode distance in the **Distance** box.

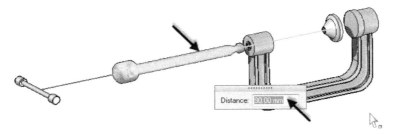

If you want to collapse an exploded part, click on it, and then click **Collapse** on the ribbon.

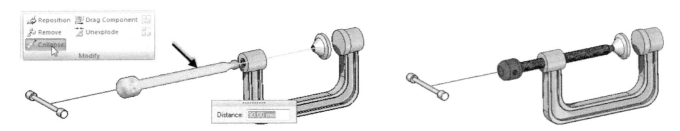

If you want to remove a part from the explosion, click on it, and then click **Remove** on the ribbon.

Assemblies

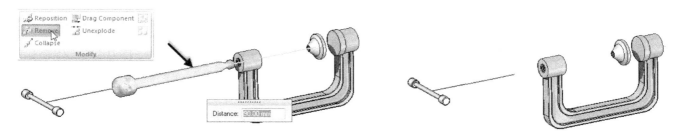

If you want to convert the explosion into a 'move component' operation, then click **Drop** on the **Flow Lines** panel. The flow lines are also converted into annotation flow lines.

If you want to modify a flow line, click **Modify** on the **Flow Lines** panel and select the flow line; two handles appears at start and end points of the flow line. Click on the start point handle, and then redefine the start point of the flow line. Similarly, redefine the end point of the flow line.

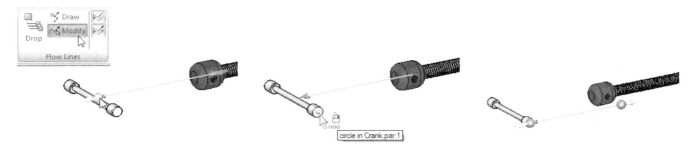

If you want to draw a new flow line, click **Draw** on the **Flow Lines** panel and select the start and end points; a flow line appears between the selected points. On the **Draw** command bar, click the **Next** icon to see different paths of the flow lines. Click **Finish** to complete the flow line creation.

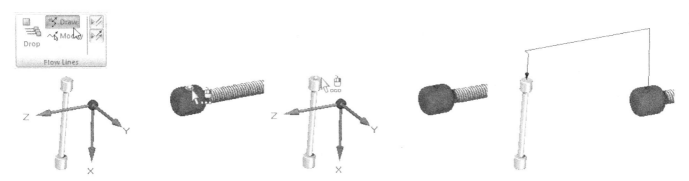

After the exploding the assembly, click **Close ERA** on the ribbon; the assembly environment appears.

Examples

Example 1 (Bottom Up Assembly)
In this example, you will create the assembly shown below.

Assemblies

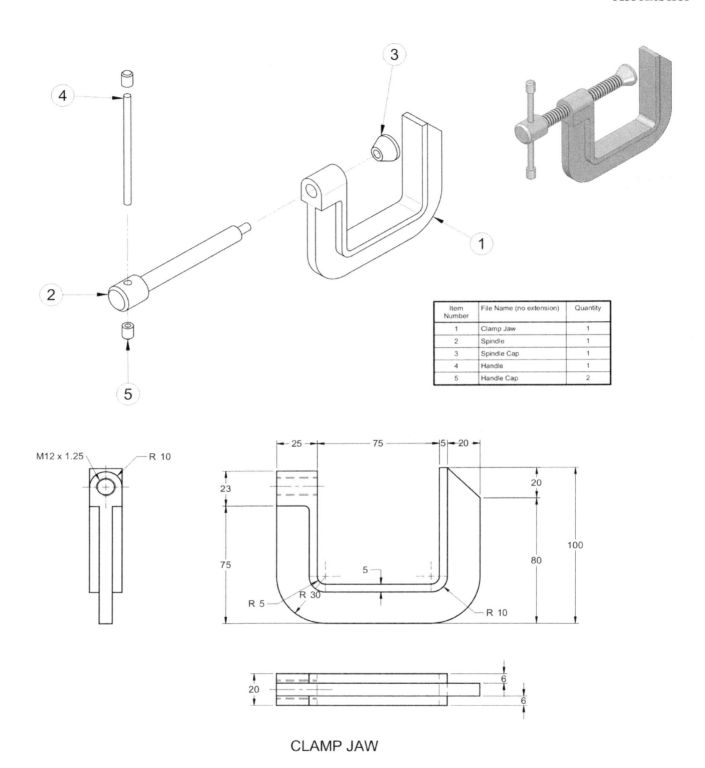

CLAMP JAW

Assemblies

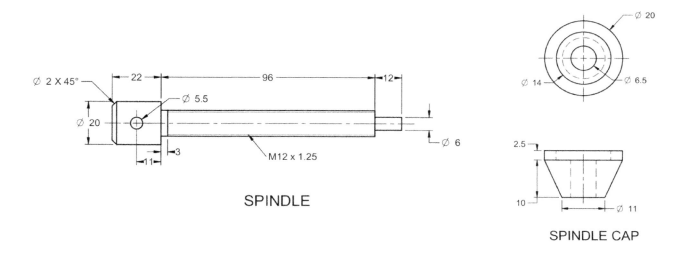

SPINDLE

SPINDLE CAP

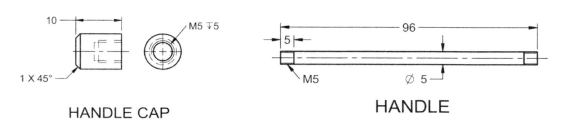

HANDLE CAP

HANDLE

1. Start **Solid Edge ST6**.
2. Create and save all the parts of the assembly in a single folder. Name this folder as *G-Clamp*.
3. On the **Application Menu**, click **New > ISO Assembly** to start an assembly file.
4. On the left side of the window, click the **Parts Library** icon to display the **Parts Library** window.
5. In the **Parts Library** window, use the drop-down menu and go to the *G-Clamp* folder.
6. In the **Parts Library** window, click *Clamp Jaw* and drag it into the assembly window.

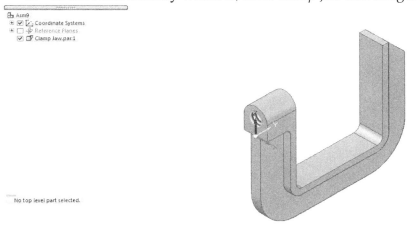

7. In the **Parts Library** window, click *Spindle* and drag it into the assembly window.

211

Assemblies

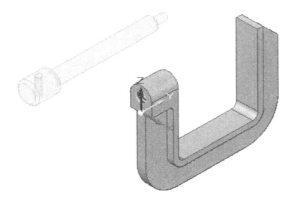

8. On the command bar, click **Relationship Types > Axial Align,** and then click the **Lock Rotation** icon.
9. Click on the cylindrical face of the *Spindle* and hole of the *Clamp Jaw*. The

10. On the command bar, click **Relationship Types > Planar Align**, and then type **-40** in the **Offset Value** box.
11. Click on the back face of the *Spindle* and rotate the view.
12. Click on the flat face of the *Clamp Jaw*, as shown in figure.

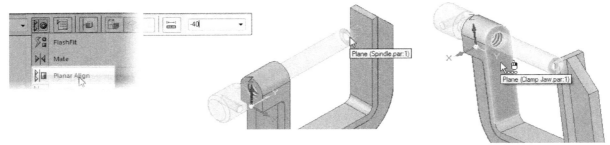

13. In the **Parts Library**, click *Spindle Cap* and drag it into the assembly window.
14. On the command bar, click the **Lock Rotation** icon, and then click on the cylindrical face of the *Spindle Cap* hole.
15. Click on the small cylindrical face of the *Spindle*. The *Spindle* and *Spindle Cap* are axially aligned.

Assemblies

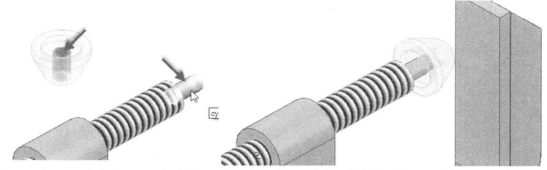

16. Rotate the model view and click on the flat face of the *Spindle Cap*, as shown in figure.
17. Click on the flat face of the *Spindle*. The *Spindle Cap* is assembled and fully constrained. But, you will notice that the part is oriented in reverse direction.

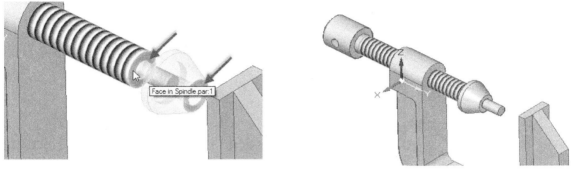

18. In the **Pathfinder**, click *Spindle Cap*. The relations associated with the part appear at the bottom of the **Pathfinder**.
19. Click on the planar align relation, and then click the **Flip** button at the bottom of the screen. The *Spindle Cap* is reversed.

20. In **Parts Library**, click *Handle* and drag it into the assembly window.
21. On the command bar, click **Relationship Types > Center-Plane** and select the axis of the *Spindle*.
22. Click on the front face and back face of the *Handle*.

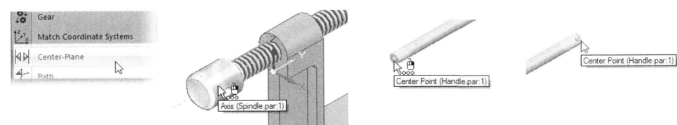

213

Assemblies

23. On the command bar, click **Relationship Types > Axial Align**. Click the **Lock Rotation** icon, and then click on the cylindrical face of the *Handle*.
24. Click on the hole of the *Spindle*. The *Handle* is axially aligned with the hole.

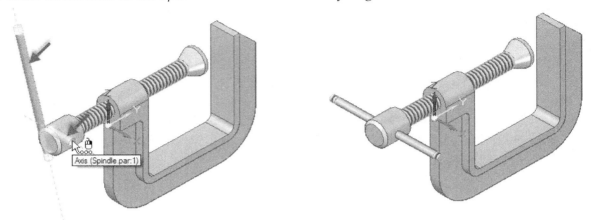

25. In the **Parts Library**, click *Handle Cap* and drag it into the assembly window.
26. On the command bar, click **Relationship Types > Insert**, and then click on a cylindrical face of the *Handle Cap*.
27. Click on the cylindrical face of the *Handle*.
28. On the command bar, type 1 in the **Offset Value** box, and then click on the flat face of the hole of the *Handle Cap*.
29. On the *Handle*, click on the end face. The *Handle Cap* is inserted into the *Handle*.

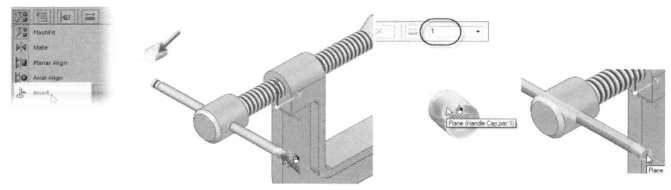

30. Save the assembly with the name **G-Clamp.asm**.
31. In the **Pathfinder**, click on the *Handle Cap*, and then click **Home > Relate > Capture Fit**. The **Capture Fit** dialog box appears. Click **OK** to close the dialog box.
32. In the **Parts Library**, click *Handle Cap* and drag it to the assembly window. The **Mate** command is activated and the flat face of the *Handle Cap* is selected.
33. Type 1 in the **Offset value** box and click on the end face of the *Handle*. The **Axial Align** command is activated and axis of the *Handle Cap* is selected.
34. Click on the axis of the *Handle* to complete the assembly.

Assemblies

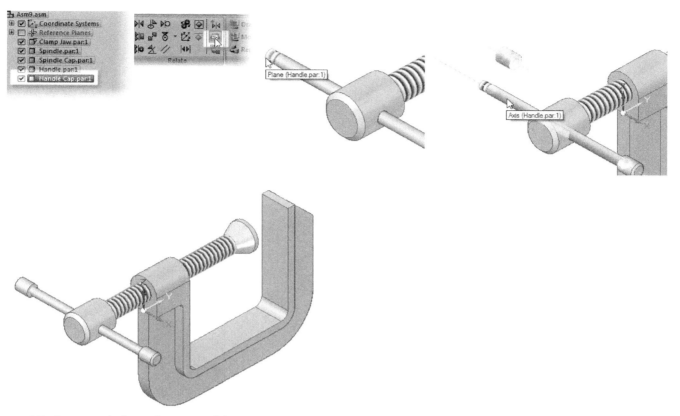

35. Save and close the assembly.

Example 2 (Top Down Assembly)
In this example, you will create the assembly shown below.

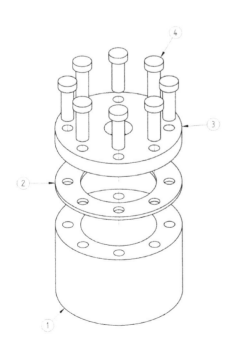

Item Number	File Name (no extension)	Quantity
1	Cylinder base	1
2	Gasket	1
3	Cover plate	1
4	Screw	8

Assemblies

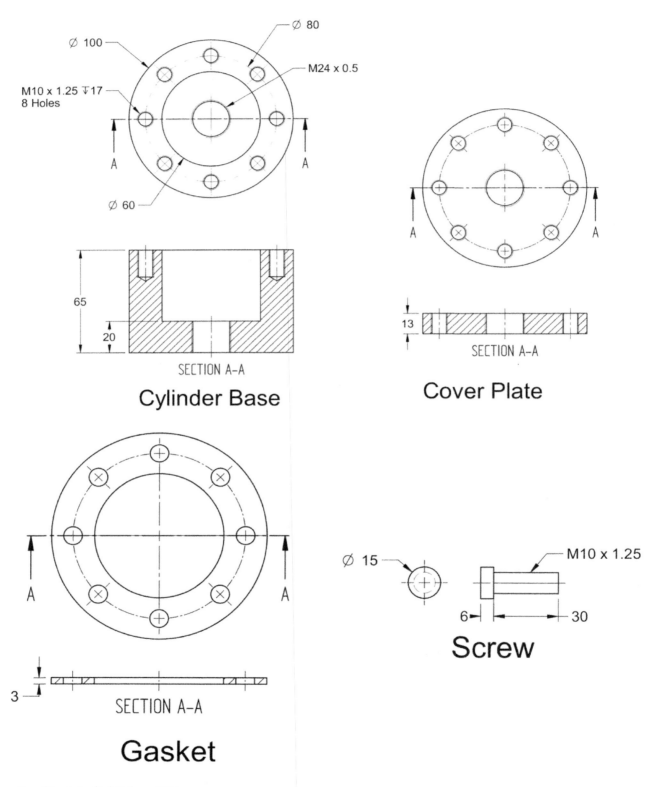

1. Start **Solid Edge ST6**.
2. Start a new part file and create the Cylinder base. Do not create the center hole.

Assemblies

3. Create a new folder with name *Pressure Cylinder*.
4. Save the file with the name *Cylinder base*.
5. On the **Application Menu**, click **New > Create Assembly**. The **Create Assembly** dialog box appears.

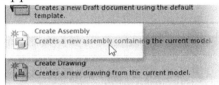

6. On this dialog box, click **OK** to start a new assembly file. The *Cylinder base* is automatically placed at the origin.
7. Save the assembly file in the *Pressure Cylinder* folder.
8. On the ribbon, click **Home > Assemble > Create Part In-Place**. The **Create Part In-Place Options** dialog box pops up on the screen.
9. On this dialog box, under the **Place the Origin** section, select the **By graphic input** option.
10. Leave the other default options on this dialog box and click **OK**. The origin of the new part is attached to the mouse cursor.
11. Place the mouse cursor on the circular edge of the Cylinder base.
12. Press **T** on your keyboard to toggle to the orientation of the origin.
13. Click when the orientation of the part origin is same as that of the assembly origin.

 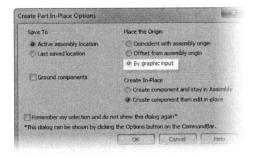  

14. On the command bar, click the green check. The **Save As** dialog box pops up.

217

Assemblies

15. Type *Gasket* in the **File name** field and click **Save**. The part file is created and Part environment is activated.
16. On the ribbon, click **Home > Draw > Project to Sketch** and lock the XY plane.
17. Click on the circular edges on the top face of the Cylinder base. The edges are projected to the locked plane.
18. Activate the **Extrude** command and click in the region enclosed by the sketch.
19. Right-click to accept the selection, and then move the mouse cursor up.
20. Type 3 in the dimension box and press Enter to create the *Extrude* feature.

 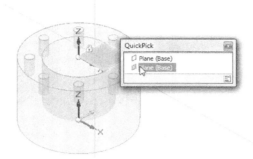 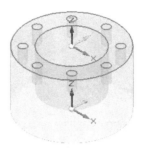 

21. On the ribbon, click **Close and Return** to return to the assembly session.
22. On the ribbon, click **Home > Assemble > Create Part In-Place**.
23. On the **Create Part In-Place** dialog box, under the **Place the origin** section, select the **Offset from assembly origin** option. Click **OK** to close the dialog box. Now, you have to enter X, Y, and Z values to specify the origin of the new part.

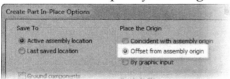 

24. Click on the circular edge of the *Gasket* to define the location of the origin.
25. On the command bar, click the green check.
26. On the **Save As** dialog box, type *Cover plate* in the **File name** field and click **Save**.
27. In the **Part** environment, activate the **Project to Sketch** command and lock the XY plane.
28. Project the outer circular edge and small circular edges.
29. Use the sketch and create an *Extrude* feature. The depth of the extrusion is 13 mm.

218

Assemblies

30. Activate the **Thread** command and add M10 x 1.25 to threads to the holes.

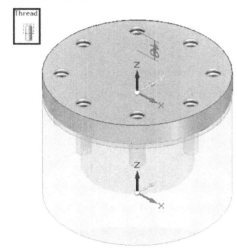

31. On the ribbon, click **Close and Return** to return back to the assembly environment.
32. Activate the **Create Part In-Place** command and create the *Screw* on the top face of the *Cover plate*.
33. In the Part environment, activate the **Project to Sketch** command and lock the XY plane.
34. Use the sketch and create an *Extrude* feature of the 30 mm depth. The direction of extrusion should be downward.

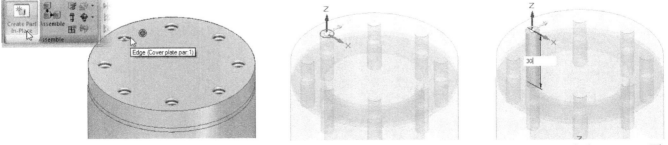

35. Create a circle of 15 mm diameter on the top face and extrude it in the upward direction. The extrude depth is 6 mm.

219

Assemblies

36. Activate the **Thread** command and add thread to the lower cylindrical face of the part. The thread size is M10 x 1.25.

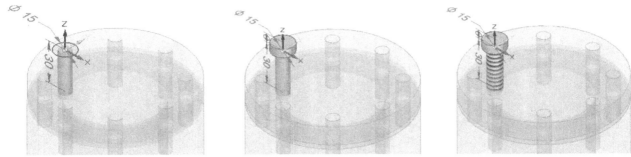

37. On the ribbon, click **Close and Return** to return back to the assembly environment. Now, you have to add relationships between parts.
38. On the ribbon, click **Home > Relate > Assembly Relationship Assistant**. The **Relationship Assistance Options** dialog box appears.
39. On this dialog box, select the **Select Set 2** option and click **OK**.
40. Click on the *Cylinder base*, and then click the green check on the command bar.
41. Click on the *Gasket*, and then click the green check on the command bar. The **Relationship Assistant Settings** dialog box pops up.

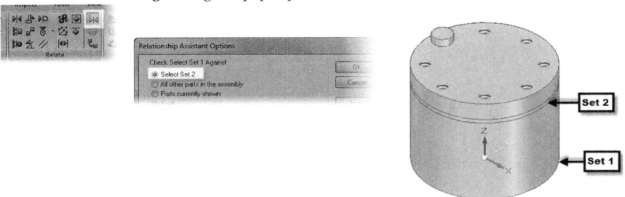

42. On this dialog box, click the **Process** button. Solid Edge automatically creates relationships between the selected parts.

220

Assemblies

43. Click on the relationships to highlight the faces associated with them.
44. Click **Accept** to create the relationships. Click **Cancel** to deactivate the command.
45. Close the dialog box and click **Finish** to complete creating the relationships.
46. In the **Pathfinder**, click on the *Gasket*, and then click on the Axial Align at the bottom.
47. At the bottom of the screen, click the **Lock Rotation** icon to arrest the rotation of the *Gasket*.

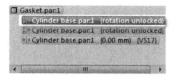 

48. Use the **Assembly Relationship Assistant** command and create relationships between the other parts of the assembly.
49. On the ribbon, click **Home > Pattern > Pattern,** and then click on the *Screw*. Click the green check on the command bar to accept the selection.
50. Click on the *Cylinder base* and select the circular pattern.
51. Click on anyone of the feature in the circular pattern.
52. On the command bar, click **Finish** to complete the pattern.

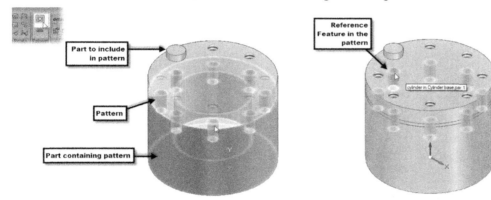 

53. On the ribbon, click **Features > Assembly Features > Hole**. The **Assembly Feature Options** dialog box pops up.
54. On this dialog box, select the **Create Part features** option, and then check the **Create Synchronous Cuts, Holes, Revolved Cuts if possible** option. Click **OK** to close the dialog box.
55. On the command bar, click the **Hole Options** dialog box and set the options, as shown below.

 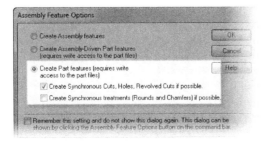 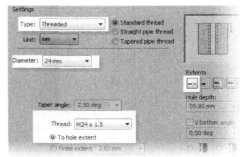

Assemblies

56. Click on the top face of the cover plate and place a hole circle at the center.
57. Click **Close Sketch** to exit the sketch.
58. Move the mouse cursor downwards and click to define the side of the hole.
59. On the command bar, click the green check to create the thread hole.

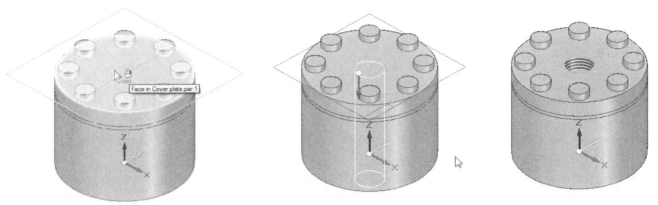

60. On the ribbon, click **PMI > Model Views > Section**.
61. Click on the XZ plane and draw the sketch, as shown in figure.

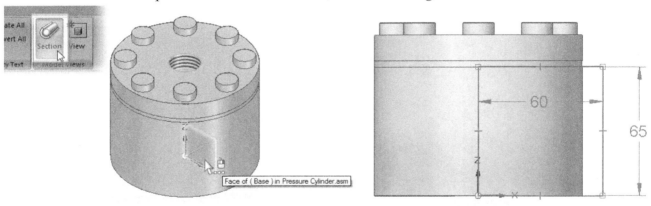

62. On the ribbon, click **Close Sketch** to close the sketch.
63. Move mouse cursor toward left and click define the side of the section cut.
64. Extrude the sketch in the forward direction to create the section cut.

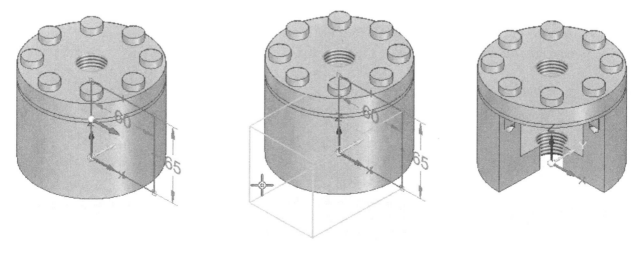

222

Assemblies

65. Explode, save and close the assembly file.

Questions

1. How to start an assembly from an already opened part?
2. What is the use of the **Capture Fit** command?
3. List the advantages of Top-down assembly approach?
4. What is a grounded part?
5. What is the use of the **Assembly Relationship Assistant** command?
6. How to create a sub-assembly in the assembly environment?
7. Briefly explain the **Edit-In Place** command.
8. Why do we prefer the **Explode** command over the **Auto Explode** command?
9. What is the difference between rigid and adjustable subassemblies?
10. How to show or hide reference planes of a part?

Exercise 1

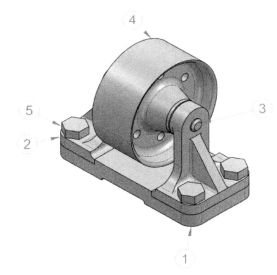

Item Number	File Name (no extension)	Quantity
1	Base	1
2	Bracket	2
3	Spindle	1
4	Roller-Bush assembly	1
5	Bolt	4

Assemblies

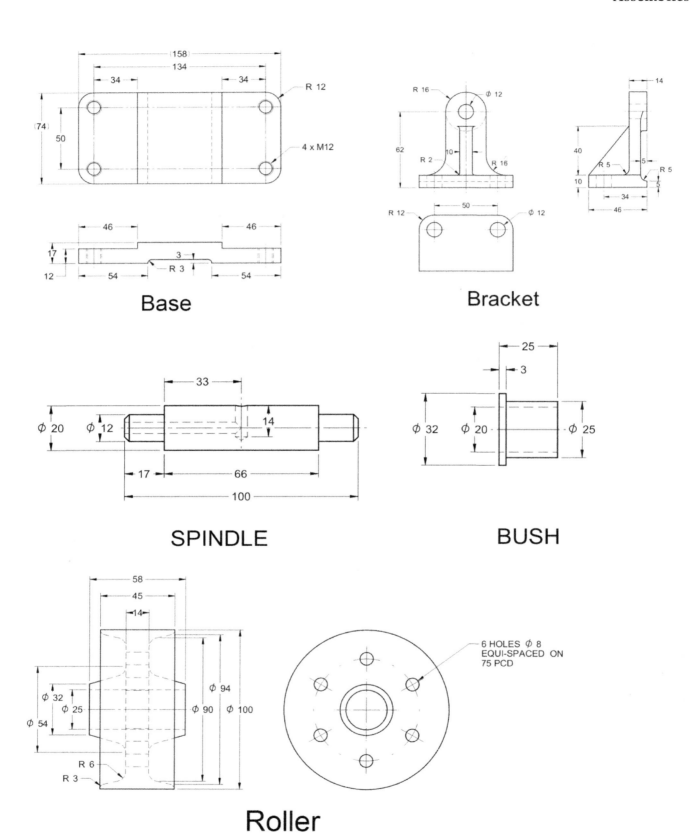

Assemblies

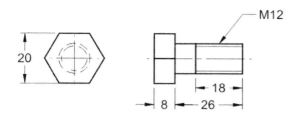

Bolt

Chapter 11: Drawings

Drawings are used to document your 3D models in the traditional 2D format including dimensions and other instructions useful for manufacturing purpose. In Solid Edge, you first create 3D models and assemblies, and then use them to generate drawings. There is a direct association between the 3D model and the drawing. When changes are made to the model, each and every view in the drawing will be updated. This relationship between 3D model and the drawing makes the drawing process fast and accurate. Because of the mainstream adoption of 2D drawings of the mechanical industry, drawings are one of the three main file types you can create in Solid Edge.

The topics covered in this chapter are:

- *Create model views*
- *Projected views*
- *Auxiliary views*
- *Sections views*
- *Detail views*
- *Broken Out views*
- *Break Lines*
- *Display Options*
- *View Alignment*
- *Parts List and Balloons*
- *Retrieve Dimensions*
- *Arrange Dimensions*
- *Maintain Alignment*
- *Remove Alignment*
- *Line Up Text*
- *Ordinate Dimensions*
- *Chamfer Dimension*
- *Center Marks*
- *Centerlines*
- *Automatic Centerlines*
- *Bolt Hole Circles*
- *Callouts and Leaders*
- *Notes*

Starting a Drawing

To start a new drawing, click the **ISO Draft** option on the starting screen (or) click the **New** icon on the **Quick Access Toolbar**, and then double-click on the **iso draft.dft** template on the **New** dialog box. If you want to start the drawing in any other sheet template, click the **More** tab and select the required template.

Drawings

 OR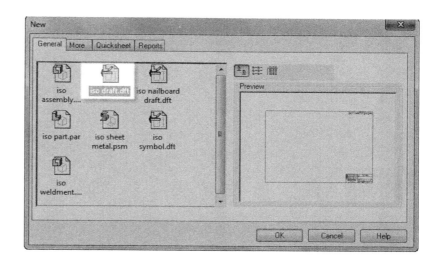

If you already have a part opened, you can click **Application Menu > New > Create Drawing**; the **Create Drawing** dialog box appears. On this dialog box, click the **Browse** button to access different sheet templates. Select anyone of the sheet templates and click **OK**. On the **Create Drawing** dialog box, check the **Run Drawing View Creation Wizard** option to start creating drawing views. If you uncheck this option, the drawing views will be created automatically. Click **OK** on the **Create Drawing** dialog box to start a new drawing.

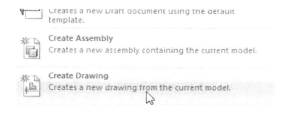 

View Creation

There are different standard views available in a 3D part such as front right top that isometric. In Solid Edge, you can create these views using the **View Wizard** command. This command is activated automatically, if you have created a drawing from an already opened part. If it is not activated, click **Home > Drawing Views > View Wizard** on the ribbon. The **Select Model** window appears. Browse to the location of the part or assembly and double-click on it; a model view will be attached to the pointer. Also, the **View Wizard** command bar pops up on the screen.

Click the **Drawing View Layout** icon on the command bar; the **Drawing View Creation Wizard** dialog box pops up on the screen. On this dialog box, select the first view from the **Primary View** list. Next, click on the icons that represent the standard views that are to be created. After selecting the standard views, click **OK** on the **Drawing View Creation Wizard** dialog box. Click the **Set View Scale** icon to adjust the sizes of the views to sheet size. Click on the sheet to create views. Click and drag the views to position them.

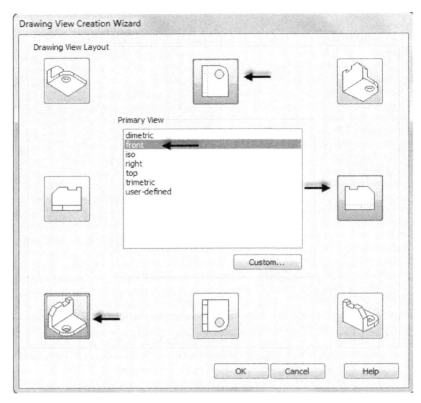
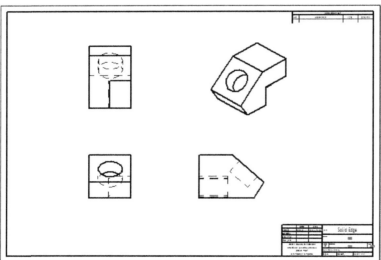

Principal View

After you have created the first view in your drawing, a principal view is one of the simplest views to create. Activate the **Principal View** command (click **Home > Drawing Views > Principal View** on the ribbon). After activating the command, select a view you wish to project from and move the pointer in the direction you wish to have the view to be projected. Next, click on the sheet to specify the location; the projected view will be created. Click the right mouse button to deactivate this command.

Drawings

 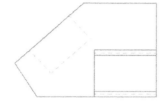 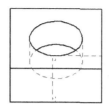 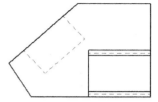

Auxiliary View

Most of the parts are represented by using orthographic views (front, top and/or side views). But many parts have features located on inclined faces. You cannot get the true shape and size for these features by using the orthographic views. To see an accurate size and shape of the inclined features, you need to create an auxiliary view. An auxiliary view is created by projecting the part onto a plane other than horizontal, front or side planes. To create an auxiliary view, activate the **Auxiliary** command (click **Home > Drawing Views > Auxiliary** on the ribbon). Click the angled edge of the model to establish the direction of the auxiliary view. Next, move the cursor to the desired location and click to locate the view.

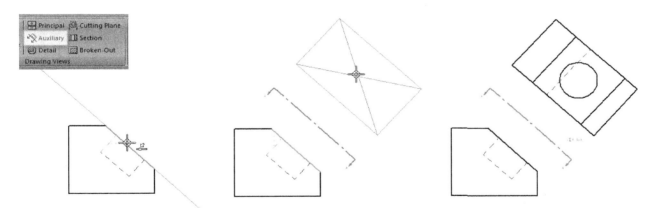

Section View

One of the more common views used in 2D drawings is the section view. Creating a section view in Solid Edge is very simple. Once a view is placed on the drawing sheet, you need to draw a line where you want to section the drawing view. Activate the **Cutting Plane** command (click **Home > Drawing Views > Cutting Plane** on the ribbon) and click on a drawing view. Now, you have to draw a line to define the cutting plane. You can use the geometry of the drawing view to draw the line. After drawing a line, click **Close Cutting Plane** on the ribbon. Next, click on either side of the cutting plane to indicate the view direction.

Drawings

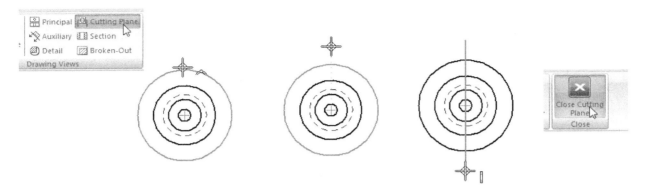

Activate the **Section** command (click **Home > Drawing Views > Section** on the ribbon) and click on a cutting plane. Move the cursor and click to position the section view.

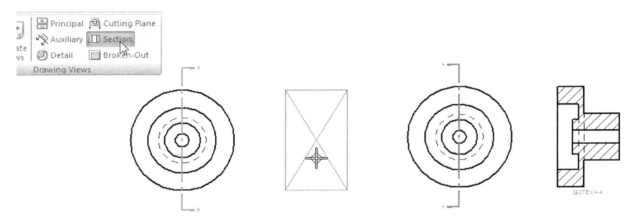

You can also use a multi-segment cutting line to create a section view.

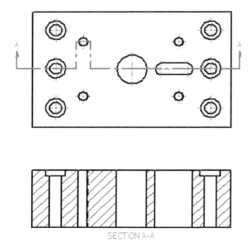

Use the **Section Only** option to display only the geometry on the cutting plane.

Drawings

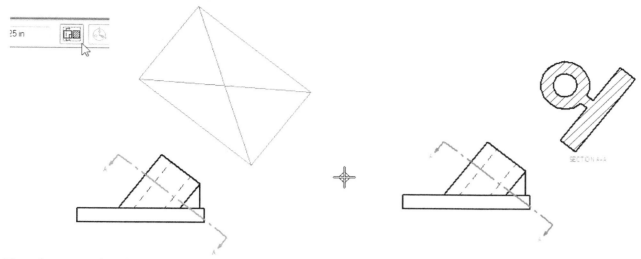

Use the **Revolved Section View** option to create a revolved section view. First draw a multiple segment cutting plane using the **Cutting Plane** command. Next, activate the **Section** command and select the multi-segment cutting plane. Click on a segment to define the fold angle of the section view. Click the **Revolved Section View** icon on the command bar. Move the cursor and click to position the revolved section view.

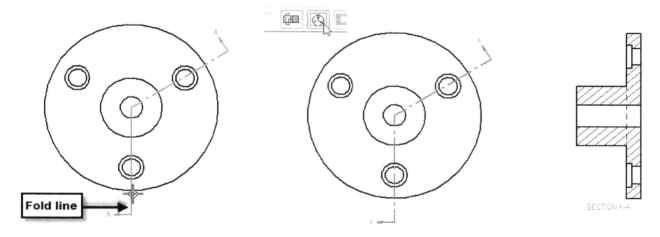

When creating a section view of an assembly, you can choose to exclude one or more components from the section cut. For example, to exclude the piston of a pneumatic cylinder, click the **Model Display Settings** icon on the command bar; the **Drawing View Properties** dialog box pops up on the screen. On this dialog box, select **piston** from the **Parts list** and uncheck the **Section** option. Click **OK** and locate the section view. You will notice that the piston is not cut.

Drawings

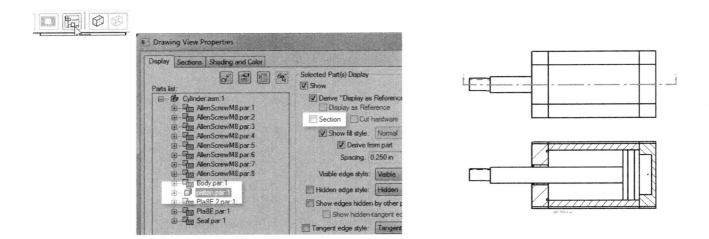

Detail View

If a drawing view contains small features that are difficult to see, a detailed view can be used to zoom in and make things clear. To create a detailed view, activate the **Detail** command (click **Home > Drawing Views > Detail** on the ribbon); this automatically activates the circle tool. Draw a circle to identify the area that you wish to zoom into. Once the circle is drawn, set the Scale value on the command bar. Next, move the cursor and click to locate the view; the detail view will appear with a label.

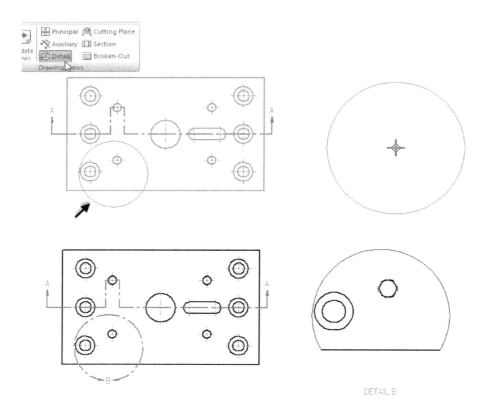

Drawings

Add Break Lines

Break lines are added to a drawing view which is too large to fit on the drawing sheet. They break the view so that only important details are shown. To add break lines, select the view and click the right mouse button. Select **Add Break Lines** from the popup menu; the **Add Break Lines** command bar pops up. On this command bar, click the **Vertical Break** or **Horizontal Break** icon and define the **Break Line Type**. Type-in the desired value in the **Break gap** box and move your cursor to the area of the view where you would like to start the break. Click once to locate the beginning of the break, and then click again to locate the end of the break. Click **Finish** on the command bar; the view is automatically broken.

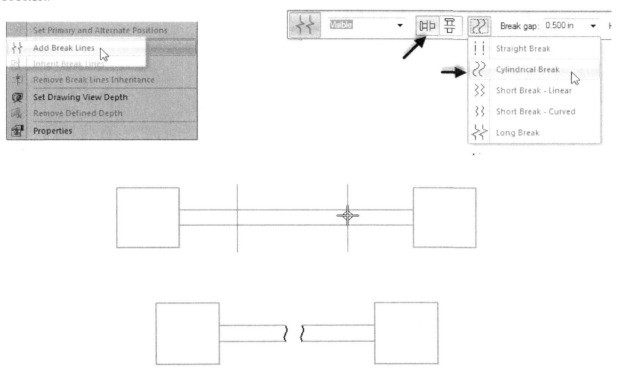

Broken Out

The **Broken-Out** command alters an existing view to show the hidden portion of a part or assembly. This command is very useful to show the parts which are hidden inside an assembly view. You need to have a closed profile to break-out a view. For example, if you want to show the piston inside a pneumatic cylinder, activate the **Broken-Out** command (click **Home > Drawing Views > Broken-Out** on the ribbon) and select drawing view to draw the profile. Draw a closed profile on the selected drawing view, and click **Close Broken Out Section** on the ribbon.

Drawings

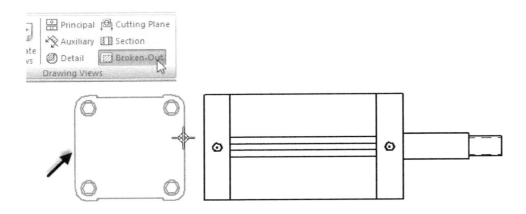

Now, move the cursor and click to specify the depth of the cutout.

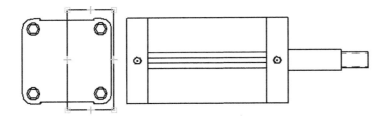

Select the drawing view to apply cutout.

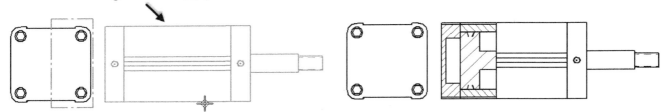

Exploded View

You can display an assembly in an exploded state as long as the assembly already has an exploded view defined. If you want to add an isometric exploded view, activate the **View Wizard** command and select the assembly from the **Select Model** dialog box. On the command bar, click the **Drawing View Wizard Options** icon; the **Drawing View Creation Wizard** dialog box pops up. On this dialog box, select **Explode** from the **.cfg, PMI model view, or Zone** drop-down menu and click **OK**. Click on the drawing sheet to locate the exploded view.

Drawings

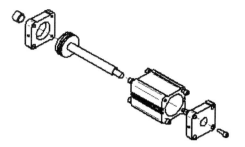

If you want to show an already existing isometric view in an exploded state, all you have to do is right-click the view and select **Properties**; the **High Quality View Properties** dialog box pops up. On this dialog box, select the explode configuration file from the **.cfg, PMI model view, or Zone** drop-down menu and click **OK**. Next, click **Update Views** on the ribbon; the view will be updated.

Display Options

When working with Solid Edge drawings, you can control the way a model view is displayed by using the display options. Select a view from the drawing sheet and click the **Shading Options** icon on the command bar; a menu appears. On this menu, select the desired shading type and click **Update Views** on the ribbon. The shading type of the view will be changed.

If you want to hide the hidden lines of a view, select it and click **Properties** on the command bar; the **High Quality View Properties** dialog box pops up. On this dialog box, uncheck the **Hidden edge style** option and click **OK**. The hidden lines will disappear from the model view.

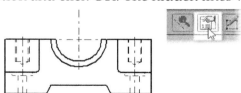
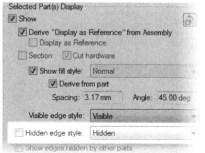
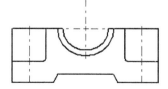

235

Drawings

View Alignment

There are several types of views that are automatically aligned to a parent view. These include section views, auxiliary views, and projective views. If you move down a view, the parent view associated with it will also move.

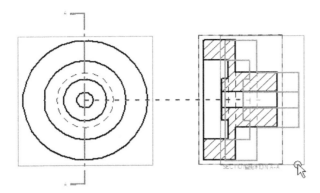

You need to break the alignment between them to move the view separately. Click the right mouse button on the view and select **Delete Alignment**. Now, click on the alignment line that appears between the two views.

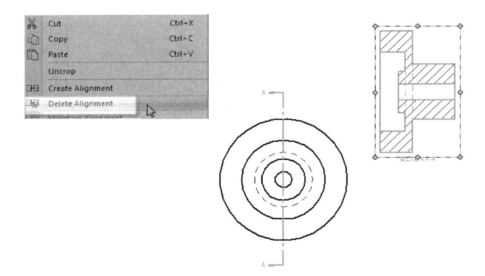

If you want to create alignment between the views, click the right mouse button on the parent view and select **Create Alignment**. On the command bar, select the required alignment option and click on the view to be aligned.

Drawings

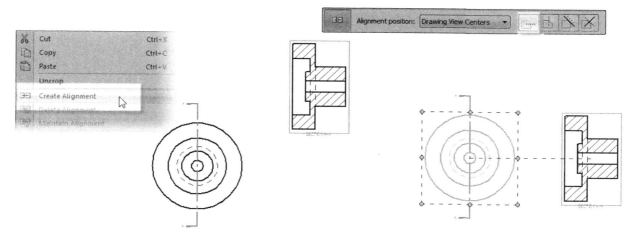

If you want to temporarily delete the alignment between the views, click the right mouse button and deactivate the **Maintain Alignment** option. Now, drag the view to a new location without affecting the position of the parent view.

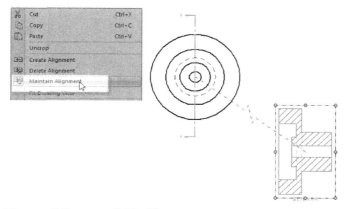

Parts List and Balloons

Creating an assembly drawing is very similar to creating a part drawing. However, there are few things unique in an assembly drawing. One of them is creating parts list. A parts list identifies the different components in an assembly. Generating a parts list is very easy in Solid Edge. First, you need to have a view of the assembly. Next, click **Home > Tables > Parts List** on the ribbon, and then click on the drawing view. On the command bar, click the **Properties** icon to open the **Parts List Properties** dialog box. On this dialog box, click the **List Control** tab and select an option from the **Global** section. You can select the **Top-level list**, **Atomic list**, or **Exploded list** option. Next, select the required configuration and click the **Columns** tab.

Drawings

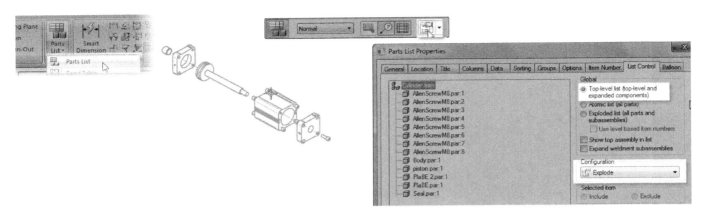

In this tab, select the column names from the **Columns** section and arrange them using the **Move Up** and **Move Down** buttons. To add a new column, select the column name from the **Properties** section and click **Add Column**. To remove a column, select the column name from the **Columns** section and click **Delete Column**. Type-in a value in the **Column width** box.

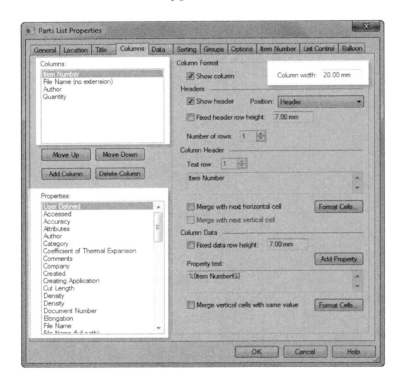

Click the **Balloon** tab and type-in a value in the **Text size** box. Click the **Shape** icon and select the desired balloon shape. If you want to hide the item count inside the balloon, uncheck the **Use Item Count for lower text** option. Under the **Auto-Balloon** section, check the **Create alignment shape** option to create magnetic lines aligning the balloons. Click on the **Pattern** button and select the alignment shape from the menu.

Drawings

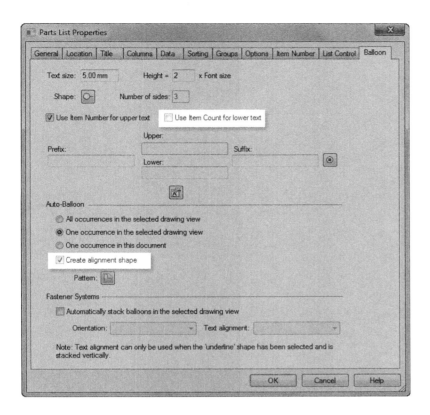

Click on the drawing sheet to place the parts list. The balloons are created automatically.

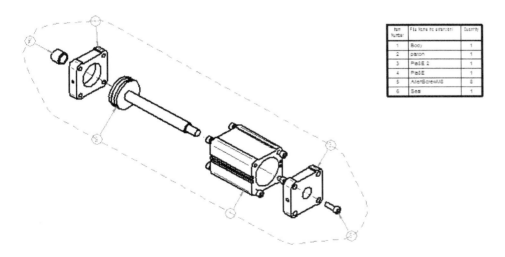

Dimensions

Solid Edge provides you with different ways to add dimensions to the drawing. One of the methods is to retrieve the dimensions that are already contained in the 3D part file. Click **Home > Dimension > Retrieve Dimensions** on the ribbon. On the command bar, select the dimension types that you want to retrieve. Click on the drawing view where you want to display the dimensions.

Drawings

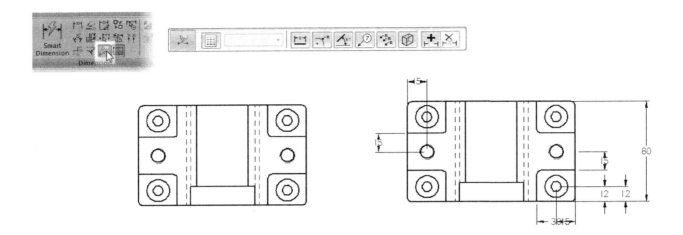

You may notice that there are some unwanted dimensions. Simply select them and press Delete to remove them. Also, the dimensions may not be positioned properly. To arrange them properly, activate the **Arrange Dimensions** command (click **Home > Dimension > Arrange Dimension** on the ribbon). Click on the dimensions, and then click the green check on the command bar. The dimensions will be arranged properly.

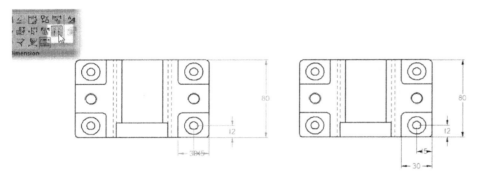

If you want to add some more dimensions which are necessary to manufacture a part, activate the **Smart Dimension** command and add them to the view. You can also use the **Distance Between** command to add linear dimensions.

Coordinate Dimensions

Coordinate dimensions are another type of dimensions that can be added to a drawing. To create them, activate the **Coordinate Dimension** command (click **Home > Dimension > Coordinate Dimension** on the ribbon), and then click on any edge of the drawing view to define the ordinate or zero reference. Now, click on the points or edges of the drawing view and place the coordinate dimensions.

Drawings

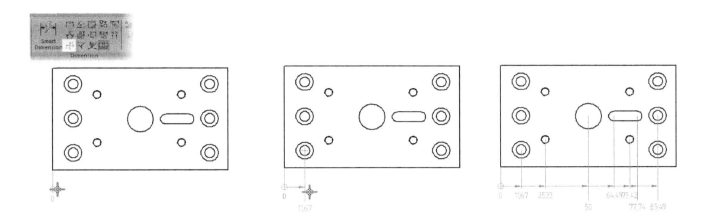

Center Marks and Centerlines

Centerlines and Centermarks are used in engineering drawings to denote hole centers and lines. To add center marks to the drawing, activate the **Center Mark** command (click **Home > Annotation > Center Mark** on the ribbon) and click on the hole circles. The centermarks are added to the circles.

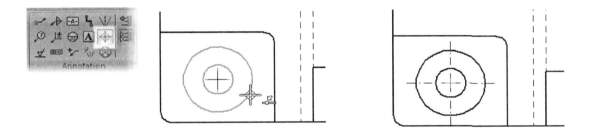

To add centerlines, activate the **Centerline** command (click **Home > Annotation > Centerline** on the ribbon). Click on two parallel edges of the drawing view. A centerline will be created between the two lines.

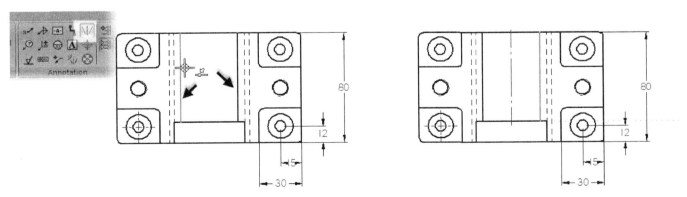

If you want to add centrelines automatically, activate the **Automatic Centerlines** command (click **Home > Annotation > Automatic Centerlines** on the ribbon). The **Automatic Centerlines** command bar pops up. On the command bar, click the **Options** icon to open the **Center Line and Center Mark Options** dialog box. On the dialog box, select the element to which the center lines and center marks

Drawings

are to be added. Click **OK** to close the dialog box. Click the drawing view to add center lines and center marks.

 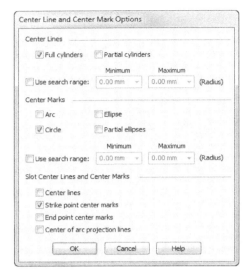 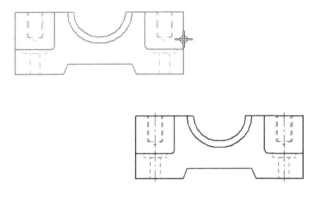

Bolt Hole Circle

The **Bolt Hole Circle** command (click **Home > Annotation > Bolt Hole Circle** on the ribbon) allows you to add center marks to the holes arranged in a circular fashion. Activate this command and click for the center of the bolt hole circle. Drag the cursor and click for the radius point of the bolt hole circle. A bolt circle will be created.

 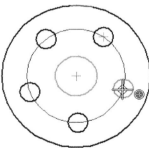 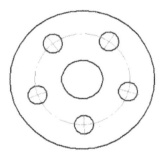

Callouts and Leaders

Callouts and leaders are an essential element in creating drawings. In this section, you will learn to add callouts and leaders to a drawing. For example, to add a counterbore hole callout, activate the **Callout** command (click **Home > Annotation > Callout** on the ribbon). On the **Callout Properties** dialog box, type-in values in the **Callout text** and **Callout text 2** boxes. You can use the **Special Character** icons available on the dialog box. Click the **OK** button and click on the hole. Drag the mouse cursor and click to place the callout.

Drawings

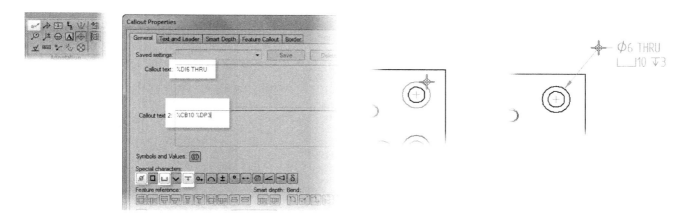

If you have multiple elements in a drawing with a same callout value, you can use leaders to connect them to an existing callout. Activate the **Leader** command (click **Home > Annotation > Leader** on the ribbon) and click on an element. Drag the mouse cursor and click on an already existing callout.

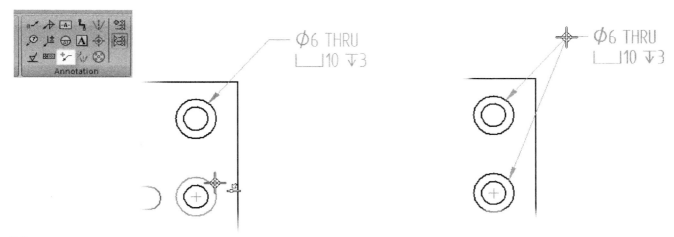

Notes

Notes are important part of a drawing. You add notes to provide additional details which cannot be done using dimensions and annotations. To add a note or text, activate the **Text** command (click **Home > Annotation > Text** on the ribbon). On the command bar, select the font and font size. Create a box and type text inside it.

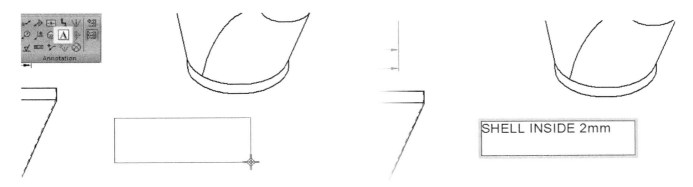

Drawings

Examples

Example 1

In this example, you will create 2D drawing of the parts shown below.

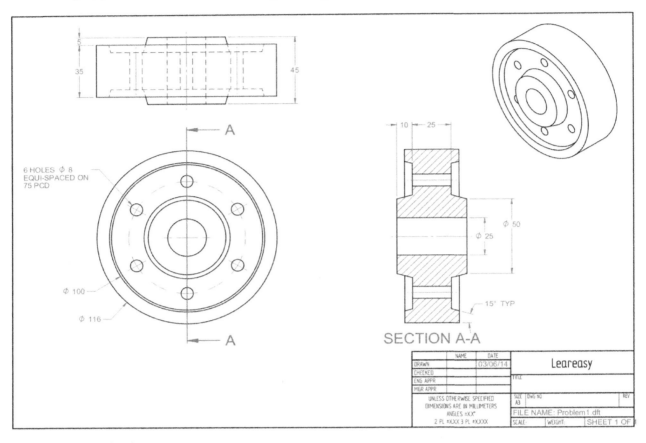

1. Start **Solid Edge ST6**.
2. On the initial screen, click **ISO Draft** to start a new drawing.
3. At the bottom of the window, right-click on the **Sheet 1** tab and select **Sheet Setup**.
4. On the **Sheet Setup** dialog box, click the **Size** tab and select the **Standard** option. Set the sheet size to **A3 Wide (420mm x 297mm)**.
5. Click the **Background** tab and set the **Background sheet** to **A3-Sheet**. Click **OK** to close the dialog box.

 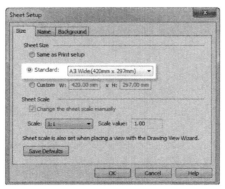 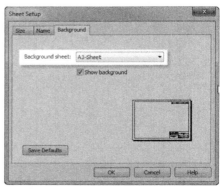

Drawings

6. On the ribbon, click **View > Sheet Views > Background** to activate the background. Deactivate the **Working** icon located below the **Background** icon.

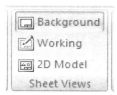

7. At the bottom of the sheet, click **A3-Sheet**.
8. Select the revision table and press Delete on your keyboard.

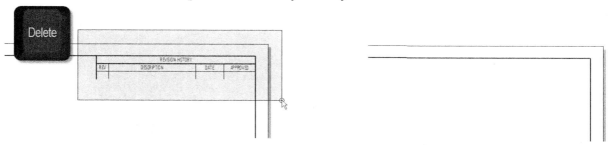

9. In the Title Block, change the company name to Larneasy.

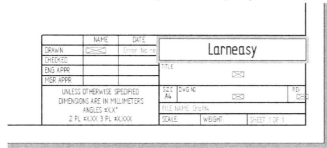

10. Activate the **Working** icon on the **Sheet views** panel, and then deactivate the **Background** icon.
11. On the **Application Menu**, click the **Solid Edge Options** button. On the **Solid Edge Options** dialog box, click the **Drawing Standards** tab. Set the **Projection Angle** to **Third** and click the **OK** button.

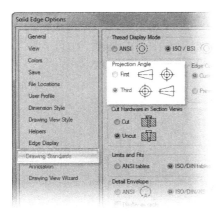

Drawings

12. Activate the **Styles** command (click **Home > Dimension > Styles** on the ribbon). On the **Style** dialog box, set the **Style type** to **Dimension**. Select **ISO** from the **Styles** box and click the **Modify** button.

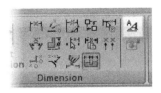
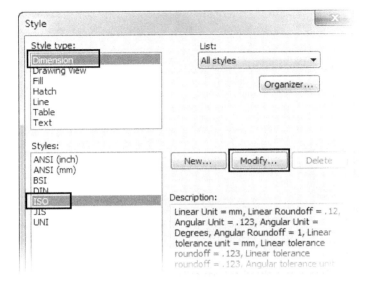

13. On the **Modify Dimension Style** dialog box, click the **Text** tab and set the **Font** type to **Arial**. Set the **Orientation** to **Horizontal** and **Position** to **Embedded**.

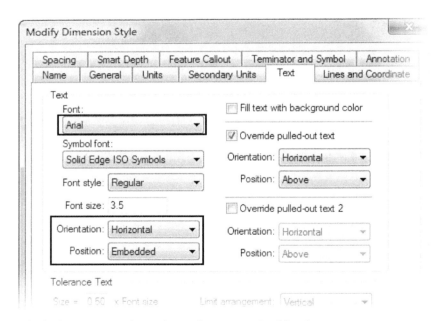

14. Click the **Units** tab and set the **Round-off** value to **1**.

Drawings

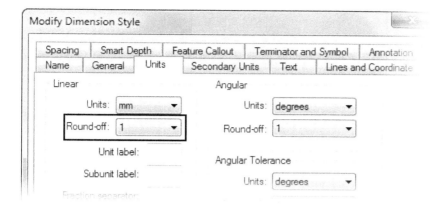

15. Click the **Lines and Coordinate** tab and set the **Element gap** to 0.5 x Font Size. Under **Dimension Lines**, uncheck the **Connect** option. Click **OK** and then **Apply** to make changes to the dimension style.

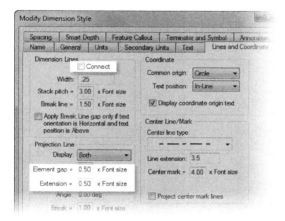

16. On the **Quick Access Toolbar**, click the **Save** icon and browse to the location C:\Program files\Solid Edge ST6\Template. Type **Larneasy** in the **File name** box and click **Save**. Close the file.
17. On the **Application Menu**, click the **New** icon to open the **New** dialog box. On this dialog box, click **User** tab and select **Larneasy.dft**. Click **OK** to start a new drawing file.

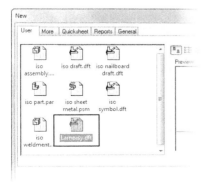

Drawings

18. Activate the **View Wizard** command (click **Home > Drawing Views > View Wizard** on the ribbon).
19. Browse to the location of Exercise 1 of Chapter 5 and click on the part file. Click the **Open** button.
20. On the command bar, click the **Drawing View Layout** icon.
21. On the **Drawing View Creation Wizard** dialog box, set the **Primary View** to **front**. Click on the top view and isometric view icons. Click the **OK** button to close the dialog box.

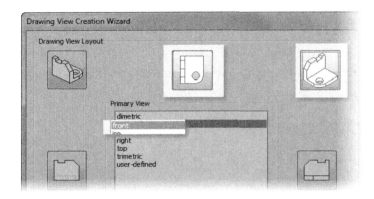

22. On the command bar, set the **Scale** to **1:1**
23. Click the left portion of the sheet to place the drawing views. Drag the isometric view and position it at the top right corner.

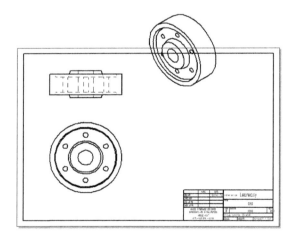
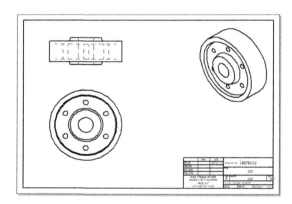

24. Click on the isometric view to activate the command bar. On the command bar, type-in **0.75** in the **Scale** box and press Enter.

Drawings

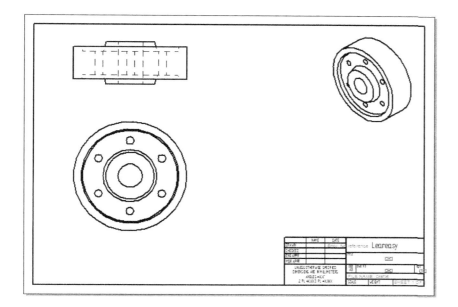

25. Activate the **Cutting Plane** command (click **Home > Drawing Views > Cutting Plane** on the ribbon) and create a cutting plane passing through the center of the front view.

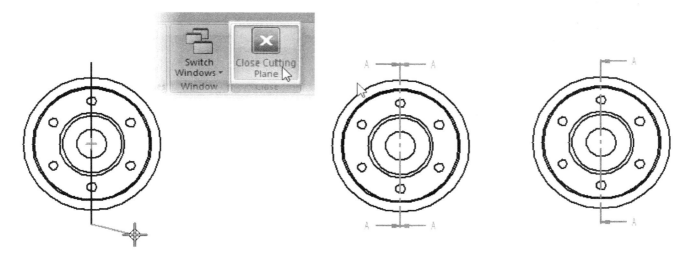

26. Activate the **Section** command (click **Home > Drawing views > Section** on the ribbon) and click on the cutting plane.
27. On the command bar, click the **Model Display Settings** icon. On the **Drawing View Properties** dialog box, uncheck the **Hidden edge style** option and click **OK** twice.

Drawings

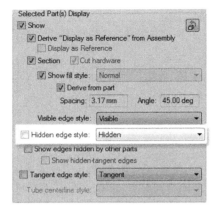

28. Drag the mouse cursor toward right and click to position the view.

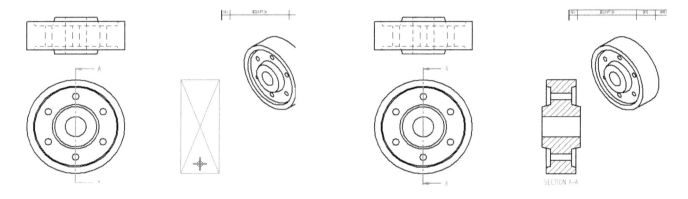

29. Activate the **Automatic Centerlines** command (click **Home > Annotation > Automatic Centerlines** on the ribbon). Click on the top view to apply centerlines.

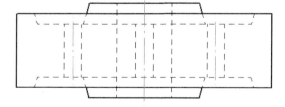

30. Activate the **Centerline** command (click **Home > Annotation > Centerline** on the ribbon). On the command bar, select **By 2 Lines** from the **Placement Options** drop-down menu.
31. On the section view, click on the horizontal line of the holes. The centerlines are created between the hole lines.

Drawings

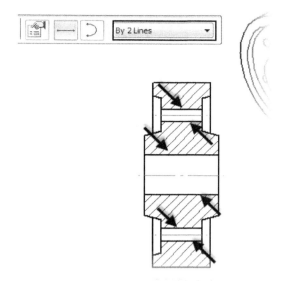

32. Activate the **Center Mark** command (click **Home > Annotation > Center Mark** on the ribbon)
33. On the command bar, set the **Orientation** to **Horizontal/Vertical** and click on the hole located at the center of the front view.
34. Activate the **Bolt Hole Circle** command (click **Home > Annotation > Bolt Hole Circle** on the ribbon) and click on the hole located at the center of the front view. Drag the mouse cursor and click on anyone of the small holes. A bolt hole circle is created.

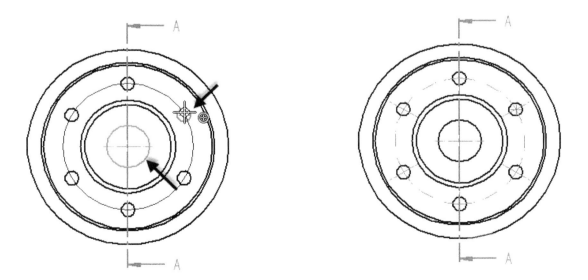

35. Activate the **Smart Dimension** command and apply dimensions to the top view.

Drawings

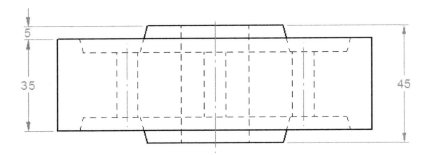

36. Activate the **Symmetric Diameter** command (click **Home > Dimension > Symmetric Diameter** on the ribbon). On the command bar, activate the **Diameter-Half/Full** icon.
37. Click the centerline of the section view and horizontal line of the large hole. Drag the mouse cursor and position the diameter dimension.

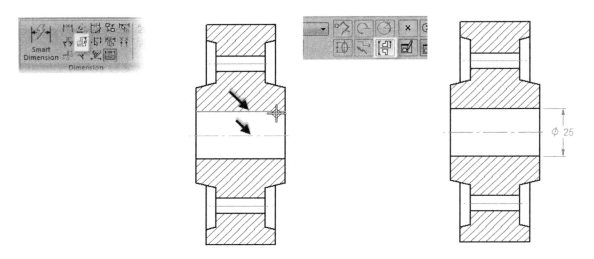

38. Click on the angled edge of the section view and create another diameter dimension.

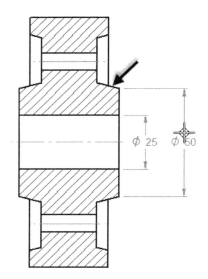

Drawings

39. Activate the **Smart Dimension** command click on the lower horizontal edge of the section view. On the command bar, activate the **Angle** icon and click on the inclined edge. Drag the cursor and click to position the angle dimension. Press Esc to deactivate the **Smart Dimension** command.

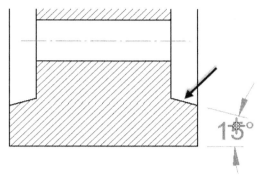

40. Click on the angle dimension and drag upward. On the command bar, click the **Prefix** icon to open the **Dimension Prefix** dialog box.
41. On the **Dimension Prefix** dialog box, type-in **TYP** in **Suffix** box and click **OK**.

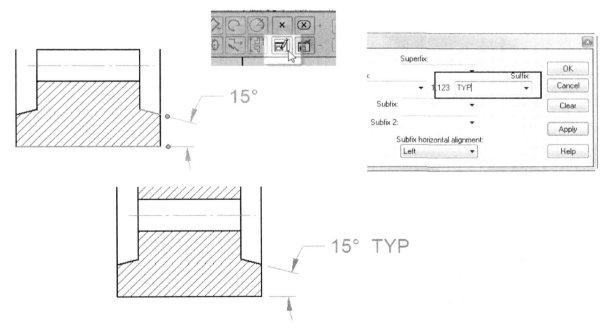

42. Activate the **Smart Dimension** command and click on the small hole of the front view. On the command bar, click the **Prefix** icon.
43. On the **Dimension Prefix** dialog box, type-in values in the **Prefix, Subfix,** and **Subfix 2** boxes. Click **OK** and position the hole dimension.

Drawings

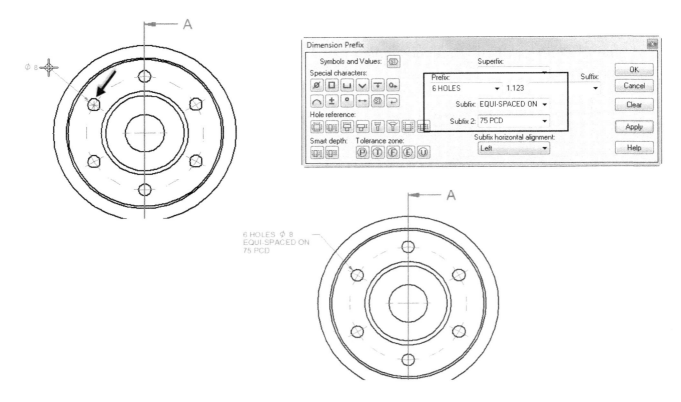

44. Activate the **Smart Dimension** command and open the **Dimension Prefix** dialog box. On this dialog box, empty the **Prefix**, **Subfix**, and **Subfix 2** boxes and click **OK**.
45. Create the other dimensions in the drawing.

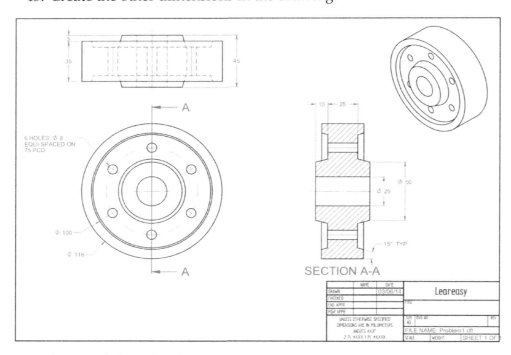

46. Save and close the drawing.

Drawings

Example 2

In this example, you will create an assembly drawing shown below.

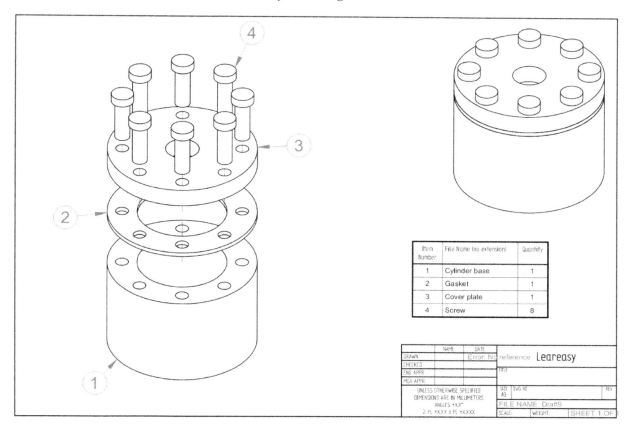

1. Start **Solid Edge ST6**.
2. On the **Quick Access Toolbar**, click the **New** icon. On the **New** dialog box, click on the **Larneasy.dft**, and then click **OK**.
3. Activate the **View Wizard** command (click **Home > Drawing Views > View Wizard** on the ribbon).
4. Browse to the location of Example 2 of Chapter 10 and click on the assembly file. Click the **Open** button.
5. Click on the top right corner to place the isometric view of the assembly. Press Esc to stop view projection.
6. Again, activate the **View Wizard** command. On the **Select Attachment** dialog box, set the **Configuration** to **explode, Solid Edge**. Click **OK**.
7. On the command bar, set the **Scale** to 1:1. Click on the drawing sheet to position the exploded view.

Drawings

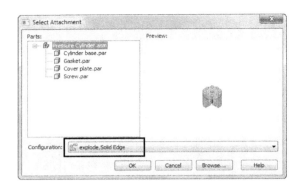
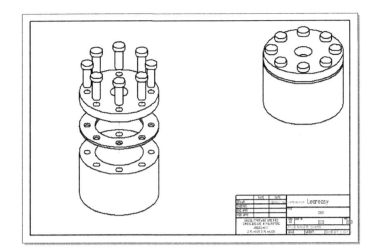

8. Activate the **Parts List** command (click **Home > Tables > Parts List** on the ribbon) and click on the exploded view.
9. On the command bar, click the **Properties** icon to open the **Parts List Properties** dialog box.
10. On this dialog box, click the **Column** tab. In the **Columns** box click on the **Author** option, and then click the **Delete Column** button.
11. On the **Data** tab, press Shift key and select all the cells of the table. Change the **Font** type to **Arial**.

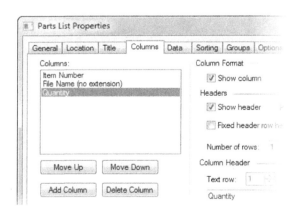
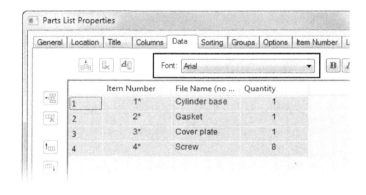

12. On the **Balloon** tab, set the **Text Size** to 8 and uncheck the **Use Item Count for lower text** option. Click **OK**.
13. Position the parts list below the isometric view. You will notice some balloons are placed outside the sheet.
14. Click on the alignment line connecting the balloons. Square and circle grips appear on it.
15. Click on a square and reduce the size of the alignment shape.

Drawings

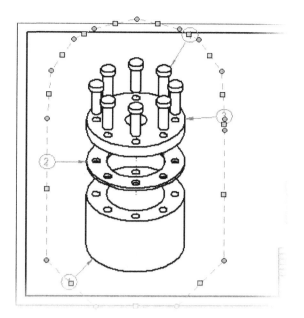 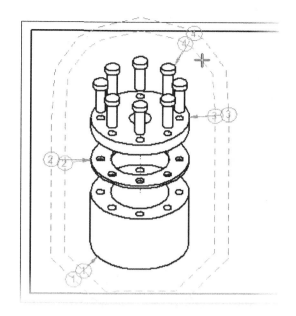

16. Save and close the drawing.

Questions

1. How to create drawing views using **View Wizard** command?
2. How to hide hidden edges of a drawing view?
3. How to change the display style of a drawing view?
4. How to drawing views when the part is edited?
5. How to control the properties of dimensions and annotations?
6. List the commands used to create centerlines and center marks?
7. How to add symbols and texts to a dimension?
8. How to add break lines to drawing view?
9. How to create revolved section views?
10. How to create exploded view of an assembly?

Exercises
Exercise 1
Create orthographic views of the part model shown below. Add dimensions and annotations to the drawing.

Drawings

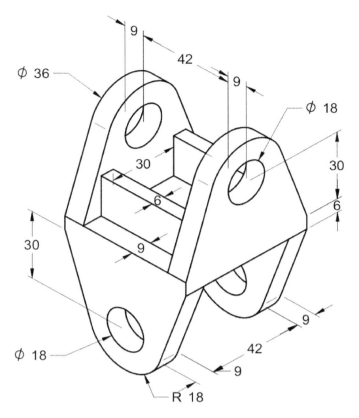

Exercise 2
Create orthographic views and an auxiliary view of the part model shown below. Add dimensions and annotations to the drawing.

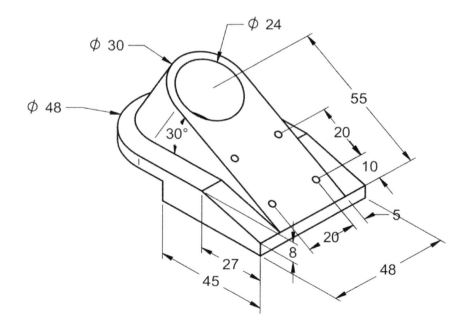

Drawings

Chapter 12: Sheet Metal Design

Sheet metal parts are made by bending and forming flat sheets of metal. In Solid Edge, sheet-metal parts can be folded and unfolded enabling you to show them in the flat pattern as well as their bent-up state. There are two ways to design sheet-metal parts in Solid Edge. You can either start the sheet-metal part from scratch using sheet-metal features throughout the design process or you can design it as a regular solid part and later converted to a sheet-metal part. Most commonly, sheet-metal parts are designed in Sheet Metal environment from the beginning. In this chapter, you will learn both the approaches.

The topics covered in this chapter are:

- *Tabs*
- *Flanges*
- *Bend Allowance*
- *Bend Tables*
- *Counter Flanges*
- *Hems*
- *Close 2-Bend Corners*
- *Bends*
- *Jogs*
- *Dimples*
- *Louvers*
- *Drawn Cutouts*
- *Beads*
- *Gussets*
- *Etches*
- *Embosses*
- *Cuts*
- *Convert to Sheet Metal*
- *Rip Corners*
- *Flat Pattern*
- *Export to DXF or DWG*

Starting a Sheet Metal part

To start a new sheet metal part, click the **ISO Sheet Metal** option on the starting screen (or) click the **New** icon on the **Quick Access Toolbar**, and then double-click on the **iso sheet metal.psm** template on the **New** dialog box. If you want to start the sheet metal part using any other template, click the **More** tab and select the required template.

Sheet Metal Design

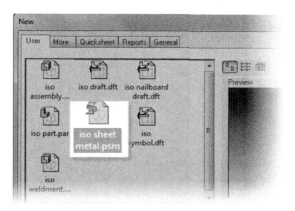

Tab

The tab is a basic type of sheet metal feature. To create a tab, create a closed sketch on plane and click inside it. An arrow handle appears along with the command bar. On the command bar, click the **Material Table** icon to open the **Solid Edge Material Table** dialog box. On this dialog box, open the **Material** tab and select define the material properties of the part. You can assign a material to the sheet metal part from the **Material** drop-down menu.

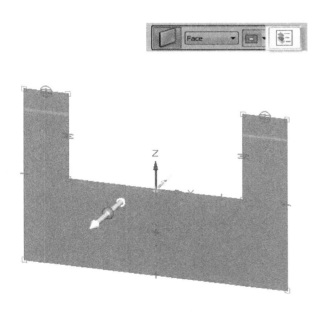

Open the **Gage** tab and define the gage properties of the sheet metal part. Type-in values in the **Material thickness**, **Bend radius**, **Relief depth**, **Relief width** boxes.

Sheet Metal Design

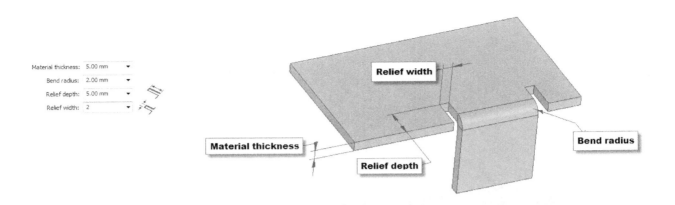

You can also use a spread sheet to define these values. Check the **Use Excel file** option and select a gage table from the **Use Gage Table** drop-down menu. You can edit the gage table values by clicking the **Edit** button. In the spread sheet, modify the values, and then save and close the file. You can also define the sheet metal properties by selecting anyone of the sheet metal gages available in the **Sheet metal gage** drop-down menu.

Next, type-in a value in **Neutral Factor** box. The **Neutral Factor** is the ratio that represents the location of neutral sheet measured from the inside face with respect to the thickness of the sheet-metal. It defines the bend allowance of the sheet metal part. The standard formula that calculates the bend allowance is given below.

$$BA = \frac{\pi(R + KT)A}{180}$$

BA = Bend Allowance $\qquad\qquad\qquad$ R = Bend Radius

Sheet Metal Design

K = Neutral Factor = t/T

T = Material Thickness

t = Distance from inside face to the neutral sheet

A = Bend Angle

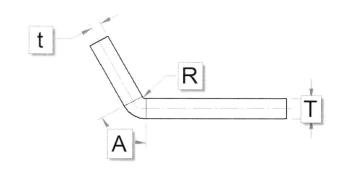

You can also define the bend allowance by using your own formula. Select the **Custom formula** option and type-in a value in the **ProgramID.ClassName** box. Click the **Apply to Model** button to apply the material and gage properties to the model. Now, click on the arrow handle to define the side of the tab feature. Click the right mouse button to create the tab feature.

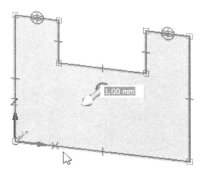
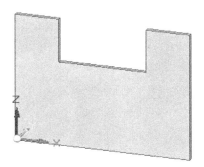

Flange

The second feature after creating a tab is flange. This feature can be created along an edge or multiple edges of a sheet metal part. In order to create a flange, all you need is to click an end face of the tab feature. The flange handle appears on the selected face. Click the small arrow and drag the cursor. A flange feature appears attached to the mouse cursor.

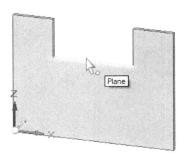

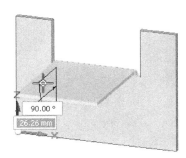

On the command bar, click the **Flange Options** icon to open the **Flange Options** dialog box. On this dialog box, you can override the gage properties by checking the **Override global value** options available next to each of the gage property.

Sheet Metal Design

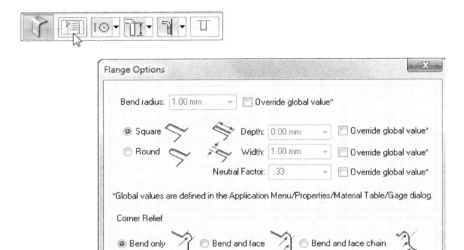

Under the **Corner Relief** section, select an option to define the type of corner relief. The three types of corner reliefs are shown below. Click **OK** to close the dialog box.

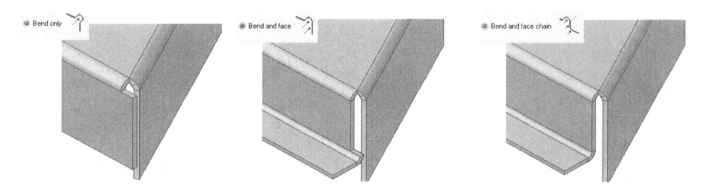

On the command bar, select an option from the **Measurement Point** drop-down menu. Both the measurement points are explained in the illustration below.

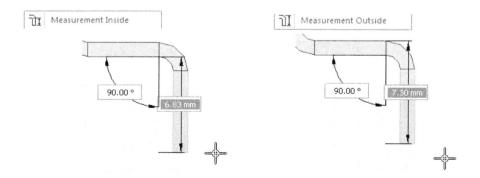

Sheet Metal Design

Define the material side using the **Material Side** drop-down menu. The three types of material sides are shown below.

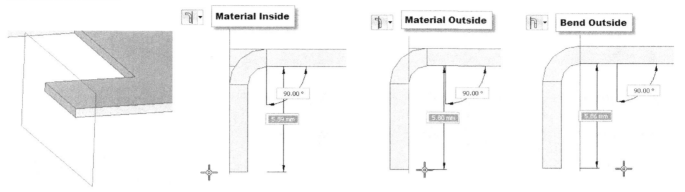

Click the **Partial Flange** icon to create the flange at the middle of the selected edge.

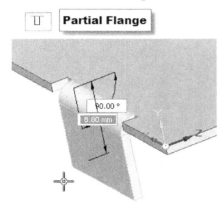

Type-in values in the distance and angle boxes that are attached to the flange. Click the right mouse button to create the flange.

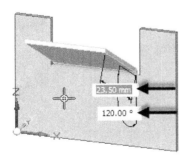 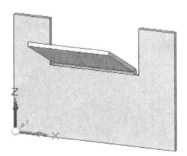

Close 2-Bend Corner

The **Close 2-Bend Corner** command allows you to control the appearance of sheet metal seams. For example, when two flanges meet at a corner, this command allows you to close the gap between them. In addition to that, it applies a corner treatment. Activate this command (click **Home > Sheet Metal > Close 2-Bend Corner** on the ribbon) and click on two bends that meet at a corner. On the command bar, select the required corner treatment.

Sheet Metal Design

There are seven types of corner treatments available in the **Corner Treatment** drop-down menu, as shown below.

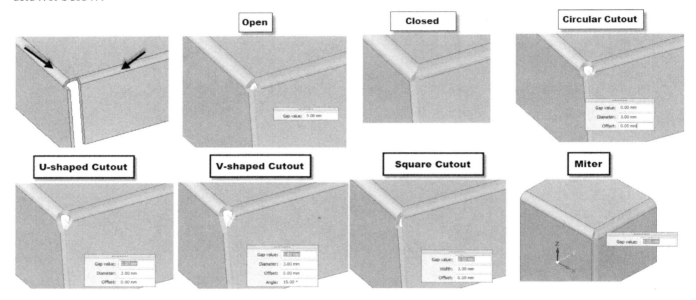

Note: the **Miter** corner treatment can be created only when the flanges are similar and perpendicular to each other.

On the command bar, click the **Overlapping Corner** icon to overlap one flange on the other. Next, type-in a value in the **Overlap ratio** box. Click the **Flip** icon to change the overlapping side.

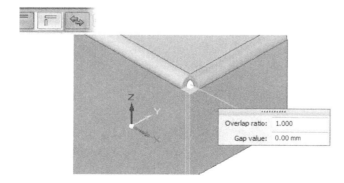

Sheet Metal Design

Contour Flange

The contour flange is another basic type of sheet metal feature. To create a contour flange, you need to have an open sketch. Activate the **Contour Flange** command (click **Home > Sheet Metal > Contour Flange** on the ribbon) and click on the open sketch. Drag the mouse cursor and type-in a value in the distance box that is attached to the preview. Press Enter to create the contour flange feature.

You can also add contour flanges to a base tab. Activate the **Line** command and lock the end face of the tab feature. On the locked face, draw an open sketch, and then activate the **Contour Flange** command. Click on the sketch, and then click on the arrow pointing towards the model. The contour flange preview appears. You will notice that the contour flange is created along face perpendicular to the sketch. You can click on multiple faces to add contour flanges to them. You can also use the **Chain** option to select multiple faces at a time.

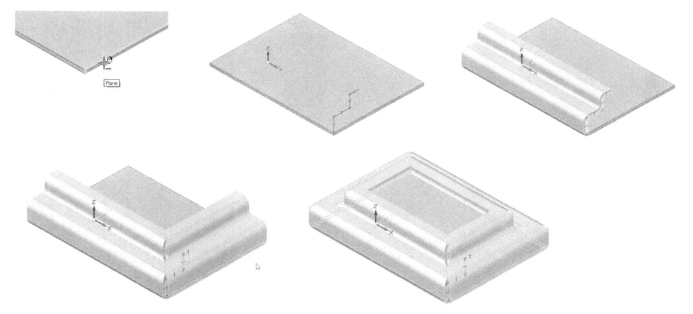

If you want to create a contour flange only upto a certain distance, then click the **Partial Flange** icon on the command bar and type-in the distance value.

Sheet Metal Design

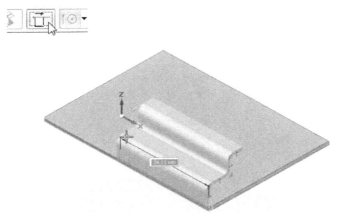

On the command bar, click the **Contour Flange Options** icon to open the **Contour Flange Options** dialog box. On this dialog box, click the **Miters and Corners** tab and check the **Miter** option to apply miter to the ends of the contour flange. Under the **Interior Corners** section, check the **Close Corner** option to apply treatment to the corners.

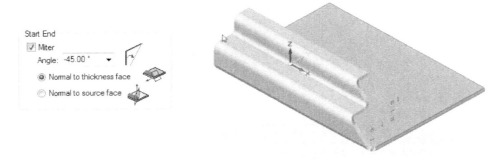

Hem

The **Hem** command is used to fold an edge of a sheet metal part. To add a hem, activate the **Hem** command (click **Home > Sheet Metal > Contour Flange > Hem** on the ribbon) and select the edge you need to fold over. On the command bar, the **Material Setback** drop-down menu controls whether the material is added to inside or outside the existing edge.

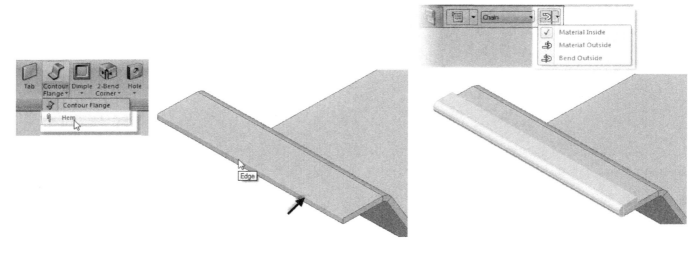

Sheet Metal Design

On the command bar, click the **Hem Options** icon to open the **Hem Option** dialog box.

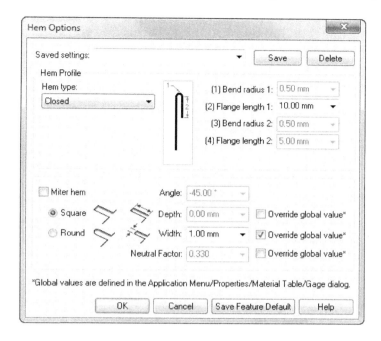

On this dialog box, select a hem type from the **Hem type** drop-down menu and define its parameters. Different hem types are shown below.

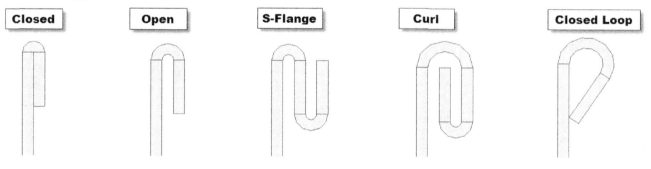

If you want to bevel the end faces of the hem, check the **Miter** option and type-in a value in the **Angl**e box. Click the **OK** button to close the dialog box, and then right-click to complete the hem feature.

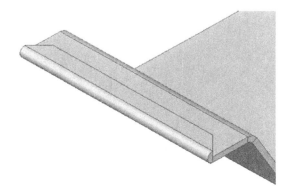

Bend

In addition to adding flanges and contour flanges, you can also bend to a flat sheet using the **Bend** command. First, draw a sketch line on the flat sheet. Activate the **Bend** command (click **Home > Sheet Metal > Bend** on the ribbon) and click on the sketched line. A two-sided arrow appears on the line. Click on the either side of the arrow to define the side to be folded. Type-in a value in the angle box to change the folding angle. Click on the arrow attached to the folded face to reverse the folding direction. Click the right mouse button to complete the feature.

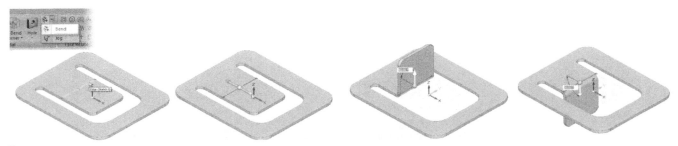

Jog

The **Jog** command is used to add a jog or offset to a flat sheet. To add a jog to sheet metal part, first you must define its location. You can do this by drawing a sketch line. Next, activate the **Jog** command (click **Home > Sheet metal > Jog** on the ribbon) and click on the sketched line. A two-sided arrow appears on the selected line. Click on either side of the arrow to define the side of bend.

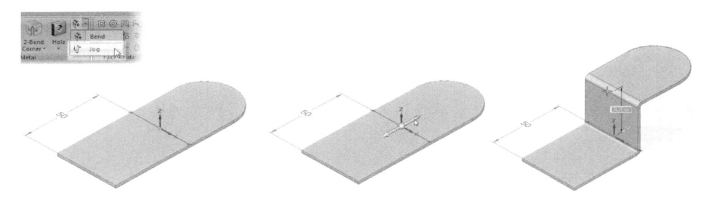

On the command bar, select a measurement point from the **Measurement Point** drop-down menu. Both the measurement points are illustrated below.

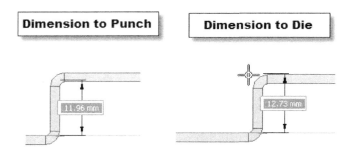

Sheet Metal Design

Type-in a value in the distance box and press Enter to add a jog to the sheet metal part.

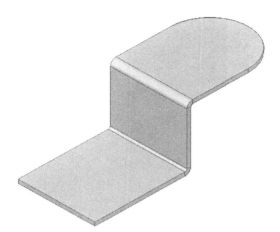

Dimple

The **Dimple** command is used to add a dimple to a flat sheet by deforming it. To add a dimple to sheet metal part, first you must define its shape, size, and location. You can do this by drawing a closed sketched. Next, activate the **Dimple** command (click **Home > Sheet Metal > Dimple** on the ribbon) and click in the sketch region. The sketch will be converted into a dimple shape. Click the arrow that appears on the dimple to change its direction.

On the command bar, click the **Dimple Options** icon to open the **Dimple Options** dialog box. On this dialog box, type-in the values of taper angle, punch radius, die radius, and corner radius. Click **OK** to close the dialog box.

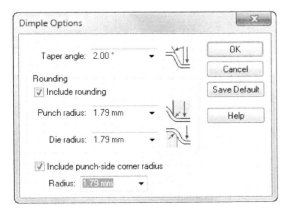

271

Sheet Metal Design

On the command bar, define the representation of the profile. You can select **Profile Represents Die** or **Profile Represents Punch**. Type-in a value in the distance box that is attached to the feature, and then press Enter to create the drawn cutout.

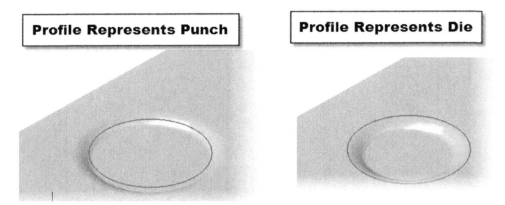

Drawn Cutout

The drawn cutout and dimple feature are almost alike, except that an opening is created in case of drawn cutout. In order to create a drawn cutout, first you must have closed sketch. Next, activate the **Drawn Cutout** command (click **Home > Sheet Metal > Drawn Cutout** on the ribbon) and click inside the sketch region. Click on the arrow that appears on the drawn cutout feature to change its direction.

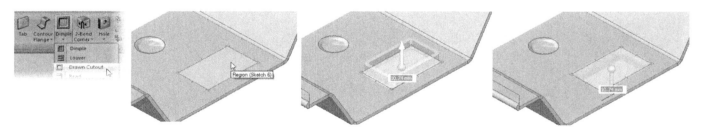

On the command bar, click the **Drawn Cutout Options** icon to open the **Drawn Cutout Options** dialog box. Type-in values of taper angle, die radius, and corner radius. Click **OK** to close the dialog box. Next, on the command bar, click the **Profile Represents Die** or **Profile Represents Punch** icon. This determines whether the side walls are placed inside or outside the sketch profile. Next, type-in a value in the distance box attached to the feature and press Enter.

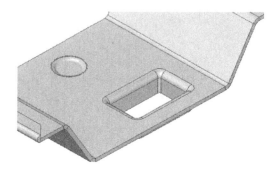

Sheet Metal Design

Bead

The **Bead** command creates bead feature which stiffens the sheet metal part. To create a bead feature, first you must have a sketch which defines its size and shape. If the sketch is having curved edges, then ensure that they are tangent continuous. Next, activate the **Bead** command (click **Home > Sheet Metal > Dimple > Bead** on the ribbon) and click on the sketch. Click on the arrow that appears on the bead feature to change its direction.

On the command bar, click the **Bead Options** icon to open the **Bead Options** dialog box. On this dialog box, under **Cross Section**, select the cross section type and define the size parameters. Check the **Include Rounding** option to apply rounds to the edges of the bead feature. Under the **End Conditions** section, select the desired option and click **OK** to close the dialog box. Click the right mouse button to complete the bead feature.

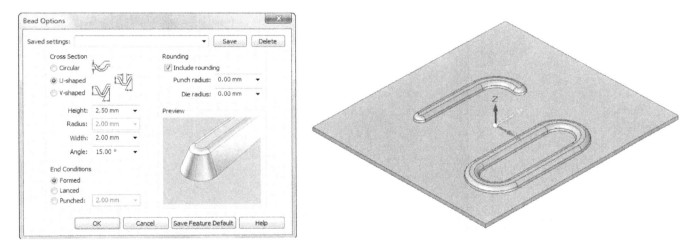

Louver

Solid Edge provides you with the **Louver** command, which makes it easy to create louvers. Activate this command (click **Home > Sheet Metal > Dimple > Louver** on the ribbon) and place the mouse cursor on a face. You will notice that a louver appears parallel to an edge. Press N or B on your keyboard to change the orientation of the louver. Press F3 on your keyboard to lock the face, and then place the mouse cursor on an edge and press E to a add location dimension.

Sheet Metal Design

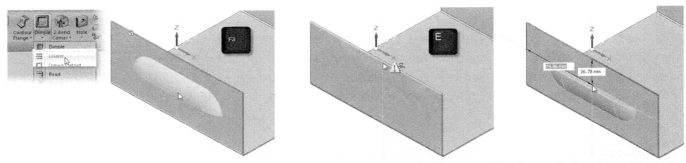

On the command bar, click the **Louver Options** icon to open the **Louver Options** dialog box. On this dialog box, select the end condition of the louver. The two types of end conditions are shown in figure.

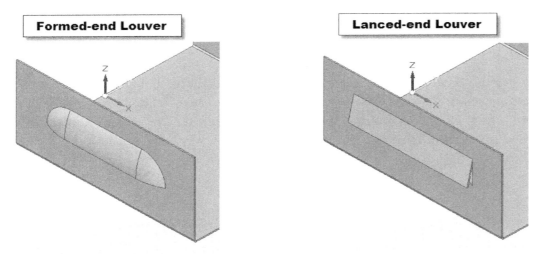

Type-in the values of the length, depth, and height. Check the **Include rounding** option to round the edges of the louver. Type-in values in the **X** and **Y** boxes to shift the default origin of the louver. Click **OK** to close the dialog box.

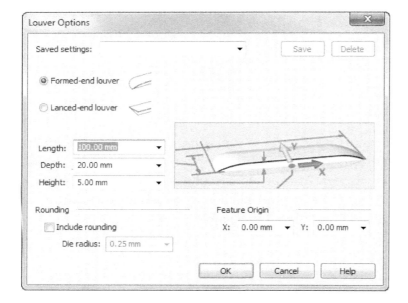

274

Sheet Metal Design

Type-in values in dimension boxes that are attached to the louver, and press Enter to complete the louver feature.

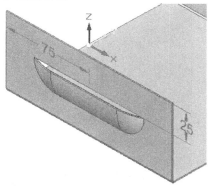

Gusset

Gussets are stiffening features created across a bend to reinforce the sheet metal part. To create a gusset, activate the **Gusset** command (click **Home > Sheet Metal > Dimple > Gusset** on the ribbon) and click on a bend face. A gusset feature appears along with a dimension box attached to it.

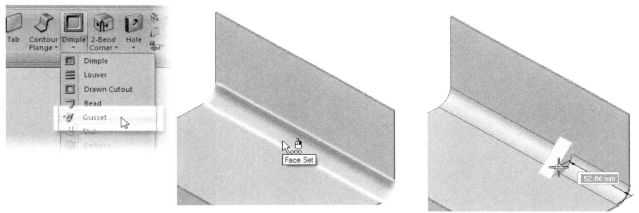

On the command bar click the **Gusset Options** icon to open the **Gusset Options** dialog box. On this dialog box, select the gusset shape and type-in a value in the **Depth** box. Type-in values of taper angle, width, and radius. Check the **Include rounding** option to round the edges of the gusset, and then click **OK** to close the dialog box.

Sheet Metal Design

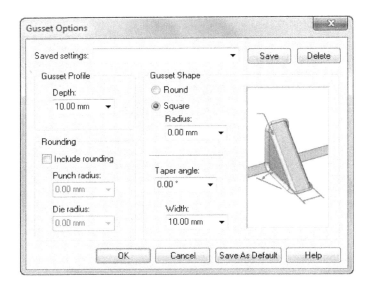

On the command bar, select a patterning option from the **Pattern** drop-down menu. The **Fit** option creates pattern along the total length of the bend by using the count value that you specify. The **Fill** option creates a pattern along the total length of the bend by using the spacing value that you specify. The **Fixed** option creates a pattern by using the spacing value and the count that you specify.

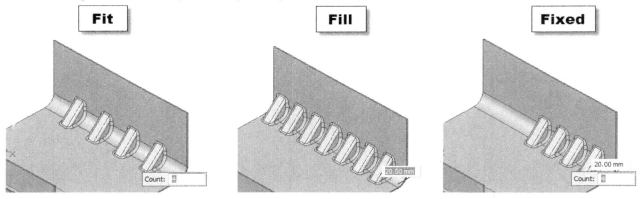

Cut

When it is necessary to remove material from a sheet metal part, you must use the **Cut** command. First, draw a sketch and click inside it; a two sided arrow appears. Click on this arrow and drag the mouse cursor into the geometry. On the command bar, the select the extent type from the **Extents** drop-down menu. Click the right mouse button to create the cut.

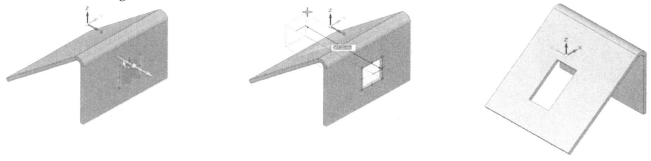

Sheet Metal Design

Creating Cut across Bends

If you need to create a cut across a bend, you must use the **Wrapped Cut** option. First, you must create a closed sketch across a bend. Press the Shift key and click inside the sketch region. On the command bar, activate the **Wrapped Cut** icon, and then click on the arrow handle. You will notice that the sheet metal part is flattened and cut is created across the bend. Click the right mouse button to complete the cut.

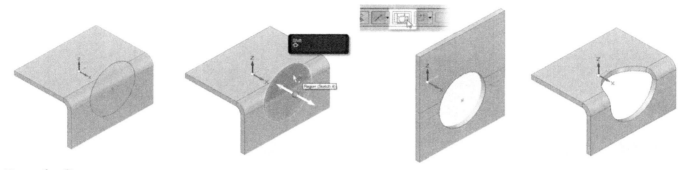

Break Corner

The **Break Corner** command is used to round or chamfer the sharp corner of a sheet metal part. Activate this command (click **Home > Sheet Metal > Break Corner** on the ribbon) and click on the corner edges of the sheet metal part. If you want to break all the corners of the sheet metal part, then drag a window across the geometry. All the corners of the sheet metal part will be selected.

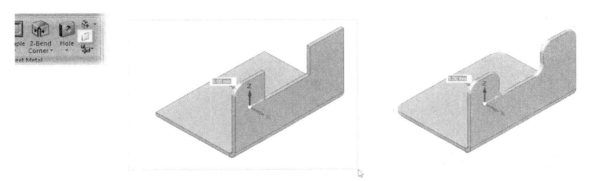

On the command bar, click the **Chamfer Corner** icon to apply chamfers to the corner edges. Type-in a value in the box that is attached to the round or chamfer. Press Enter to complete the break corner feature.

Flat Pattern

The **Flat Pattern** command flattens the part so that the manufacturing information can be displayed easily. To create a flat pattern, activate the **Flat Pattern** command (click **Tools > Model > Flatten** on the ribbon) and click on a base sheet. Next, click on an edge to define the x-axis of the flat pattern. Click the right mouse button to create the flat pattern.

Sheet Metal Design

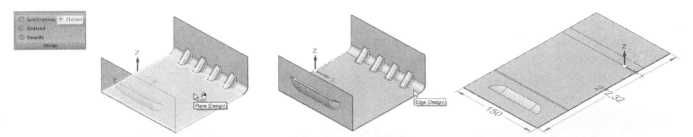

You will notice that a new entry 'Flat Pattern' is created in Pathfinder. You can switch back to the modeling mode by clicking **Tools > Model > Synchronous** on the ribbon.

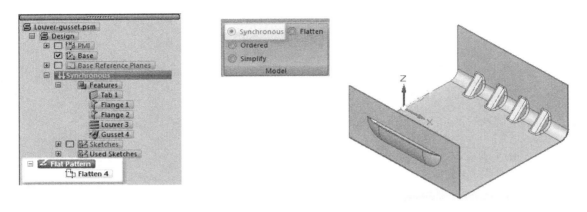

Lofted Flange

The **Lofted Flange** command allows you to create a lofted flange that can be unfolded into flat pattern. In Solid Edge ST6, the **Lofted Flange** command is available only in the **Ordered** environment. Transit to the **Ordered** environment and create two sketches on planes parallel to each other. Ensure that the sketches are not closed. Also, the openings should be in the same direction.

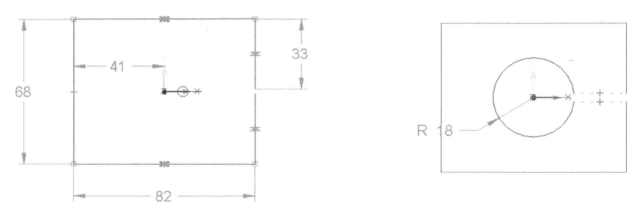

Activate the **Lofted Flange** command (click **Home > Sheet Metal > Contour Flange > Lofted Flange** on the ribbon) click on the first cross section. Click the green check on the command bar to accept the selection. Click on the second cross section and click the green check.

Sheet Metal Design

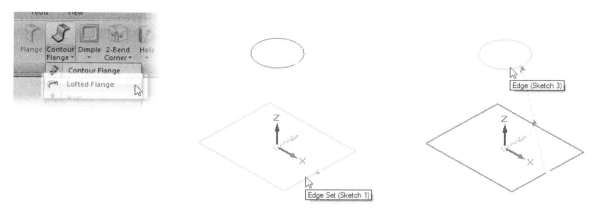

On the command bar, type-in a value in the **Thickness** box. Click inside or outside the sketch to define the side of sheet metal. Click **Finish** to complete the lofted flange feature.

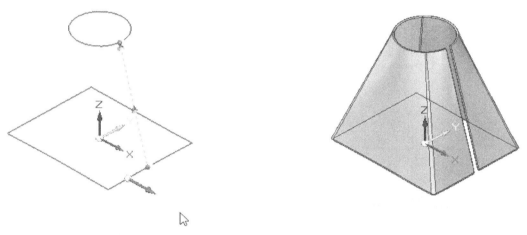

Create the flat pattern of the sheet metal part.

Transition to Synchronous Sheet Metal

Solid Edge has a special command which automates the process of converting an already existing part into a sheet metal part. This command is called **Transition to Synchronous Sheet Metal**. First, create a part in the Synchronous environment, and then shell it using the **Thin Wall** command. Next, click **Application Menu > Transform to Synchronous Sheet Metal**.

Sheet Metal Design

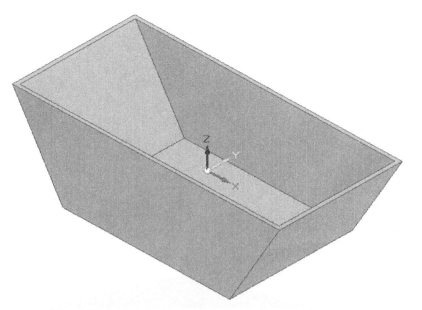

On the command bar, click the **Options** icon to open the **Transform to Sheet Metal Options** dialog box. On this dialog box, set the relief depth and width, bend radius, and neutral factor. Click **OK** to close the dialog box.

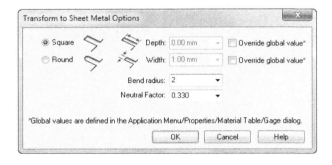

Click on a face of the part geometry to define the base face. A message pops up asking you to rip the edges of the part.

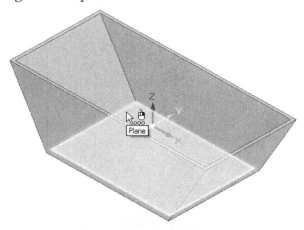
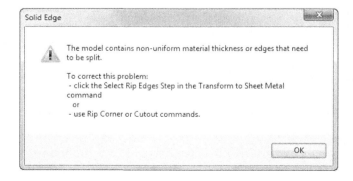

Sheet Metal Design

On the command bar, click the **Select Rip Edges Step** icon and click on the side edges of the part. Click the green check to complete the conversion process. Now, you can save and close the file.

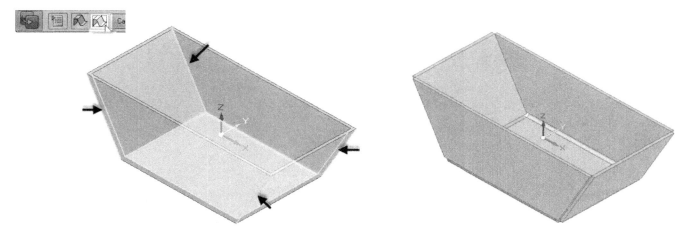

Sheet Metal Drawings

Creating drawings of a sheet metal part is same as any other drawing. However, there are some settings specific to sheet metal flat pattern. You can access these settings in the **Annotation** tab of the **Solid Edge Options** dialog box.

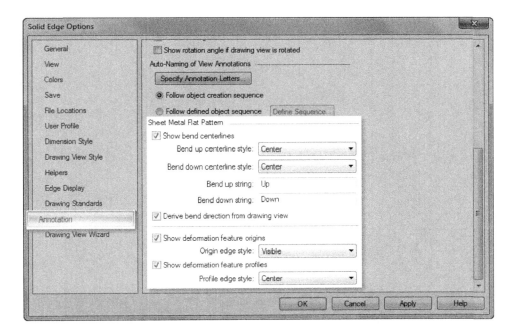

To create a flat pattern view, activate the **View Wizard** command and select the sheet metal part. On the command bar, click the **Drawing View Wizard Options** icon to open the **Drawing View Creation Wizard** dialog box. On this dialog box, select the **Flat pattern** option and click **OK**.

Sheet Metal Design

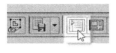 

On the command bar, set the **Scale** value and click to place the view. You will notice that the bends are represented by centrelines.

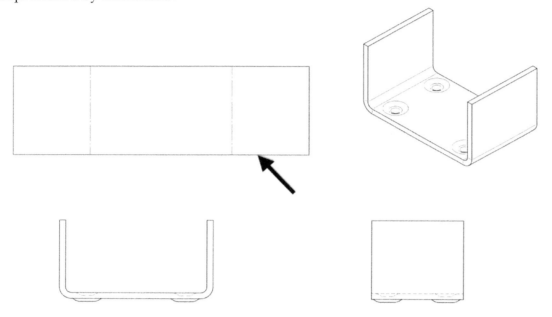

To add a bend table, click **Home > Table > Parts List > Bend Table** on the ribbon, and then click on the flat pattern view. Click on the sheet to position the bend table.

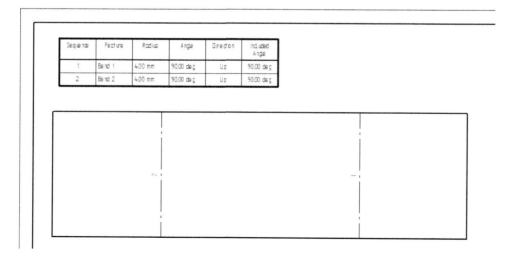

Sheet Metal Design

Export to DWF

In addition to creating drawings, you can directly export a sheet metal to DWF format which can be opened in AutoCAD. All you have to do is click **Application Menu > Save As > Save As Flat**. On the **Save As Flat** dialog box, click the **Options** button to open the **Save As Flat DXF Options** dialog box. On this dialog box, set the layer properties and bend data, and then click **OK**. Type-in a name in the **File name** box and click **Save**. Now, you can open the DWF file in AutoCAD.

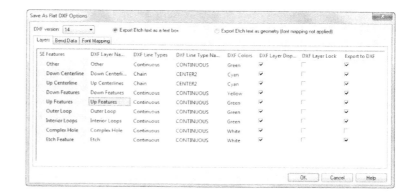

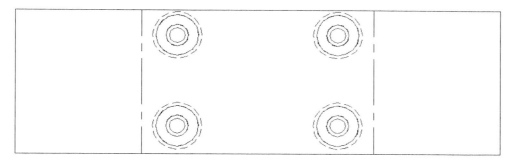

Examples
Example 1
In this example, you will construct the sheet metal part shown below.

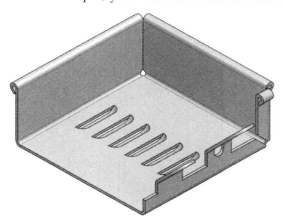

283

Sheet Metal Design

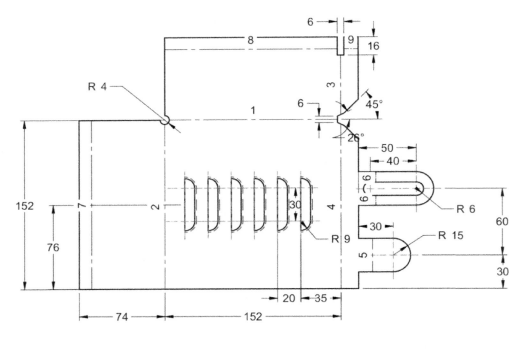

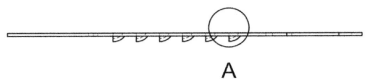

A

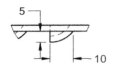

DETAIL A

Sequence	Feature	Radius	Angle	Direction	Included Angle
1	Bend 1	2.77 mm	90.00 deg	Up	90.00 deg
2	Bend 2	2.77 mm	90.00 deg	Up	90.00 deg
3	Bend 4	2.77 mm	90.00 deg	Up	90.00 deg
4	Bend 3	2.77 mm	90.00 deg	Up	90.00 deg
5	Bend 5	2.77 mm	45.00 deg	Down	135.00 deg
6	Bend 9	2.77 mm	45.00 deg	Down	135.00 deg
7	Bend 12	2.00 mm	136.44 deg	Down	43.56 deg
8	Bend 11	2.00 mm	136.44 deg	Down	43.56 deg
9	Bend 10	2.00 mm	136.44 deg	Down	43.56 deg

Sheet Metal Design

1. Start **Solid Edge ST6**.
2. On the initial screen, click **ISO Sheet Metal** to start a new sheet metal file.
3. Create a sketch on the top (XY) plane. Change the orientation of the model to the ISO View.

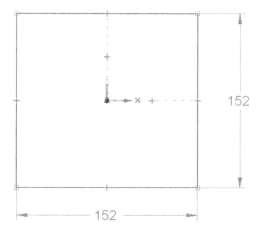

4. Click inside the region enclosed by the sketch. On the command bar, click the **Material Table** icon to open the **Material Table** dialog box. On this dialog box, open the **Gage** tab and set the **Sheet metal gage** to **12 gage**. Set the **Neutral Factor** to 0.5. Click **Apply to Model** to close the dialog box.
5. Click on the arrow handle to make it point upwards. Click the right mouse button to complete the tab feature.

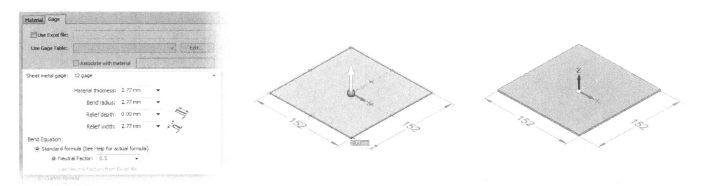

6. Click on the end face at back to display the flange handle on it. On the flange handle, click the arrow pointing upwards, and then drag the mouse cursor.
7. On the command bar, set the **Measurement Point** to **Measurement Outside**. Set the **Material Side** to **Material Outside**.
8. Move the mouse cursor up and type-in **65** in the distance box. Press Enter to create the flange.

Sheet Metal Design

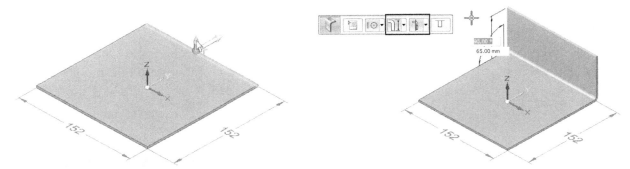

9. Create another flange on the left side. The flange length is 65 mm.

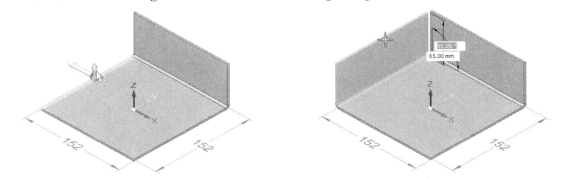

10. Lock the front end face and draw a line of **15** mm length. Activate the **Contour Flange** command (on the ribbon, click **Home > Sheet Metal > Contour Flange**) and click on the line.
11. Click the arrow pointing toward right.

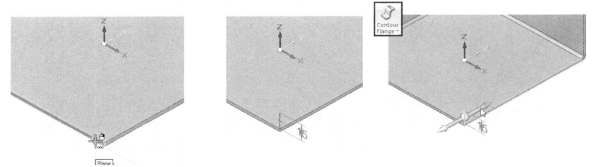

12. Select the end face of the flange perpendicular to the tab feature. Click the right mouse button to create the contour flange.

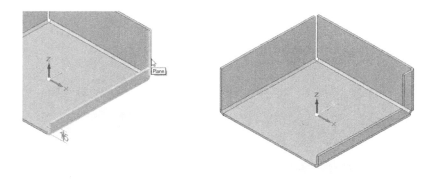

Sheet Metal Design

13. Lock the outer face of the contour flange and draw the sketch shown below. Create a tab feature using the sketch.

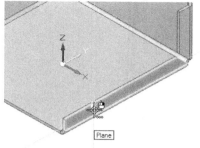 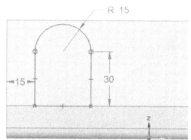 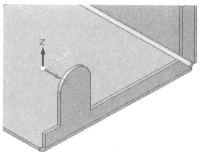

14. Draw a line on the outer face of the tab. Activate the **Bend** command (click **Home > Sheet Metal > Bend** on the ribbon) and click on the line.
15. Click on the arrow pointing upwards. Type-in **135** in the angle box and press Enter to bend the tab feature.

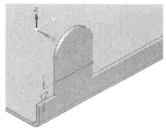 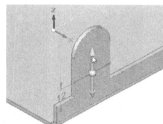 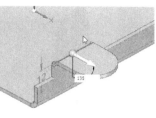 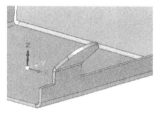

16. Draw another sketch on the outer face of the contour flange.
17. Activate the **Tab** command and create a tab feature using the sketch.

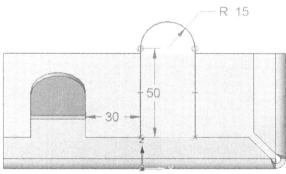 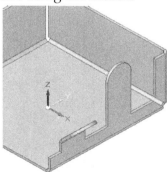

18. Draw a line on the outer face of the tab feature. Activate the **Bend** command (click **Home > Sheet Metal > Bend** on the ribbon) and click on the sketched line.
19. Click on the arrow pointing upwards. Type-in **135** in the angle box and press Enter to bend the tab feature.

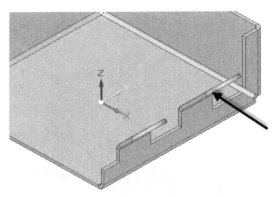

20. On the vertical face of the bend feature, create the sketch shown in figure.
21. On ribbon, click **Home > Sheet Metal > Hole > Cut**.
22. Click inside the regions enclosed by the sketch. Click the right mouse button to accept the selection.
23. On the command bar, click the **Wrapped Cut** icon, and then click the right mouse button.

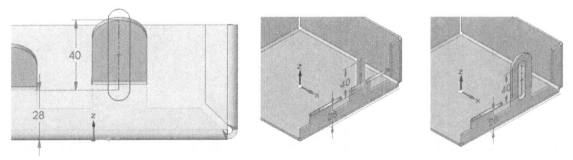

24. Again, click the right mouse button to complete the cut feature.

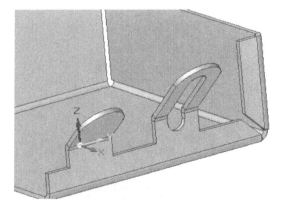

25. Activate the **Close 2-Bend Corner** command (click **Home > Sheet Metal > Close 2 Bend Corner** on the ribbon) and click on the bends of the flange features.
26. On the command bar, set the **Corner Treatment** to **Circular Cutout**. Set the **Diameter** value to 8 mm. Click the right mouse button to close the bends.

Sheet Metal Design

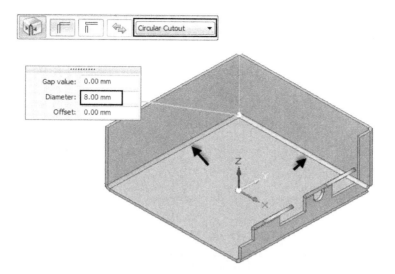

27. Activate the **Hem** command (click **Home > Sheet Metal > Contour Flange > Hem** on the ribbon).
28. On the command bar, click the **Hem Options** icon to the open the **Hem Options** dialog box. On this dialog box, set the **Hem type** to **Closed Loop**. Set the **Bend radius1** to 2 and **Flange length1** to 8. Click **OK** to close the dialog box.

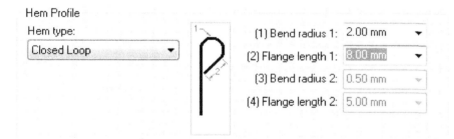

29. Click on the outer edges of the flange features. Click the right mouse button to create the hem features.

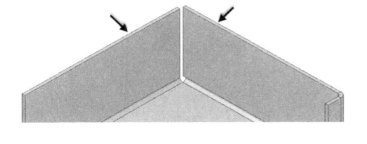
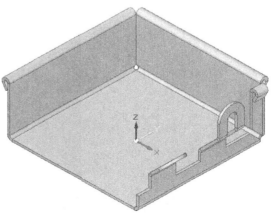

30. Rotate and orient the model, as shown below.

289

Sheet Metal Design

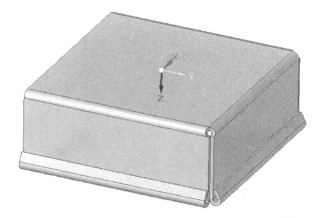

31. Activate the **Louver** command (click **Home > Sheet Metal > Dimple > Louver** on the ribbon) place the mouse cursor on the top face. Press F3 on your keyboard to lock the plane.
32. On the command bar click the **Louver Options** icon to open the **Louver Options** dialog box. On this dialog box, set the **Length**, **Depth** and **Height** values to 50, 10, and 5, respectively. Click **OK** to close the dialog box.

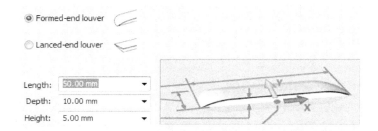

33. Place the mouse cursor on the left edge and press E twice. The location dimensions appear.
34. Type-in 76 and 120 in the dimension boxes. Press Enter to create the louver feature.

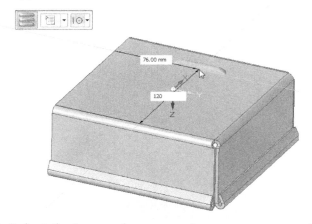

35. Select the louver feature and create a rectangular pattern.

Sheet Metal Design

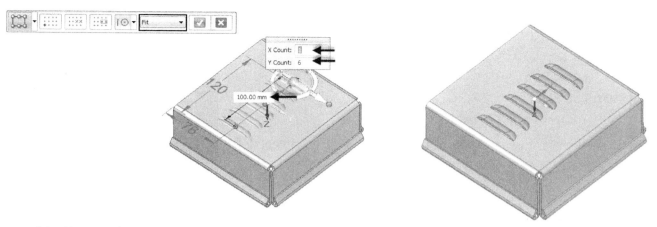

36. Change the view orientation of the sheet metal to ISO.
37. On the ribbon, click **Tools > Model > Flatten** on the ribbon. The **Flat Pattern** command is activated.
38. Click on the top face of the tab feature.
39. Click on the front edge of the tab feature to define the x-axis of the flat pattern. The flat pattern is created.

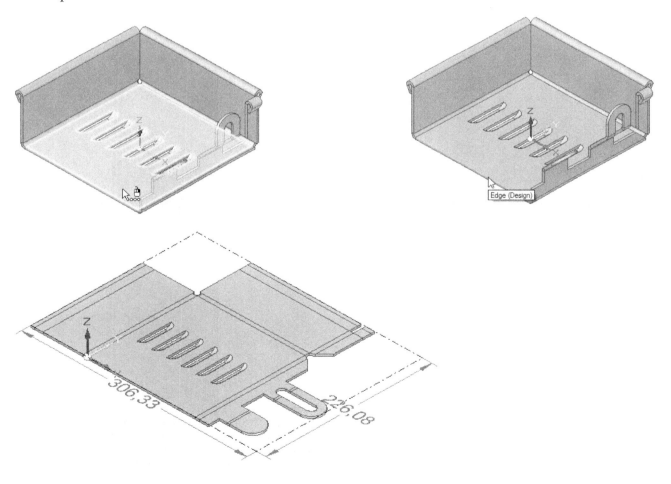

40. On the ribbon, click **Tools > Model > Synchronous** to switch back to the Synchronous environment.
41. Save and close the sheet metal part.

Questions

1. How to insert a flat pattern into a drawing?
2. Describe parameters that can be specified on the **Material Table** dialog box.
3. Define the term 'Neutral Factor'.
4. List any two parameters settings of a gage table that can be overridden when creating a feature.
5. What is the use of the **Cut** command?
6. Which command is used to apply rounds and chamfers to the corners of a sheet metal part?
7. List the types of hems that can be created in Solid Edge?
8. What does the **Close 2-Corner** command do?
9. What are the corner treatment options when closing a corner?
10. What is the difference between a dimple and drawn cutout?

Exercises

Exercise 1

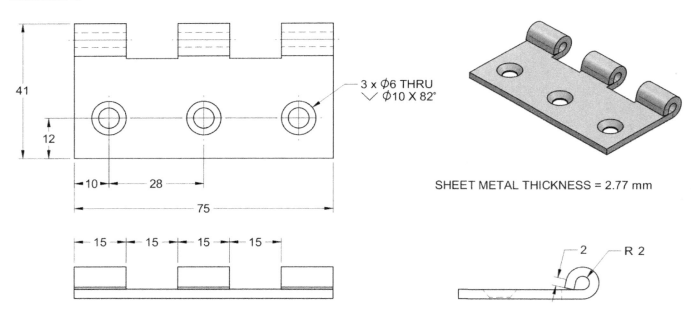

Sheet Metal Design

Exercise 2

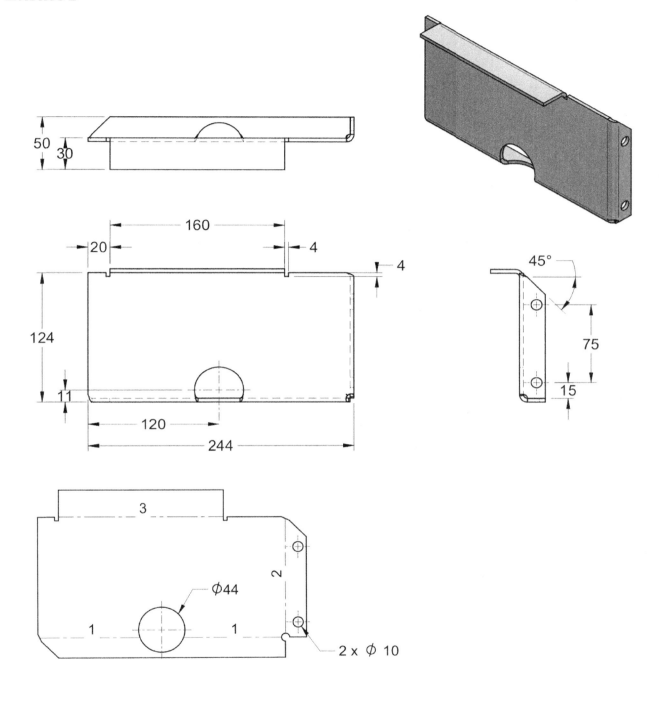

Sequence	Feature	Radius	Angle	Direction	Included Angle
1	Bend 1	3.58 mm	90.00 deg	Down	90.00 deg
2	Bend 2	3.58 mm	90.00 deg	Down	90.00 deg
3	Bend 3	3.58 mm	90.00 deg	Up	90.00 deg

Printed in Great Britain
by Amazon